Futures Past.
Economic Forecasting in the 20th and 21st Century

LITERATUR — KULTUR — ÖKONOMIE

LITERATURE — CULTURE — ECONOMY

Herausgegeben von / Edited by
Christine Künzel, Axel Haunschild, Birger P. Priddat,
Thomas Rommel, Franziska Schößler und / and Yvette Sánchez

VOLUME 5

Zu Qualitätssicherung und Peer Review der vorliegenden Publikation

Die Qualität der in dieser Reihe erscheinenden Arbeiten wird vor der Publikation durch einen externen, von der Herausgeberschaft benannten Gutachter im Double Blind Verfahren geprüft. Dabei ist der Autor der Arbeit dem Gutachter während der Prüfung namentlich nicht bekannt; der Gutachter bleibt anonym.

Notes on the quality assurance and peer review of this publication

Prior to publication, the quality of the work published in this series is double blind reviewed by an external referee appointed by the editorship. The referee is not aware of the author's name when performing the review; the referee's name is not disclosed.

Ulrich Fritsche / Roman Köster /
Laetitia Lenel (eds.)

Futures Past. Economic Forecasting in the 20th and 21st Century

PETER LANG

Bibliographic Information published by the Deutsche Nationalbibliothek
The Deutsche Nationalbibliothek lists this publication in the Deutsche Nationalbibliografie; detailed bibliographic data is available online at http://dnb.d-nb.de.

Library of Congress Cataloging-in-Publication Data
A CIP catalog record for this book has been applied for at the Library of Congress.

We acknowledge support by the Open Access Publication Fund of Humboldt-Universität zu Berlin.

Cover Illustration: @iStock.com/MissTuni

Printed by CPI books GmbH, Leck
ISSN 2364-1304
ISBN 978-3-631-79316-9 (Print)
E-ISBN 978-3-631-81869-5 (E-Book)
E-ISBN 978-3-631-81870-1 (EPUB)
E-ISBN 978-3-631-81871-8 (MOBI)
DOI 10.3726/b16817

Peter Lang – Berlin · Bern · Bruxelles · New York · Oxford · Warszawa · Wien

This publication has been peer reviewed.

www.peterlang.com

Table of Contents

List of Authors

Jörg Döpke teaches economics and empirical research methods at the University of Applied Sciences, Merseburg. Before joining this institution, he has been affiliated with the Kiel Institute of World Economics and the German central bank. Research interests include empirical macroeconomics and business cycle forecasting.
Contact: joerg.doepke@hs-merseburg.de.

Ulrich Fritsche is an economist and Full Professor of Economics, esp. Applied Economics at Universität Hamburg. His research interests include forecasting methods, macroeconomic expectation formation of households and experts, and time series econometrics.
Contact: ulrich.fritsche@uni-hamburg.de.

Roman Köster is currently Visiting Professor at the Bundeswehr University in Munich. His research interests include economic and environmental history with focus on the 20th century. Among other topics he has written about the "Crisis" of German economics during the 1920s ("Die Wissenschaft der Außenseiter," 2011) and the history of waste management after 1945 in West Germany ("Hausmüll. Abfall und Gesellschaft in Westdeutschland 1945–1990," 2017).
Contact: roman.koester@unibw.de.

Laetitia Lenel is a Ph.D. candidate at the Department of History at Humboldt-Universität zu Berlin. Her research focuses on economic knowledge practices and the history of capitalism. Her research project, which is part of the Priority Programme 1859 "Experience and Expectation. Historical Foundations of Economic Behaviour" funded by the German Research Foundation, explores the Euro-American history of business forecasting in the 20th century.
Contact: laetitialenel@hu-berlin.de.

Jan Logemann is assistant professor (Wissenschaftlicher Mitarbeiter and Privatdozent) at the Institute for Economic and Social History, Georg August University of Göttingen. He explores modern U.S. American and German economic history from a transnational perspective. He

most recently published "Engineered to Sell: European Emigrés and the Making of Consumer Capitalism" (Chicago University Press, 2019) and is co-editor (with Gary Cross and Ingo Köhler) of "Consumer Engineering, 1920s–1970s: Marketing between Expert Planning and Consumer Responsiveness" (Palgrave Macmillan, 2019).
Contact: jan.logemann@wiwi.uni-goettingen.de.

Olivier Pilmis is a Research Fellow in Sociology at the French National Center for Scientific Research (CNRS) and a member of the Centre de Sociologie des Organisations (Sciences Po - CNRS). His research applies economic sociology, organizational sociology, and sociological theory to the study of macroeconomic forecasting.
Contact: olivier.pilmis@sciencespo.fr.

Werner Reichmann is a sociologist and Privatdozent at the University of Konstanz. He analyzes economics and economic forecasting from a sociological perspective, works on human interaction under digital conditions, and investigates the connections between architecture and society. Further information can be found at www.wernerreichmann.net.
Contact: werner.reichmann@uni-konstanz.de.

Marion Ronca is currently Ph.D. candidate and scientific researcher at the University of Zurich. She writes her Ph.D. thesis on the history of economic observation in Switzerland. Her research interests are among others the history of economic thought, quantitative rationalization as modern ideal, and managerial practices of the nation state.
Contact: marion_ronca@kulturversus.net.

Tara M. Sinclair is an associate professor of economics and international affairs at the George Washington University in Washington, DC. Sinclair is also co-director of the H. O. Stekler Research Program on Forecasting where she evaluates real time economic data and forecasts. Much of Sinclair's research has focused on the role of recessions in economic models and forecasts. Her research and commentary is covered regularly by the media including the New York Times, the Wall Street Journal, and the Washington Post.
Contact: tsinc@gwu.edu.

Gabi Waldhof is interested in social (group) behaviour and moral behaviour. At the Economic Ethics Chair in Halle, and at IAMO, Halle, she is currently working on her Ph.D. on moral values and their impact on biotechnology acceptance. Prior to starting her Ph.D., Waldhof worked in the DFG priority program "Experience and Expectation. Historical Foundations of Economic Behaviour." Additionally, she worked as a research assistant at the Department of Experimental Psychology of the University of Oxford, at the Saïd Business School of Oxford, at the Halle Institute of Economic Research, and in the Laboratory of Experimental and Behavioural Economics in Moscow.
Contact: waldhof@iamo.de.

Timo Walter is currently a visiting research fellow at the University of Edinburgh. His current research is on the history and sociology of finance, focusing in particular on the formalization and financialization of economic rationality. He has published on the financialization of central banking, qualitative methodology, and the semiotics of financial markets.
Contact: timo.walter@graduateinstitute.ch.

Laetitia Lenel (Humboldt-Universität zu Berlin), Roman Köster (Universität der Bundeswehr München), and Ulrich Fritsche (Universität Hamburg)

Introduction

Over the last years, the history of economics has received broad attention. As a side-effect of the financial crisis of 2008, much of this research has served a critical purpose: By investigating the history of economic thought, scholars aimed at unveiling how economics helped bringing into being the world of ruthless capitalism we inhabit. Aside from rather "popular" explorations in the history of economic thought, which targeted the entire field of economics (Sedláček 2011; Vogl 2016), the financial crisis also spawned a broad research on the history and impact of economic statistics. Research has especially focused on the history of the Gross Domestic Product (GDP). Scholars have, for example, investigated how the GDP became what has been called "the world's most powerful number" and how it has helped making economic growth a priority among social scientists and politicians alike (Fioramonti 2013; Speich Chassé 2013; Lepenies 2016; Schmelzer 2016).

Despite this newly awakened interest in the history of economics and economists' impact on economic and political decision-making, the history of economic forecasting has received only little attention until now. This finding is surprising, as economic forecasting has often been perceived as one of the most important fields of economic expertise (Zarnowitz 1992, 519; Köster 2016). Also, economists' failure to predict the financial crisis was one of the strongest points of public criticism towards economics after 2008. Journalists attested economists a "collective failure," and accused them of three sins: "That macro and financial economists helped cause the crisis, that they failed to spot it, and that they have no idea how to fix it" (Nienhaus 2009; "What Went Wrong with Economics. And How the Discipline Should Change to Avoid the Mistakes of the Past" 2009; cf. also Jorion 2012). These highly emotional reactions, which take the value of economic forecasts as a yardstick for evaluating the performance of the entire economics profession, is contrasted by a comparatively silent stance of the scientific community. The academic interest in the history of economics that the financial crisis has brought about has, it seems, not yet spread to the field of economic forecasting. There are still very few case studies that investigate the creation and the impact of economic forecasts (Friedman 2014; Lenel 2018; J. Pietruska 2018; Reichmann 2018).

This volume is an attempt to change this. We believe that economic forecasting presents a unique opportunity to study the development of economic statistics and modelling and other forecasting practices and the changing relationship between economics, economic policy, and the public over time. Forecasting constitutes an important activity carried out by institutes of economic research, central banks and international organizations. Economic forecasts receive extensive media coverage and attain great public attention. Policy institutions and private companies rely to a high degree on economic forecasts. Notwithstanding the challenges and difficulties economic forecasting faces, it apparently inhabits a crucial place in modern industrial societies. This raises pressing questions. Why does the reliance on economic forecasting not seem to be shattered by forecasting failures and the severe disappointments they yield? How do economic forecasting services adapt their forecasting techniques and presentations to practical purposes? How do they deal with wrong predictions and economic crises? Is it true, what some critics say, that forecasters stay with their models regardless of empirical failure? Or are there practices of critical self-evaluation at work which contribute to the refinement and (sometimes) paradigm change of forecasting techniques? Finally, what is the impact of forecasts on economic expectations and behavior and how do the expectations of economic and political decision-makers, in turn, affect the epistemic process of economic forecasting?

In approaching the history of economic forecasting, we try to avoid what appears to us as one of the biggest problems of the research on the history of economics today: The issues at play are normally discussed among economists, historians, and sociologists, but these disciplines rarely reach out to each other. Despite repeated calls for a synthesis (cf., e.g., Abbott 1991; Siegenthaler 1999), interdisciplinarity is more than underdeveloped in this field. This is unfortunate, as a greater cooperation would prove beneficial for all three disciplines. Economists could gain from a greater historical contextualization of economic knowledge. As historians and sociologists have shown, economics is not a uniform science, but differs among historical and geographical contexts (cf., e.g., Fourcade 2009). Also, historians' and sociologists' focus on the practices of knowledge production, their sites and multilayered effects, could help economists broaden the all too narrow perspective of the so-called *Dogmengeschichte* or *History of Economic Thought* (Dommann, Speich Chassé, and Suter 2014; on the field of the history of knowledge more general, see Dupré and Somsen 2019). Historians and sociologists, on the other hand, could benefit from economists' broader knowledge and their better understanding of the relevant issues. And while historians could caution sociologists against drawing too broad generalizations from small sample sizes, historians, on the other hand, could gain from using sociological theories and models. This might not only counteract historians' deplorable inclination to marginalize their own work, but also make their case studies and their underlying premises and methods more comprehensible and more comparable to others.

One of the goals of the conference "Futures Past. Economic Forecasting in the 20th and 21st Century," hosted at the University of Hamburg in October 2018 and funded by the German Research Foundation Priority Program 1859 "Experience and Expectation. Historical Foundations of Economic Behavior," was to encourage such exchanges. We wanted to bring together scholars from different disciplines to discuss the history of economic forecasting in the 20th and 21st century, its changing practices, its roles in society, and the multilayered interactions between forecasters, economic and political decision-makers and the public. The conference demonstrated that the different perspectives on the subject provoked fruitful discussions, confrontations, and clarifications of perspectives. The successful "experiment" of the conference motivated us to edit this volume, which seeks to give an impulse to a field of research which deserves more attention and more collaboration.

1. A Very Short History of Economic Forecasting

People have always tried to forecast the future. For the longest time, however, the main target of prophecy were cataclysmic events in the context of Christian eschatology. During the 18th century, in the course of the development of a "modern" society, attempts to forecast the future became more important and systematic. The shift in the relationship between experience and expectation, which the historian Reinhard Koselleck described as one of the main features of the onset of modernity, brought about a consciousness of a future that was fundamentally different from the past (Koselleck 2004). The semantics of political and social communication were more and more transformed to target a future that was now understood as open (Luhmann 1980). At the same time, political thinkers started to outline conceptions about the historical development and the future prospects of civil society. These were not actually forecasts, as especially utopian endeavors were generally meant as a criticism of present conditions (Saage 1991). They did, however, constitute first attempts to bridge the separation of space of experience and horizon of expectation.

The late 19th century, then, saw the emergence of professional forecasting, as trading at stock exchanges and speculative market practices of all kinds grew in importance, especially in grain trade. This brought about a growing demand for all kinds of forecasts such as to predict, for example, weather conditions and market fluctuations. As Jamie Pietruska has shown in her work on the culture of prediction in the second half of the 19th century in the United States, a new quest for certainty led to the establishment of numerous forms of prediction. Utopian novelists, crop forecasters, and business prophets competed for scientific authority and professional credibility (J. Pietruska 2018). Interestingly, despite their different fields and techniques, these forecasters often shared certain semantics such as a "meteorological" language, which has remained important in economic forecasting up to this day, thus testifying to meteorology's lasting influence (Anderson 2005; J. L. Pietruska 2011; J. Pietruska 2018).

With regards to economics, the "discovery" of the business cycle in the mid-19th century played a major role in the development of forecasting. In the 1860s, the French physician and economists Clément Juglar studied time series of economic data and identified a cycle of roughly ten years' duration. Juglar distinguished different phases of economic fluctuations, thereby abandoning the long-held notion of random events and shocks as the sole cause for economic crises (Juglar 1862). As the first to define a pattern of periodic fluctuations, Juglar has been referred to as the "ancestor" of business cycle research (Schumpeter [1954] 1997).

Numerous economic crises in the late 19th and early 20th century seemed to testify to the periodic character of economic fluctuations, thereby prompting economists and entrepreneurs to study business cycles in a more systematic fashion. The economic crisis of 1907 led to the establishment of a multitude of forecasting services in the United States (Friedman 2014). Some relied on "common sense," extrapolations of past developments, or simple statistical correlations. Others claimed to apply sophisticated mathematical methods and models to predict future economic developments. The "Harvard barometer," established in 1919, especially captured contemporaries' attention for its seemingly sophisticated technical approach, spurring the establishment of economic services and institutes of business cycle research in Europe, Australia, and South-America throughout the 1920s (Friedman 2009; 2014; Lenel 2018). However, as recent research has shown, failures of the Harvard index led members of the Harvard group to increasingly abandon the use of the index in the early 1920s, instead basing their forecasts on the expectations and plans of American manufacturers as well as Federal Reserve authorities and other bankers (Lenel 2018). Widely unnoticed by the public, an unofficial practice of "foretalk" with economic and political decision-makers replaced the seemingly "mechanical" means of forecasting.

The unforeseen October 1929 crash and the following Great Depression greatly shook the economic forecasting community. As a reaction to their forecasting failures and the severe loss of reputation that these failures brought about, forecasting services like the Harvard Economic Service had to shut their doors in the aftermath of the Great Depression. At the same time, the unprecedented economic crisis revealed the importance of economic forecasting and prevention measures. With government intervention in the economy increasing throughout the 1930s, administrations' demand for economic forecasts rose.

This demand was further spurred by the publication and wide reception of John Maynard Keynes' *General Theory of Employment, Interest, and Money* (Keynes [1936] 2013). The claim for deficit spending and work creation schemes to maintain economic growth and minimize price changes required a close monitoring of monetary, fiscal and economic conditions. Keynes' *General Theory* therefore provided a framework to expand the statistical coverage and to develop national accounting systems. As a reaction, the 1930s and 1940s saw a second wave of establishments of institutes of business cycle research in Europe and the U.S., with institutes becoming the nucleus for the development of empirically based and theoretically informed forecasting techniques to predict future economic developments.

Forecasting could mean very different things, though. Which time span should be predicted? Which data, which theories, which techniques should be used and applied? These were hotly debated issues in the postwar decades, as the somewhat dramatic American "measurement without theory" debate exemplifies (Koopmans 1947; Fourcade 2009, 86). With the IS/LM model interpretation of Keynes' *General Theory* (Hicks 1937) and the development of dynamic macro models (e.g. Samuelson 1939) based on the description of business cycles as reactions to stochastic shocks in a system of difference equations, macroeconomic theory began to replace old-style business cycle theories (M. S. Morgan 2012, 217–55) with endogenously arising economic fluctuations. While descriptive and "intuitive" techniques of forecasting lost in reputation, economists began to model the economy as a system of simultaneous economic equations with stochastic influences. By manipulating their models, they could testify their hypotheses about relationships represented in the model and demonstrate some answer with the model (M. S. Morgan 2012). This procedure promised to yield "objective" future knowledge that seemed urgently needed at a time of a growing quest for economic policy advice (M. S. Morgan and Rutherford 1998).

This quest was fostered by a growing planning euphoria. Two decennia of relatively stable economic growth since the late 1940s, which had led contemporaries in the 1960s ask if the business cycle was obsolete (Bronfenbrenner 1969), had created the notion of a "programmability" of the future (Plitzko 1964). The planning optimism was further fueled by the Cold War context, in which the future became a battleground as predictions could serve as weapons (Connelly et al. 2012; Andersson 2012; Seefried 2015; Andersson 2018).

In the following decade, however, sharp economic fluctuations, the "oil shocks" of 1973 and 1979, the "comeback" of unemployment, and the structural changes which were a result of industrial restructuring and a serious competition from East Asian countries, created a new feeling of uncertainty which pushed back the optimism of the 1960s. Already in 1971, a reviewer explained that it "is hard to imagine that the question of the possible obsolescence of the business cycle would be chosen as the theme for a conference held today" (Allsopp and Bronfenbrenner 1971, 951). Keynesian macroeconomics came under attack, as critics blamed it for the phenomenon of "stagflation," as the seemingly paradoxical coexistence of economic stagnation and a high inflation rate characteristic of Western industrial countries during this decade was called (Nützenadel 2005). Not surprisingly, the 1970s also brought economic forecasting under fire, as forecasters delivered more and more false predictions (Graff 1977). While some observers in the 1960s had considered long-term forecasts of more than ten years possible, forecasters now even grappled with the accuracy of short-term predictions. Two phenomena were striking: that forecasters had enormous problems to predict economic downswings, and that they had a tendency to underestimate upswings. In the German case, these shortcomings even led to "backbiting" from scholars of the German Democratic Republic, who perceived the forecasting problems as indicative for the unstableness of the free market system in general (Kuczynski 1970).

And forecasters? Critics often stated that forecasters stayed with their "wrong" methods at all costs and simply ignored their "failures." The reality was different, though: Forecasters undertook big efforts to improve their methods, to broaden their statistical basis, and to develop computer programs (and the appropriate computers) to process the gigantic data volume. Forecasters furthermore developed sophisticated evaluation methods to assess and improve the quality of forecasts. Some of them also started to apply different kinds of forecasting techniques during the 1970s – especially autoregression equations – to overcome some of the mentioned shortcomings. The 1980s and 1990s brought substantial improvements in time series methods: vector autoregressions, models for non-stationary data and models to handle co-integrated systems (Elliott, Granger, and Timmermann 2006; 2013). Although this often simply caused other (just different) problems, it demonstrates that forecasters undertook great efforts to improve their forecasts. This also entailed the cooperation of economic institutes and forecasting services, which led for instance to a "Gemeinschaftsdiagnose" (joint prognosis) by the leading economic research institutes in Germany, aiming to enhance the authority of forecasts by achieving a consensus (Reichmann 2018, 34–35).

But fundamental problems remain (Fildes and Stekler 2002). As Tara Sinclair shows in her contribution to this volume, forecasters are still facing severe challenges when predicting economic downswings. Unfortunately, this is exactly what the public demands from them. But this inaptitude is certainly not caused by unwillingness or ideological ignorance of forecasters (Döpke, Fritsche, and Waldhof 2019). The simple truth is that "correct" forecasting is a very complicated, to some degree unsolvable task. But this has more to do with the complexity of the task itself and the challenges it has to tackle.

2. The Social Fabrication of Forecasts: Some Aspects

As already mentioned, the financial crisis of 2008 also plunged forecasters into a crisis ("What Went Wrong with Economics. And How the Discipline Should Change to Avoid the Mistakes of the Past" 2009). As a reaction, forecasters began to overthink their forecasting habits. Some forecasters openly admitted that their models were unable to predict financial crises (Heuser 2008; Hartmann and Vogel 2010). However, the loss in reputation does not seem to have had lasting effects. As other crises before, the financial crisis of 2008 has not diminished the public interest in economic forecasts. Forecasts are still eliciting broad media coverage, and institutes of business cycle research are still receiving public funds. This indicates that the accuracy of economic forecasts is not the only criterion determining their demand. Rather, forecasting seems to constitute a dynamic means of observing current developments that helps actors to coordinate and stabilize their expectations of an uncertain future in the present. As the sociologist Werner Reichmann has argued, economic forecasts are anchored in the present, not in the future. By influencing the variables they predict, forecasts can validate or invalidate themselves. "True" or "false" are therefore no fitting categories for judging the quality of economic forecasts (Reichmann 2018, 286).

This is of course highly controversial, as the accuracy of forecasts seems to constitute the most important "currency" within the field of forecasting. As Oskar Morgenstern has argued in 1928, "Every forecast must become true, otherwise it is entirely worthless" (Morgenstern 1928, 95). But Reichmann's observation rightly points to the fact that the epistemic status of forecasts in the social sciences is different from their status in the natural sciences, as economic forecasts have the potential to create the conditions of their own fulfillment (Morgenstern 1928, 92–108; Merton 1948, 195; Reichmann 2018, 286–87). They can become "self-fulfilling prophecies," which the sociologist Robert Merton described as false definitions of a situation that evoke a new behavior which makes the originally false prediction come true (Merton 1948, 195), or act as "self-disfulfilling prophecies": The prediction of a recession can lead to countercyclical measures by the government, thereby preventing or at least postponing the predicted recession.

The potential of economic forecasts to shape actors' expectations and thereby influence their economic behavior makes economic forecasting and its potential impacts both a challenging and a highly relevant topic. How actors form expectations is a hotly debated question in economics, even more so since the 2008 financial crisis, which presented a severe challenge for the standard theory of rational expectations. According to the rational expectations theory, economic actors form decisions on the basis of all available information. They are therefore able, on average, to accurately predict the future; deviations from perfect foresight are only random. Recently, the sociologist Jens Beckert presented a different account of economic expectations. Alluding to the fundamental uncertainty of the future, Beckert described economic expectations as "communicatively established imaginaries" of the future (Beckert 2016, 42). According to Beckert, actors base their behavior on these "fictional expectations" *as if* they did actually describe future states of the world (Beckert 2014, 9–10; 2016, 10). This allows them to act and coordinate their economic actions.

In this picture, economic forecasts play a crucial role. They offer stories on which economic actors can base their fictional expectations and thus their behavior. By this means, forecasts are persuasive and performative utterances that are inherently political. But forecasts are not only a means to create and stabilize expectations. They also provide what Luhmann called a "symbolic cover," which allows actors to coordinate their expectations and thereby overcome the threshold of uncertainty. Only by agreeing on shared expectations, agents can counteract the double contingency which is present in all social interactions. Forecasts thus justify and legitimate action despite the uncertainty of the future, thus enabling capitalism's functioning (Luhmann 1995, 127–28; 1994, 74; Beckert and Bronk 2018; Lenel 2018, 412).

This might explain why forecasts are the outcome of not only statistical calculations and mathematical models, but also of an interactive negotiation process. As Werner Reichmann has shown in his research on current forecasting practices in German-speaking countries, forecasters are embedded in various formal and informal networks (Reichmann 2013; 2018). They consult with economic and political decision-makers and, as demonstrated by the German *Gemeinschaftsdiagnose*, also with other forecasters. By this means, economic and political decision-makers as well as other economists can participate in the epistemic process of forecasting (Reichmann 2013). Similar networks have already existed in the 1920s, thus questioning the vision of a purely technical forecast, which was brought forward, among others, by the Harvard index (Lenel 2018, 398–405). Drawing on a term introduced by the American sociologist David Gibson in his research on political decision-making during the Cuban missile crisis, Reichmann describes the exchange between two or more actors about possible futures as "foretalk:" Here, actors negotiate their expectations to produce a consensus on the future (Gibson 2011b; 2011a; 2012; Reichmann 2013).

As these observations forcefully remind us, we need to rethink our common understanding of economic forecasts. Forecasts are not well-founded statements about the future, but only judgments of likelihood, which are the outcome of communicative acts of imagination. As Jamie Morgan explained, their translation into number gives the impression of precision and thus "makes us think of economic forecasting as more than simply complicated guesswork, […] a science and not an art of numbers" (J. Morgan 2013; on the process of translation, see Svetlova 2012). In fact, however, economic forecasts are mere anticipations of possible futures, or "foresights" (on this term, see J. Morgan 2013; Priddat 2016). Through the process of negotiation and by being circulated, however, they can create "convergences of beliefs" and expectations and by that means gain currency (Arrow 1979). Their communication engineers agreement on a shared narrative of the future and thereby fosters the realization of this version of the future (Priddat 2016).

The importance of the social fabrication of forecasts should, however, not be overstressed. The future is not just made of expectations. There are "objective facts" in economic life. People have money or have not, have marketable goods or not, have suitable technologies at hand or not. These facts may be perceived as "constructed" as well, but they are, and this is important here, not negotiable. They simply do not change if actors have different expectations. They, too, influence actors' expectations. The hard to disentangle mixture of economic facts and stories, material conditions and fabricated expectations demonstrates that economic forecasting is certainly not physics, but at the same time not made out of thin air.

Economic forecasts are the result of very different practices. They are derived by a set of different statistical, mathematical and social techniques, thus entailing both calculative and non-calculative practices. By presenting contributions from economists, historians, and sociologists, this volume wants to highlight the multifacetedness of economic forecasting. While by no means representative in geographical or periodical scale, this volume seeks to start a discussion on the multilayered, intricate practices which form the basis of economic forecasts and their impacts on futures past.

3. This Volume

The contributions in this volume look at the history and present state of forecasting, the practices involved and the impacts they yield(ed).

Tara Sinclair opens the volume with an overview of the state and historical record of economic forecasting and an analysis of some explanations and the implications of this record. In her chapter, "Continuities and Discontinuities in Economic Forecasting," Sinclair demonstrates that until this day and despite the seeming advances in forecasting techniques, forecasters have serious problems to predict economic downturns. As Sinclair argues, this finding testifies to the necessity for policy makers and the public to use economic forecasts with caution and improve and quicken their reactions to recessions as they are occurring. Forecasters, on the other hand, should be encouraged to publish warning signals of recessions in advance as the social costs of recessions are huge.

The historian Jan Logemann in his chapter, "Measuring and Managing Expectations: Consumer Confidence as an Economic Indicator,

1920s–1970s," investigates the origins and the application of consumer confidence measurements as a prognostic tool. Stimulated by a new understanding of consumers and their vital importance for economic growth, economists and market experts working in the mid-20th century developed new techniques to track consumers' changing expectations. From the 1950s onwards, corporate and government officials used these techniques to forecast and engineer consumer-driven economic growth in the United States and in Europe. Logemann argues that European émigré scholars like George Kantona played a crucial role in this development. Drawing on insights of continental European social and Gestalt psychology, they presented new ideas about the expectations of consumers and their impacts and developed innovative tools to measure these "soft" factors and derive forecasts from them. Logemann's chapter not only sheds light on the origins and the history of an important forecasting variable, but also provides a fascinating account of the central importance of transnational knowledge transfers in economics, whose history and place in 20th century economics is astonishingly unexplored up to this date.

In her contribution, "The economist as futurologist. The making and the public reception of the *Perspektivstudien* in Switzerland, 1964–1975," historian Marion Ronca investigates the emergence and the history of the "Perspektivstudien" in the 1960s, which aimed at providing long-term forecasts of the economic development in Switzerland. As a reaction to the opposition of vested interests and its unique form of government, Switzerland had long abstained from economic planning and the development and expansion of a statistical infrastructure. In the 1960s, however, the Swiss government assigned a group of economists headed by the futurologist Francesco Kneschaurek to investigate the long-term development of Switzerland. Ronca argues that the "Perspektivstudien" excluded social and political factors in their outlooks and thus conveyed a new conception of the economy as a separated, ahistorical sphere. As such, the "Perspektivstudien" were contributing to widespread expectations of an infinite post-war prosperity that were, however, heavily shaken during the 1970s.

Timo Walter offers a sociological analysis of the problems of inflation targeting, which is premised on the assumption that future inflation rates can be ensured by shaping economic expectations in the present. In his chapter, "The Janus Face of Inflation Targeting: How Governing Market Expectations of the Future Imprisons Monetary Policy in a Normalized Present," Walter draws on recent interventions in the fields of sociology and anthropology to investigate the conditions on which the success of this future-oriented and expectations-based form of monetary policy depends and the limitations these conditions imply. Walter shows that inflation targeting has become an "expectations game," which is played out entirely within a "present future" (the future as it is imagined and projected from the present) and decoupled from the "future present" as it materializes at a later point in time. Through increasingly sophisticated models for forecasting inflation, central banks can construct a present future in terms of which they can coordinate expectations. This procedure, Walter argues, is problematic as it reduces central bank's control of the future present and thus their power to govern the future.

In his chapter, "Social Interaction, Emotion, and Economic Forecasting," sociologist Werner Reichmann points to the social fabrication of forecasting. Drawing on surveys conducted with forecasters at business cycle research institutes in Germany, Austria and Switzerland since 2004, Reichmann distinguishes two epistemic resources that help economic forecasters to issue forecasts *despite* the radical uncertainty of the future. First, Reichmann shows that forecasters do not work alone, but are entangled in a vast network of other forecasters, business professionals, and politicians who participate in the epistemic process of economic forecasting. Second, Reichmann emphasizes the vital role of emotions in economic forecasting. By developing a "feeling" for numbers and an intuitive understanding of economic trends, forecasters try to overcome the shortcomings of pure reasoning, economics theory, and econometric models. Pointing to these findings, Reichmann forcefully argues that economic forecasting is not merely a technical matter, but also depends on social interaction and the mobilization of emotions.

Oliver Pilmis, too, takes a sociological perspective on forecasting. Contrasting Reichmann's qualitative approach, Pilmis' contribution, "The Dynamics of Expectations: A Sequential Perspective on Macroeconomic Forecasting," exploits a huge database of historical inflation and growth forecasts and investigates the heterogeneity across forecasters by the means of quantitative analysis. Pilmis reaches the conclusion that economic forecasting is mainly data-driven. This means that a fundamental homogeneity of forecasting methods and applied models exists and a certain characteristic of forecasts depending on the forecasting institutions cannot be easily identified. Interestingly, Pilmis reports a tendency for all forecasts under investigation to return to a certain "normal stance" in the medium run with higher and stronger adjustments in the short run.

The chapter by the economists Jörg Döpke, Ulrich Fritsche, and Gabi Waldhof, "Never Change a Losing Horse?: On Adaptations in German Forecasting after the Great Financial Crisis," presents the result of a broad empirical survey investigating how macroeconomic forecasters have reacted to the dire accuracy of forecasts before and in the first phase of the financial crisis. Building on surveys and questionnaires among German forecasters in 2017, they demonstrate that despite occasionally contrary statements, forecasters' behavior has changed surprisingly little since the financial crisis. There is, however, increased awareness of forecast uncertainty. Also, forecasters whose forecasts proved erroneous in the past seem to be more prone to adopt other methods and theories.

References

Abbott, Andrew. 1991. "History and Sociology: The Lost Synthesis." *Social Science History* 15 (2): 201–38. https://doi.org/10.1017/S014555320002109X.

Allsopp, Christopher J., and Martin Bronfenbrenner. 1971. "Is the Business Cycle Obsolete?" *The Economic Journal* 81 (324): 951. https://doi.org/10.2307/2230339.

Anderson, Katharine. 2005. *Predicting the Weather: Victorians and the Science of Meteorology*. Chicago, IL: University of Chicago Press.

Andersson, Jenny. 2012. "The Great Future Debate and the Struggle for the World." *The American Historical Review* 117 (5): 1411–30.

Andersson, Jenny. 2018. *The Future of the World: Futurology, Futurists, and the Struggle for the Post Cold War Imagination*. New York, NY: Oxford University Press.

Arrow, Kenneth J. 1979. "Rational Discourse and Conflicts in Value & Judgment." In *Recent Approaches to the Social Sciences*, edited by H. K. Betz, 3–16. Calgary, Alberta: The University of Calgary.

Beckert, Jens. 2014. "Capitalist Dynamics. Fictional Expectations and the Openness of the Future." MPifG Discussion Paper 14/7, March.

Beckert, Jens. 2016. *Imagined Futures: Fictional Expectations and Capitalist Dynamics*. Cambridge, MA: Harvard University Press.

Beckert, Jens, and Richard Bronk, eds. 2018. *Uncertain Futures: Imaginaries, Narratives, and Calculation in the Economy*. Oxford; New York: Oxford University Press.

Bronfenbrenner, Martin. 1969. *Is the Business Cycle Obsolete?* New York; London: Wiley.

Connelly, Matthew, Matt Fay, Giulia Ferrini, Micki Kaufman, Will Leonard, Harrison Monsky, Ryan Musto, Taunton Paine, Nicholas Standish, and Lydia Walker. 2012. "'General, I Have Fought Just as Many Nuclear Wars as You Have': Forecasts, Future Scenarios, and the Politics of Armageddon." *The American Historical Review* 117 (5): 1431–60.

Dommann, Monika, Daniel Speich Chassé, and Mischa Suter. 2014. "Einleitung: Wissensgeschichte ökonomischer Praktiken." *Berichte zur Wissenschaftsgeschichte* 37 (2): 107–11. https://doi.org/10.1002/bewi.201401683.

Döpke, Jörg, Ulrich Fritsche, and Gabi Waldhof. 2019. "Theories, Techniques and the Formation of German Business Cycle Forecasts." *Jahrbücher Für Nationalökonomie Und Statistik* 239 (2): 203–41. https://doi.org/10.1515/jbnst-2018-0018.

Dupré, Sven, and Geert Somsen. 2019. "The History of Knowledge and the Future of Knowledge Societies." *Berichte Zur Wissenschaftsgeschichte*, August, bewi.201900006. https://doi.org/10.1002/bewi.201900006.

Elliott, Graham, Clive Granger, and Allan Timmermann, eds. 2006. *Handbook of Economic Forecasting*. 1st ed. Vol. 1. Elsevier. https://EconPapers.repec.org/RePEc:eee:ecofor:1.

Elliott, Graham, Clive Granger, and Allan Timmermann, eds. 2013. *Handbook of Economic Forecasting*. 1st ed. Vol. 2. Elsevier. https://EconPapers.repec.org/RePEc:eee:ecofor:2.

Fildes, Robert, and Herman Stekler. 2002. "The State of Macroeconomic Forecasting." *Journal of Macroeconomics* 24 (4): 435–68. https://doi.org/10.1016/S0164-0704(02)00055-1.

Fioramonti, Lorenzo. 2013. *Gross Domestic Problem: The Politics behind the World's Most Powerful Number*. Economic Controversies. London; New York: Zed Books.

Fourcade, Marion. 2009. *Economists and Societies: Discipline and Profession in the United States, Britain, and France, 1890s to 1990s*. Princeton Studies in Cultural Sociology. Princeton, NJ: Princeton University Press.

Friedman, Walter A. 2009. "The Harvard Economic Service and the Problems of Forecasting." *History of Political Economy* 41 (1): 57–88. https://doi.org/10.1215/00182702-2008-037.

Friedman, Walter A. 2014. *Fortune Tellers: The Story of America's First Economic Forecasters*. Princeton, NJ: Princeton University Press.

Gibson, David R. 2011a. "Speaking of the Future: Contentious Narration During the Cuban Missile Crisis." *Qualitative Sociology* 34 (4): 503–22. https://doi.org/10.1007/s11133-011-9206-0.

Gibson, David R.. 2011b. "Avoiding Catastrophe: The Interactional Production of Possibility during the Cuban Missile Crisis." *American Journal of Sociology* 117 (2): 361–419. https://doi.org/10.1086/661761.

Gibson, David R. 2012. *Talk at the Brink: Deliberation and Decision during the Cuban Missile Crisis*. Princeton, NJ: Princeton University Press.

Graff, Peter. 1977. *Die Wirtschaftsprognose. Empirie Und Theorie, Voraussetzungen Und Konsequenzen*. Tübingen: J.C.B. Mohr (Paul Siebeck).

Hartmann, Heinrich, and Jakob Vogel. 2010. "Prognosen: Wissenschaftliche Praxis Im Öffentlichen Raum." In *Zukunftswissen. Prognosen in Wirtschaft, Politik Und Gesellschaft Seit 1900*, edited by Heinrich Hartmann and Jakob Vogel, 7–29. Frankfurt; New York: Campus Verlag.

Heuser, Uwe Jean. 2008. "Kassandras Albtraum." *DIE ZEIT*, December 23, 2008.

Hicks, John R. 1937. "Mr. Keynes and the 'Classics'; A Suggested Interpretation." *Econometrica* 5 (2): 147–59.

Jorion, Paul. 2012. *Misère de La Pensée Économique*. Paris: Fayard.

Juglar, Clément. 1862. *Des Crises Commerciales et de Leur Retour Périodique En France, En Angleterre et Aux États-Unis*. Paris: Guillaumin.

Keynes, John Maynard. (1936) 2013. *The General Theory of Employment, Interest and Money*. Vol. 7. The Collected Writings of John Maynard Keynes. Cambridge: Cambridge University Press.

Koopmans, Tjalling C. 1947. "Measurement Without Theory." *The Review of Economics and Statistics* 29 (3): 161–72.

Koselleck, Reinhart. 2004. *Futures Past: On the Semantics of Historical Time*. New York, NY: Columbia University Press.

Köster, Roman. 2016. "Prognosen." *Merkur. Deutsche Zeitschrift Für Europäisches Denken* 70 (802): 49–54.

Kuczynski, Jürgen. 1970. *Propheten Der Wirtschaft. Studien Zum Problem Der Wirtschaftsprognose Im Kapitalismus*. Berlin: Dietz Verlag.

Lenel, Laetitia. 2018. "Mapping the Future. Business Forecasting and the Dynamics of Capitalism in the Interwar Period." *Jahrbuch Für Wirtschaftsgeschichte/Economic History Yearbook* 59 (2): 377–413.

Lepenies, Philipp. 2016. *The Power of a Single Number: A Political History of GDP*. New York: Columbia University Press.

Luhmann, Niklas. 1980. "Temporalisierung von Komplexität: Zur Semantik Neuzeitlicher Zeitbegriffe." In *Gesellschaftsstruktur Und Semantik. Studien Zur Wissenssoziologie Der Modernen Gesellschaft* 1, 235–300. Frankfurt am Main: Suhrkamp.

Luhmann, Niklas. 1994. *Die Wirtschaft der Gesellschaft*. Frankfurt am Main: Suhrkamp.

Luhmann, Niklas. 1995. *Social Systems*. Stanford, CA: Stanford University Press.

Merton, Robert K. 1948. "The Self-Fulfilling Prophecy." *The Antioch Review* 8 (2): 193. https://doi.org/10.2307/4609267.

Morgan, Jamie. 2013. "Forecasting, Prediction and Precision: A Commentary." In *Ungewissheit Als Herausforderung Für Die Ökonomische Theorie. Nichtwissen, Ambivalenz Und Entscheidung*, edited by Birger P. Priddat and Alihan Kabalak, 281–97. Marburg: Metropolis-Verlag.

Morgan, Mary S. 2012. *The World in the Model: How Economists Work and Think*. Cambridge; New York: Cambridge University Press.

Morgan, Mary S., and Malcolm C. Rutherford. 1998. "American Economics: The Character of the Transformation." In *From Interwar Pluralism to Postwar Neoclassicism*, edited by Mary S. Morgan and Malcolm C. Rutherford, 30, 1–26. Annual Supplement to History of Political Economy. Durham/London: Duke University Press.

Morgenstern, Oskar. 1928. *Wirtschaftsprognose. Eine Untersuchung Ihrer Voraussetzungen Und Möglichkeiten*. Wien: Julius Springer.

Nienhaus, Lisa. 2009. *Die Blindgänger: Warum Die Ökonomen Auch Künftige Krisen Nicht Erkennen Werden*. Frankfurt/Main: Campus.

Nützenadel, Alexander. 2005. *Stunde Der Ökonomen: Wissenschaft, Politik Und Expertenkultur in Der Bundesrepublik 1949–1974*. Kritische Studien Zur Geschichtswissenschaft, Bd. 166. Göttingen: Vandenhoeck & Ruprecht.

Pietruska, Jamie. 2018. *Looking Forward. Prediction and Uncertainty in Modern America*. Chicago/London: The University of Chicago Press.

Pietruska, Jamie L. 2011. "US Weather Bureau Chief Willis Moore and the Reimagination of Uncertainty in Long-Range Forecasting." *Environment and History* 17 (1): 79–105. https://doi.org/10.3197/096734011X12922359172970.

Plitzko, Alfred, ed. 1964. *Planung Ohne Planwirtschaft: Frankfurter Gespräch Der List Gesellschaft, 07.-09. Juni 1963*. Basel: Kyklos-Verlag.

Priddat, Birger P. 2016. *Erwartung, Prognose, Fiktion, Narration: Zur Epistemologie Des Futurs in Der Ökonomie*. Reihe Wirtschaftsphilosophie, Band 4. Marburg: Metropolis-Verlag.

Reichmann, Werner. 2013. "Epistemic Participation: How to Produce Knowledge about the Economic Future." *Social Studies of Science* 43 (6): 852–77. https://doi.org/10.1177/0306312713498641.

Reichmann, Werner. 2018. *Wirtschaftsprognosen: eine Soziologie des Wissens über die ökonomische Zukunft*. Frankfurt New York: Campus Verlag.

Saage, Richard. 1991. *Politische Utopien Der Neuzeit*. Darmstadt: Wissenschaftliche Buchgesellschaft.

Samuelson, Paul A. 1939. "Interactions between the Multiplier Analysis and the Principle of Acceleration." *The Review of Economics and Statistics* 21 (2): 75–78.

Schmelzer, Matthias. 2016. *The Hegemony of Growth: The OECD and the Making of the Economic Growth Paradigm.* Cambridge: Cambridge University Press.

Schumpeter, Joseph A. (1954) 1997. *History of Economic Analysis.* Reprint. London: Routledge.

Sedláček, Tomáš. 2011. *Economics of Good and Evil: The Quest for Economic Meaning from Gilgamesh to Wall Street.* Oxford; New York: Oxford University Press.

Seefried, Elke. 2015. *Zukünfte: Aufstieg Und Krise Der Zukunftsforschung 1945–1980.* Quellen Und Darstellungen Zur Zeitgeschichte, Band 106. Berlin: De Gruyter Oldenbourg.

Siegenthaler, Hansjörg. 1999. "Geschichte Und Ökonomie Nach Der Kulturalistischen Wende." *Geschichte Und Gesellschaft* 25 (2): 276–301.

Speich Chassé, Daniel. 2013. *Die Erfindung des Bruttosozialprodukts: globale Ungleichheit in der Wissensgeschichte der Ökonomie.* Kritische Studien zur Geschichtswissenschaft, Bd. 212. Göttingen: Vandenhock & Ruprecht.

Svetlova, Ekaterina. 2012. "Talking about the Crisis: Performance of Forecasting in Financial Markets." *Culture and Organization* 18 (2): 155–69. https://doi.org/10.1080/14759551.2011.636618.

Vogl, Joseph. 2016. *Das Gespenst des Kapitals.* 7. Auflage. Zurich: Diaphanes.

"What Went Wrong with Economics. And How the Discipline Should Change to Avoid the Mistakes of the Past." 2009. *The Economist*, July. http://www.economist.com/node/14031376.

Zarnowitz, Victor. 1992. *Business Cycles: Theory, History, Indicators, and Forecasting.* A National Bureau of Economic Research Monograph, no. 27. Chicago, IL: University of Chicago Press.

Tara M. Sinclair (George Washington University)

Continuities and Discontinuities in Economic Forecasting[1]

"The cost of a recession is so great that a forecaster should never miss one."

Herman O. Stekler (11/4/1932 - 9/4/2018)[2]

Abstract: Throughout the history of macroeconomic forecasting, several major themes have remained surprisingly consistent. The failure to forecast economic downturns ahead of time is perhaps the most significant of these. Forecasting approaches have changed, but forecasts for recessions have not improved. What can we learn from past evaluations of macroeconomic forecasts? Is it possible to predict major economic shocks or is it a fool's errand? This chapter discusses how forecasting techniques have evolved over time and yet the record on forecasting recessions remains dismal. There are several competing hypotheses for why forecasters fail to foresee recessions, but little evidence any of them are going to be addressed before the next recession occurs. This suggests planners and policymakers should expect to be surprised by the arrival of downturns and develop ways to be prepared for recessions without having clear warning of their coming.

Keywords: Forecast evaluation, recessions

---

1 The author thanks Jacob Jones for excellent research assistance; Fred Joutz, Prakash Loungani, James Morley, Adrian Pagan, and Nigel Ray, for insightful discussions; and participants in the Futures Past: Economic Forecasting in the 20th and 21st Century Conference at the University of Hamburg and the Second Macroeconomic Modelling Workshop at the University of Tasmania for helpful comments. This chapter is dedicated to my colleague, co-author, mentor, and friend, Herman Stekler, whose passion for forecast evaluation was so incredibly contagious. He left a lasting imprint on the profession and is greatly missed.

2 Quote from Joutz, Loungani, and Sinclair (2015).

1. Introduction

One of the key tenets of economic theory is that decisions are forward-looking. Economic forecasts are used in all sorts of planning and in particular are relevant for policymakers who are charged with preventing recessions. Unfortunately the record is not good for forecasting recessions. Ahir and Loungani (2014) and An, Jalles, and Loungani (2018) document that forecasters have a poor record of predicting recessions across countries and for both private and official sectors. Does this poor record reveal that forecasting recessions is a fool's errand? Or are improvements possible? This chapter provides an overview of the historical record of economic forecasting focused on recessions, considers some common explanations of this poor record, and discusses the implications of this record for future planning and policymaking.

2. The Historical Record of Economic Forecasting

Economic forecasts before and through the Great Depression tended to focus on qualitative predictions: would the economy get better or worse? This qualitative nature made them difficult to evaluate until textual analysis approaches were introduced by Goldforb, Stekler, and David (2005) and Mathy and Stekler (2017). According to Hardy and Cox (1927), three common forecasting methods were used: (1) a "cross cut" approach of judgemental comparison and weighting of positive and negative news, (2) modeling the economy as following a regular rhythm, and (3) forecasting by analogy, comparing current events to past events to predict future outcomes. These forecasting approaches led to what Goldfarb, Stekler, and David (2005) called "egregious errors" where forecasters in 1930 predicted 1931 would show a recovery in the U.S. Instead the economy contracted for two more years.

Many new forecasting techniques have been introduced since the Great Depression. They have been predominantly quantitative and have focused on continuous rather than binary or directional forecasts. Two broad camps have evolved over time: (1) theory-based and (2) data-driven. The theory-based approaches started with large-scale macroeconomic models which have since been replaced by Dynamic Stochastic General Equilibrium (DSGE) models. The appeal of theory-based models is that they provide structure and stories to explain the patterns in the forecasts. They can also be used to analyze the impact of different proposed policies on the forecasts. In terms of forecast quality, however, the theory-based models typically cannot out-perform simple benchmarks such as autoregressive models (Chauvet and Potter 2013).

Data-driven approaches have focused on mostly time series econometric models such as autoregressive integrated moving average (ARIMA), vector autoregressive (VAR), and factor models of various kinds. New techniques are being developed now using "Big Data," machine learning, and artificial intelligence. Data-driven approaches, however, cannot consistently beat judgemental forecasts, particularly the average forecast from forecast surveys (Ang, Bekaert, and Wei 2007).

With all the advances in forecasting techniques, it would be reasonable to expect that forecasts would have improved over time. Unfortunately there is little evidence that there has been substantial improvement, particularly if focused on predicting recessions. The Global Financial Crisis of 2007–2008 and the associated Great Recession took economic forecasters by surprise. Culbertson and Sinclair (2014) document how both private sector forecasters and policymakers completely failed to predict the Great Recession in the U.S. And this is not just a U.S. story. In a response to a question from Her Majesty the Queen of England about why everyone missed the Global Financial Crisis, Besley and Hennessy wrote: "the exact form that it would take and the timing of its onset and ferocity were foreseen by nobody" (2009, page 8). Ahir and Loungani (2014) found that around the world, *none* of the 62 recessions in 2008–2009 was predicted by September of the previous year by the consensus of professional forecasters.

For an example of how economic forecasts perform around recessions, Fig. 1 presents a graph of U.S. real Gross Domestic Product (GDP) growth and the median of the four quarter ahead forecasts for US real GDP growth from the Philadelphia Fed's Survey of Professional Forecasters (SPF). Median forecasts from surveys, particularly from the SPF, tend to out-perform other forecasting methods (see Ang, Bekaert, and Wei 2007; similar results are true for Europe using the European Central Bank SPF, see Genre et al. 2013). Fig. 1 shows that the forecasts perform fairly well outside of recessions, but there is little to no anticipation of a downturn a year in advance of recessions.

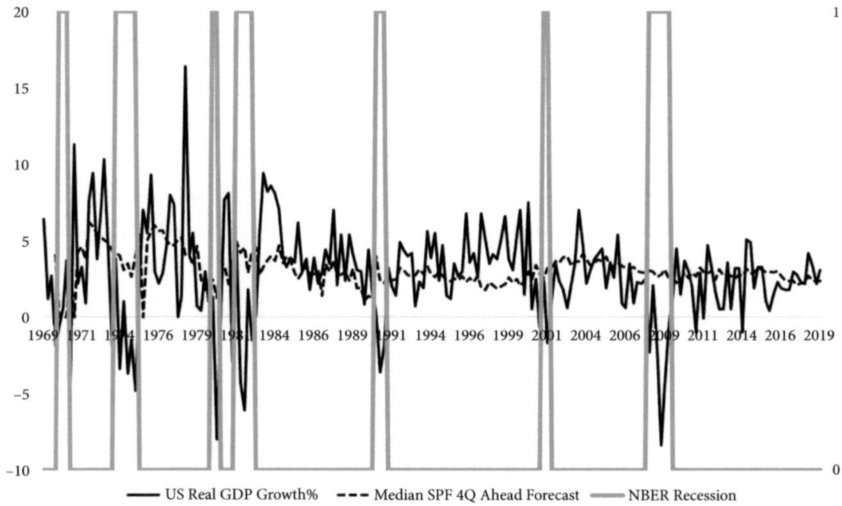

Fig. 1: U.S. Real GDP Growth and 4 Quarter Ahead SPF Forecasts

Perhaps a year ahead is asking too much of forecasters, but it is a relevant horizon for planning and policymaking. Even if we look at forecasts just one quarter ahead, forecasters miss the arrival of the downturn in the next quarter, although once in a recession they do adjust their forecasts downward. They consistently miss the turning point and the depth of recessions, however, even at this short horizon, as can be seen in Fig. 2.

One interpretation of these figures is that forecasters focus on predicting normal times and ignore recessions, at least until the recession has arrived. In their study of 19 advanced economies, Dovern and Jannsen (2017) provide evidence that forecasters produce forecasts that are unbiased conditional on being in an expansion and therefore neglect recessions in their models and forecasts. Fildes and Stekler (2002) similarly conclude that forecasters are better when economic conditions are relatively stable. This might reflect the standard training for economists to fill in the status quo when other information is not available. Forecasting recessions may therefore still be out of reach for our existing models and knowledge. There are however, various potential reasons why forecasters consistently miss recessions, described in the next section.

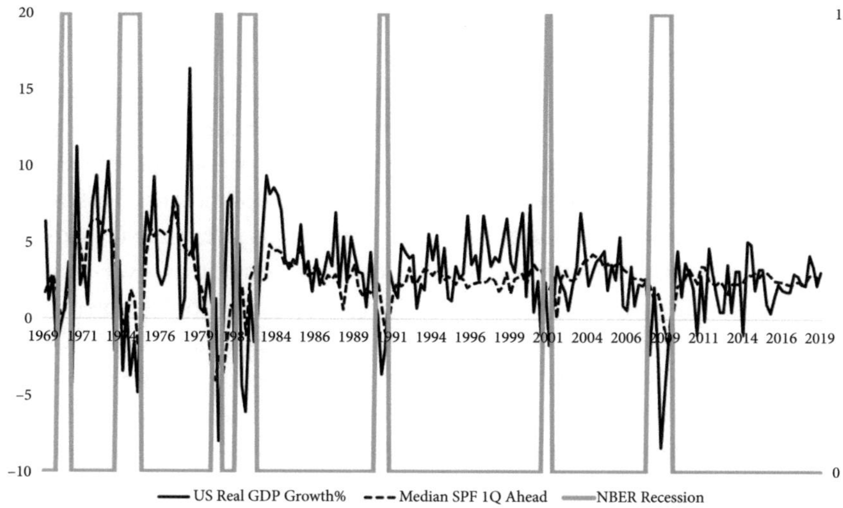

Fig. 2: U.S. Real GDP Growth and 1 Quarter Ahead SPF Forecasts

3. Why Do Forecasters Miss Recessions

A number of different explanations have been put forward as to why forecasters consistently miss recessions. Some suggest we need better models or better/more timely data sources. Others suggest that falsely predicting a recession when one does not occur is much worse than missing a recession entirely, which explains why forecasters are conservative in forecasting recessions. Still others suggest that by their very nature recessions are inherently unpredictable.

In a sense these explanations range from optimistic to completely pessimistic. The solution in the case of poor models, methods, or data is to invest further in these directions. The new methods and data sources coming from the Big Data revolution may help us to forecast future recessions. Historical experience, however, tempers this optimism since there have been substantial improvements in these directions to date without noticeable improvement in forecasting recessions.

Despite the under-prediction of recessions, it is still a common joke that forecasters over-predict recessions, which suggests economists are very sensitive to over-prediction. For example, Paul Samuelson said in

1966 that the stock market predicted nine of the past five recessions.[3] This might mean that forecasters could predict recessions, but they do not have the right incentives to do so. If it is an issue of forecaster reputation, where predicting a recession when one does not occur is more costly than missing one entirely, then we might see forecasters only slowly respond to new information, particularly around downturns. This might look like forecasters are smoothing their predictions over time (Nordhaus 1987). But recent research suggests forecasters sometimes over-respond to new information, not always smoothing (e.g. Azeredo da Silveira and Woodford 2019; Bordalo et al. 2018; Messina, Sinclair, and Stekler 2015; Dovern and Weisser 2011). Similarly we might expect forecasters to herd, i.e. to produce forecasts similar to their peers, to protect their reputation. Rülke, Silgoner, and Wörz (2016), however, find evidence of anti-herding across an international set of business cycle forecasters, particularly in times of increased uncertainty. These findings suggest that even if we could find a way to change forecaster incentives around predicting recessions, that may not improve their record on forecasting recessions.

Thus we are left with the most dismal explanation, that recessions may be caused by purely random shocks, which by their nature are impossible to forecast (e.g. Drautzburg 2019). Consistent with this explanation, we see forecasters adjust their models after a downturn so that they would have better predicted the past, but do no better at predicting the future. This was particularly obvious after the Global Financial Crisis where forecasters added financial and housing sectors into their models so they would have been able to forecast the Great Recession with those models. Only time will tell if these improvements help predict the next recession.

To give a sense of the challenge facing forecasters, Fig. 3 provides an example using 3-month decline in the industrial production index. This

---

3 Samuelson, Paul (September 19, 1966), "Science and Stocks," *Newsweek*, p. 92. Herman Stekler proudly claimed to have "predicted n + x of the last n recessions" (recorded by Joutz, 2010, in an interview of Stekler for the *International Journal of Forecasting*), but he saw this as in contrast to the profession that typically missed recessions completely. If policymakers were predicting and preventing some recessions then we would see a poor forecasting record coming from predicting more recessions than occur, but unfortunately the record is too few recessions forecasted by policymakers rather than too many.

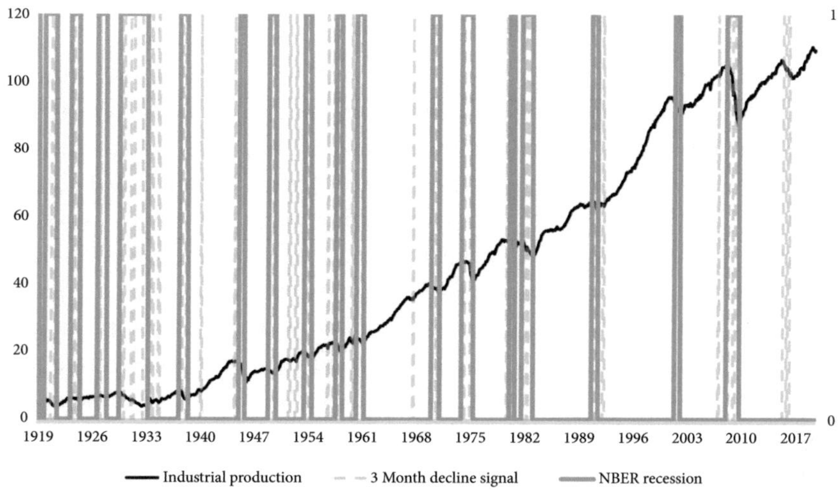

Fig. 3: Industrial Production Index and Recession Signal

was a leading indicator originally proposed in the 1950s (Alexander and Stekler 1959; Stekler 1972).[4] Every US recession identified by the NBER[5] is signaled by this indicator in some way, but there are both false signals of recession and false indications of expansions. Perhaps the most disconcerting is that we miss the start of many recessions, not by much, typically just one to two months, but it suggests that we cannot breathe easy even when this indicator is in positive territory. Indicators are often maligned for falsely predicting recessions, but we might be willing to take some false signals if we consistently had an accurate prediction of the timing of recessions. Unfortunately no model, forecaster, or indicator has yet achieved that standard.

4 Board of Governors of the Federal Reserve System (US), Industrial Production Index [INDPRO], retrieved from FRED, Federal Reserve Bank of St. Louis; https://fred.stlouisfed.org/series/INDPRO, June 23, 2019. Note that because this series is revised, it is important to evaluate it in real time (Stark and Croushore 2002). This simple example, however, uses the latest available data.

5 https://www.nber.org/cycles/

4. Nowcasting Recessions

The record for identifying a recession once it's occurring (nowcasting) is much better than predicting one even one quarter ahead. There is evidence that policymakers such as the Federal Reserve are able to identify recessions once they are in progress (Sinclair, Joutz, Stekler 2010). Giusto and Piger (2017) have shown that several approaches identify recessions in real time. These approaches provide faster identification of recessions than waiting for the NBER business cycle dating committee to provide official classification of the turning point, but for monetary policy with its long and variable lags, knowing a recession is occurring only in real time may be too late. There are however, other policies that might work in a world where we can only nowcast recessions.

For example, recently there has been much attention directed to the "Sahm rule" based on Claudia Sahm's proposal (Sahm 2019) to use a 3-month moving average of the unemployment rate as a trigger for automatic stimulus payments. Sahm argues that an increase of 0.50 percentage points or more, relative to the unemployment rate's low in the prior 12 months (in order to allow for changes in the natural rate of unemployment), has historically only occurred during or closely after recessions in the US. Thus this rule does not predict recessions, but it is a simple and useful one to trigger automatic fiscal stimulus. This sort of policy approach can quickly react to a recession as it is occuring to offset some of its impact even if we cannot predict recessions in advance.

5. Conclusion

The failure of forecasters to predict past recessions does not necessarily imply we will never be able to forecast recessions. It is possible that with further development of techniques and insights into the structure of the economy along with new and more timely data sources our forecasts will improve. But it is important for the public and policymakers to understand the current state of forecasting and not rely on predictions to prepare for downturns.

Despite advances in forecasting techniques, computational power, as well as data quality and quantity, forecasters continue to systematically miss recessions. Harding and Pagan (2016) advise that we should know the limits of forecasting and focus research instead on better understanding the business cycle rather than trying to predict it We may need to accept that nowcasting recessions is the best we can do and build policy plans with that information in mind. As we continue to develop new models and methods, deepen our understanding of the structure of the economy, and build the quantity and timeliness of data sources, we need to continue to heed Stekler's (2007) advice for evaluating forecasters and remember that forecasters are responding to their own set of incentives that affect their judgement as well as the models they choose.

References

Ahir, Hites, and Prakash Loungani. 2014. " 'There Will Be Growth in the Spring': How Well Do Economists Predict Turning Points?" VoxEU. Org. April 14. https://voxeu.org/article/predicting-economic-turning-points (last access: 8/5/2019).

Alexander, Sidney S., and Herman O. Stekler. 1959. "Forecasting Industrial Production--Leading Series versus Autoregression." *Journal of Political Economy* 67 (4): 402–9. doi:10.1086/258200.

An, Zidong, João Tovar Jalles, and Prakash Loungani. 2018. "How Well Do Economists Forecast Recessions?" *International Finance* 21 (2): 100–21. doi:10.1111/infi.12130.

Ang, Andrew, Geert Bekaert, and Min Wei. 2007. "Do Macro Variables, Asset Markets, or Surveys Forecast Inflation Better?" *Journal of Monetary Economics* 54 (4): 1163–212. doi:10.1016/j.jmoneco.2006.04.006.

Azeredo da Silveira, Rava, and Michael Woodford. 2019. "Noisy Memory and Over-Reaction to News." *AEA Papers and Proceedings* 109 (May): 557–61. doi:10.1257/pandp.20191049.

Besley, Tim, and Peter Hennessy. 2009. "The Global Financial Crisis – Why Didn't Anybody Notice?" *British Academy Review* 14: 8–10.

Bordalo, Pedro, Nicola Gennaioli, Yueran Ma, and Andrei Shleifer. 2018. "Over-Reaction in Macroeconomic Expectations." Working Paper 24932. National Bureau of Economic Research. doi:10.3386/w24932.

Chauvet, Marcelle, and Simon Potter. 2013. "Forecasting Output." In *Handbook of Economic Forecasting*, Vol. 2, edited by Graham

Elliott and Allan Timmermann, 141–94. Elsevier. doi:10.1016/B978-0-444-53683-9.00003-7.

Culbertson, Daniel S., and Tara M. Sinclair. 2014. "The Failure of Forecasts in the Great Recession." *Challenge* 57 (6): 34–45. doi:10.2753/0577-5132570603.

Dovern, Jonas, and Johannes Weisser. 2011. "Accuracy, Unbiasedness and Efficiency of Professional Macroeconomic Forecasts: An Empirical Comparison for the G7." *International Journal of Forecasting* 27 (2): 452–65. doi:10.1016/j.ijforecast.2010.05.016.

Dovern, Jonas, and Nils Jannsen. 2017. "Systematic Errors in Growth Expectations over the Business Cycle." *International Journal of Forecasting* 33 (4): 760–69. doi:10.1016/j.ijforecast.2017.03.003.

Drautzburg, Thorsten. 2019. "Why Are Recessions So Hard to Predict? Random Shocks and Business Cycles." *Economic Insights* 4 (1): 1–8.

Fildes, Robert, and Herman Stekler. 2002. "The State of Macroeconomic Forecasting." *Journal of Macroeconomics* 24 (4): 435–68. doi:10.1016/S0164-0704(02)00055-1.

Genre, Véronique, Geoff Kenny, Aidan Meyler, and Allan Timmermann. 2013. "Combining Expert Forecasts: Can Anything Beat the Simple Average?" *International Journal of Forecasting* 29 (1): 108–21. doi:10.1016/j.ijforecast.2012.06.004.

Giusto, Andrea, and Jeremy Piger. 2017. "Identifying Business Cycle Turning Points in Real Time with Vector Quantization." *International Journal of Forecasting* 33 (1): 174–84. doi:10.1016/j.ijforecast.2016.04.006.

Goldfarb, Robert S., Herman O. Stekler, and Joel David. 2005. "Methodological Issues in Forecasting: Insights from the Egregious Business Forecast Errors of Late 1930." *Journal of Economic Methodology* 12 (4): 517–42. doi:10.1080/13501780500343524.

Harding, Don, and Adrian Pagan. 2016. *The Econometric Analysis of Recurrent Events in Macroeconomics and Finance*. Princeton University Press. https://muse.jhu.edu/chapter/1984459 (last access: 8/5/2019).

Hardy, Charles O., and Garfield V. Cox. 1927. *Forecasting Business Conditions*. New York: MacMillan.

Joutz, Frederick L. 2010. "Interview with Herman O. Stekler." *International Journal of Forecasting, Special Section: European*

Election Forecasting 26 (1): 195–203. doi:10.1016/j.ijforecast.2009.12.001.

Joutz, Fred, Prakash Loungani, and Tara Sinclair. 2015. "Honoring Herman: A Special Section for Stekler." *International Journal of Forecasting* 31 (1): 93–95. doi:10.1016/j.ijforecast.2014.11.001.

Mathy, Gabriel, and Herman Stekler. 2017. "Expectations and Forecasting during the Great Depression: Real-Time Evidence from the Business Press." *Journal of Macroeconomics* 53 (September): 1–15. doi:10.1016/j.jmacro.2017.05.006.

Messina, Jeffrey D., Tara M. Sinclair, and Herman Stekler. 2015. "What Can We Learn from Revisions to the Greenbook Forecasts?" *Journal of Macroeconomics* 45 (September): 54–62. doi:10.1016/j.jmacro.2015.04.002.

Nordhaus, William D. 1987. "Forecasting Efficiency: Concepts and Applications." *The Review of Economics and Statistics* 69 (4): 667–74. doi:10.2307/1935962.

Rülke, Jan-Christoph, Maria Silgoner, and Julia Wörz. 2016. "Herding Behavior of Business Cycle Forecasters." *International Journal of Forecasting* 32 (1): 23–33. doi:10.1016/j.ijforecast.2015.02.004.

Sahm, Claudia. 2019. "Direct Stimulus Payments to Individuals." *Brookings*. May 16. https://www.brookings.edu/research/direct-stimulus-payments-to-individuals/ (last access: 8/5/2019).

Sinclair, Tara M., Fred Joutz, and Herman O. Stekler. 2010. "Can the Fed Predict the State of the Economy?" *Economics Letters* 108 (1): 28–32. doi:10.1016/j.econlet.2010.04.010.

Stark, Tom, and Dean Croushore. 2002. "Forecasting with a Real-Time Data Set for Macroeconomists." *Journal of Macroeconomics* 24 (4): 507–31. doi:10.1016/S0164-0704(02)00062-9.

Stekler, Herman O. 1972. "An Analysis of Turning Point Forecasts." *American Economic Review* 62 (4): 724–29.

Stekler, Herman O. 2007. "The Future of Macroeconomic Forecasting: Understanding the Forecasting Process." *International Journal of Forecasting* 23 (2): 237–48. doi:10.1016/j.ijforecast.2007.01.002.

Jan Logemann (University of Göttingen)

Measuring and Managing Expectations: Consumer Confidence as an Economic Indicator, 1920s–1970s

Abstract: This chapter explores the origins of consumer confidence measurements as a prognostic tool. Commercial consumer studies had gained in importance since the interwar decades as a "scientific" means of predicting market developments for corporations and advertisers. In the years surrounding World War II, government economists became equally interested in forecasting consumer behavior. Such forecasts required a new understanding of consumers, their attitudes and expectations, and of the role that psychological factors play in economic behavior. The chapter focuses on George Katona and several other European émigré scholars in this field to highlight the importance of transnational knowledge transfers. Finally, it considers consumer research as a means of economic forecasting in the context of attempts to socially engineer mass consumption and to "manage" consumer expectations on both sides of the Atlantic during the middle of the twentieth century.

Keywords: Consumer confidence, consumer research, George Katona, émigré scholars, behavioral economics, economic psychology

1. Introduction

Beginning in the 1950s, consumer confidence measurements became a critical indicator of economic development in the United States.[1] In America's "consumer's republic" (L. Cohen), economists and marketing experts identified "the consumer" as a crucial link between shifting cultural attitudes and social expectations on the one hand and market developments on the other (Cohen 2003). Accordingly, the study of consumer expectations and decision-making became a focal point of new research in behavioral economics and economic psychology. Since World War II, large-scale surveys kept track of consumer outlook regarding individual finances and overall

---

1 This chapter draws on my upcoming monograph *Engineered to Sell: European Émigrés and the Making of Consumer Capitalism* (Logemann 2019).

economic development. Their responses were now compiled into indices of consumer confidence that since have become a staple of popular economic analysis as well. While economists debate the prognostic value of consumer confidence measurements, newscasts today are full of reports about swings in consumer confidence, especially in times of crisis.[2]

This chapter, however, is less concerned with the accuracy of consumer attitude measures for predicting the movements of business cycles or consumer spending. Instead, I will ask about the historical contexts in which consumer attitude measurements emerged as a predictive tool. Why and in what ways do the middle decades of the twentieth century represent a point of transition for the history of economic forecasting? A growing interest in market studies among marketing specialists had contributed to the rise of consumer surveys already since the interwar years. They drew on early, psychologically-informed research on consumer behavior, which transformed prevailing assumptions about the expectations and decision-making of consumers and economic actors more generally. In the context World War II and postwar affluence, research in consumer psychology further complicated such notions of consumer decision-making and expanded the set of variables deemed relevant in this process. In a sense, these consumer researchers presaged a shift from focusing on adaptive and rational expectations to predict economic behavior to psychologically and socially framed "fictional expectations" that informed consumer behavior (Jakob, Nützenadel and Streb 2018).

Focusing on the life and career of George Katona, the economist responsible for the original consumer sentiment index, the chapter highlights the transnational origins of consumer confidence measurements and of early consumer research more broadly. Katona, an émigré who came to America fleeing the Nazi regime in 1933, was part of a larger group of other émigrés who brought insights of continental European social and Gestalt psychology into mid-century U.S. debates about marketing and economic behavior. Katona theorized about the interplay of experiences

2 In January of 2009 the Conference Board Consumer Confidence Index fell to its lowest level since 1967 which was widely reported as a sign of additional future woes: (Clifford 2009). For a critical assessment of the predictive value see Croushore (2004).

and expectations of economic actors, drawing on psychological research to critique and supplement rational actor models of consumer behavior. Understanding and forecasting consumer behavior was a complex matter, Katona argued, involving close attention to socio-psychological dynamics.

More fundamentally, the chapter finally raises the question in what ways economic forecasting has been employed as a means of managing the expectations of consumers as economic actors and influencing their attitudes and behavior.[3] Indicators such as Katona's Index of Consumer Sentiment were intimately tied to corporate and government attempts at shaping and engineering mass consumption. Consumer research not only became a marketing tool for companies, but also a means to predict macroeconomic development used by government experts and academics. Economists such as Katona saw their work as part of larger social efforts to spur economic development and ultimately stabilize consumer capitalism. Katona was an outspoken champion of consumer-driven growth and he believed that "framing" consumer expectations was a crucial aspect of managing aggregate consumer buying and demand as well as inflation (Horowitz 1998). In bringing consumer forecasting "back" to Germany and Western Europe during the postwar decades, Katona was not simply interested in transferring economic knowledge. Instead, he believed, such indicators presented a way of fostering a collective mindset adjusted to a dawning age of affluence in which European consumers, too, would embrace consumer capitalism during the Cold War.

2. A Tool for "Scientific Marketing": Interwar Consumer Research and Psychological Transfers

The growing use of market research and consumer surveys during the interwar years constituted one important context for the emergence of consumer surveys as a prognostic tool. Early, sporadic efforts by producers, retailers and advertisers to track and survey their customers in order to improve sales and distribution date back well into the nineteenth century (Schwarzkopf 2016). After World War I, American marketing experts were actively searching for new methodological input from the academic

3 On the management of expectations in economic systems see Beckert (2013).

world and calls for "Scientific Marketing" in analogy to "Scientific Management" built on work by scholars such as Walter Dill Scott and Arch W. Shaw (Kreshel 1993; Usui 2008, Ch. 3; Ward 2009). Advertising agencies were among the first to apply new academic concepts to practical marketing research. J. Walter Thompson (JWT) emerged as the prototypical full-service agency with a "scientific" approach to advertising as they proclaimed to their clients in 1928: "Advertising must be scientifically prepared. Nothing must be taken for granted" (Kreshel 1993, 66). Predicting markets to plan marketing campaigns became increasingly important for advertisers.

At the same time, specialized market research firms began to offer market analyses to forecast consumer behavior. The A.C. Nielsen Company (est. 1923) compiled consumer demand projections based on household studies that asked consumer panels about what they stocked in their pantries. Studies in media use for marketing purposes had been pioneered by the Curtis Publishing Company (*Saturday Evening Post*, *Ladies Home Journal*), which set early standards for consumer reception research (Root and Welsh 1942; Lockley 1950; Kreshel 1993). Institutions specialized in public opinion surveys such as the firms of Archibald Crossley (est. 1926), Elmo Roper (est. 1937) and the American Institute of Public Opinion, founded in 1935 by George Gallup in cooperation with advertising executive David Ogilvy, also conducted commercial consumer research. The Market Research Corporation of America (est. 1934) likely had the largest contingent of interviewers across the United States, conducting elaborate surveys and publishing the trade journal *Market Research* (Jones and Tadajewski 2011). By the 1930s, consumer research had become part of the American marketing landscape and its significance would only grow in the wake of the Great Depression.

Interwar consumer research, however, was confined to advertising agencies and large corporations and was not particularly sophisticated in its methodology. This changed over the course of the 1930s and 1940s. Corporate marketing specialists increasingly engaged in what they termed "merchandising": they planned products based on customer expectation and demand (Usui 2008, Ch. 4). Marketing experts envisioned a "new consumption era" in which the distribution of goods would be transformed by insights from the social sciences and earlier, "spasmodic" efforts in salesmanship would give way to "more definitively and scientifically planned campaigns for the consumption of goods" (Hess 1935, 16). As forecasting increasingly became a business, claims to scientific expertise opened doors in the corporate world. The new *Journal of Marketing* closely tracked ongoing academic consumer research across universities in the United States, emphasizing the connection of commercial practitioners to academic investigation (Taylor 1936). As marketing professor Edmund McGarry observed, scientific credentials created high expectations among businessmen: "[business men] are prone to look upon a scientific expert as one who has remarkable and mysterious powers of foresight [...]. He must be a prophet who can foretell, where profits are to come from. He is expected to know the unknown, to foresee the unforeseeable" (McGarry 1936, 83).

Traditional, mechanistic models of economic forecasting, however, did not fare particularly well during the years of interwar market crisis, as historian Laetitia Lenel has recently noted (Lenel 2018). Increasingly, companies became interested in empirical consumer research, which took psychological factors into account. Historians have demonstrated the growing influence of psychology on advertising research and the linkages between consumer studies and the emergence of empirical social science research (Igo 2007; Samuel 2010). Already in the 1920s, J. Walter Thompson had employed prominent behaviorist psychologist John Watson to systematically study consumer responses to advertising. His stimulus-response research explored the possibility of not just forecasting, but of conditioning consumers to react to advertising stimuli (Benjamin 2004). Similarly, the Psychological Corporation had been established in 1921 by psychologist James Cattell.[4] Its "psychological sales barometer" drew on the expertise of 60 academic psychologists to survey changing customer preferences regarding various brands in an effort to systematically predict consumer behavior (Link and Lorge 1935). In this context, several émigré psychologists such as Paul Lazarsfeld, Ernest Dichter and George Katona from Vienna, Berlin and elsewhere in Europe were able to bring

4 Cattell had been a student of German psychologist Wilhelm Wundt at Leipzig. On consumer research before and during the Great Depression see Igo (2007) and Robinson (1999, 15–18 and 39–63).

new insights from European individual, social and Gestalt psychology to American consumer research.[5]

The émigrés contributed to a transnational exchange between academic and commercial research, which allowed them to shape American consumer psychology (Kasserdjan 1994). They helped push the field beyond behaviorist assumptions of stimulus and response mechanisms, which largely left actual decision-making processes as a "black box." Much like theoretical economists, the psychological behaviorists had subscribed to a theory of "adaptive expectations," which assumed a linear connection between past experiences (stimuli) and expected behavior (response). Building on insights from the émigrés, this notion was increasingly made more complicated in three ways:

1. Depth psychology: systematic research into (conscious and subconscious) motives by Lazarsfeld and others increasingly opened up the "black box" of decision-making processes.
2. Social psychology: the social context in which stimuli were processed and endowed with meaning received more scrutiny e.g. through the work of émigré psychologist Kurt Lewin.
3. Cognitive (Gestalt) psychology: The research of émigrés such as Kurt Koffka, Wolfgang Köhler and Max Wertheimer directed attention towards cognitive processes and the perceptions and misperceptions of stimuli as they informed decision-making processes (Logemann 2017).

Consumer expectations (and, by extension, their decisions and future behavior), these psychologists argued, could not be understood as a simple function of past experiences or of present conditions such as income. Instead, the way consumers made choices regarding the future was informed by a complex interplay of conscious and subconscious motives, of the social dynamics in which information was received and decisions processes took place and, last but not least, of the cognitive processes which (mis)guided human perception. Taken together, these three strands of psychology influenced by émigré scholars informed the way American consumer research began to reevaluate the connection between experiences

5 On interwar market research in Vienna see Fullerton (1990) and Fullerton (2013).

and expectation in consumer behavior. When the American Marketing Society published its first handbook on *The Technique of Marketing Research* in 1937, for example, Viennese émigré Paul Lazarsfeld contributed several chapters (Wheeler 1937). Beyond the field of marketing, too, the academic input of European émigrés contributed to the transformation of prevailing perceptions of consumers and to the study of their motivations, attitudes and social dynamics, which could help understand and predict consumer behavior.

3. Consumer Expectations and Decision-Making: George Katona and Wartime Attitude Research

During World War II, state actors and economists similarly developed an interest in surveying and predicting consumer behavior. Their wartime studies provide another important context for the emergence of consumer forecasting, and émigré psychologist George Katona came to play a prominent role in efforts to predict and control home front consumption. Along with Kurt Lewin, Katona was instrumental in transforming ideas regarding the social psychology of consumption. He focused on the formation and impact of consumer attitudes on inflation and macroeconomic development. Both Katona and Lewin came from within the larger orbit of the Berlin Institute for Experimental Psychology where Max Wertheimer and Kurt Koffka had been leading protagonists of Gestalt psychology before fleeing to the United States during the 1930s (Mandler 1969). Katona applied their research to problems of the psychology of mass consumption during the war, contributing to the U.S. government's fight against inflation.

An early exponent of behavioral economics, George Katona's work challenged prevailing assumptions of consumers as "rational actors" by highlighting the role of psychological attitudes in economic decision-making. His career was both transatlantic and genuinely interdisciplinary, moving between the fields of psychology and economics. He was born in Budapest in 1901 where he enrolled in the University in 1918, but moved to Germany not even a year later after the revolutionary government of Bela Kun had come to power. Katona earned his doctorate in psychology at Göttingen University, developing an interest in sensory perception and the work of the Gestalt school (Katona 1924). He subsequently moved to Frankfurt where he continued his research in experimental psychology, but also worked for a commercial bank at a time of severe economic strain in Germany. The experience of the 1923 hyperinflation was formative for Katona's pursuit of economic psychology, because it led him to explore what he saw as an intimate connection between economic developments and the collective psychology of economic actors. In Berlin, where he had moved in 1926, Katona continued to pursue his dual-track career in psychology and economics: he remained an experimental psychologist studying and working with Max Wertheimer and Kurt Lewin, but also developed a second career as a financial journalist for Gustav Stolper's *Der Deutsche Volkswirt*. Long before his emigration, Katona had thus begun to think about the relationship between social psychology and economic behavior.[6]

During the war, properly forecasting inflation presented a challenge to U.S. economists and Katona brought Gestalt psychology into the field of economics to address this problem. He had emigrated to the United States following the Nazi seizure of power in 1933. Struggling to establish himself in American academia, Katona and Stolper initially joined a New York investment office, which advised European investors on the U.S. market. Through fellowships and a lecturer position at the New School's "University in Exile," Katona also stayed in close contact with Max Wertheimer while working on the psychology of learning from a Gestalt perspective (Katona 1940). With the advent of the war Katona returned to the interplay of psychology and economics. Émigré economist Jacob Marschak invited him to Chicago where Katona conducted surveys for the Committee on Price Control and Rationing as part of the so-called Cowles Commission. Here, he used detailed interviews with opened-ended questions to probe business and retailer reactions to price controls and inflation (Katona 1945).

In 1942, Katona published *War without Inflation*, a book-length essay, which argued for the importance of utilizing psychological insights to address problems of the war economy (Katona 1942). Drawing on his prior

6 On Katona's life and career see Horowitz (1998), Curtin (1984), Freie Universität (1982), and Strumpel et al. (1972).

economic work in Germany as well as on more recent work in the psychology of learning he argued for the potential of managing consumer expectations through "social framing" as discussed by Kurt Lewin. In his social psychological experiments conducted in exile in Iowa, Lewin had demonstrated that perceptions of and reactions to various stimuli depended on the "social field" and on the "frame of reference" in which they were received. The impact and meaning given to a message directed at consumers, for example, thus varied according to the social and cultural context in which it was embedded. Its effect depended on the way the message was framed and on the means by which it was communicated (e.g. Lewin 1943a). Katona's study now claimed that it was possible to avoid inflation, if the necessity of economic measures was properly conveyed to the public, which would adapt its economic expectations and consumer behavior to match wartime conditions. Favorably received by American economists and marketing experts for its methodological innovations, the book spoke to an overarching interest in shaping consumer behavior to meet wartime needs (Katona 1942).

Wartime studies directed at the consuming public and home-front propaganda efforts still count among the largest attempts in mass persuasion in American history.[7] Between 1942 and 1945, the U.S. government spent over $200 million on propaganda activities at home and abroad (Glander 2000). State agencies became involved in surveying consumer behavior and molding consumer opinions and expectations. As hundreds of social-scientists moved to Washington, D.C., the number of researchers employed by the federal government almost doubled during the first six months of the war and included leading communications scholars such as Harold Laswell, Hadley Cantril, and Samuel Stouffer. Commissioned and coordinated especially by the Office of War Information (OWI), survey research reached new qualitative and quantitative dimensions (Converse 1987; Sudman and Bradburn 1987).

In the context of the war, many were eager to employ consumer psychology in social engineering efforts. Public relations experts, however, grew increasingly skeptical towards simplistic assumptions about the

---

7 On the home front experience in comparative perspective see Berghoff, Logemann and Römer (2017).

impact of propaganda on malleable "masses." Instead, consumers came to be seen as part of diverse and socially contextualized groups, which were not as easily swayed by mass media messages. As in market research, communications scholars increasingly understood consumer behavior and attitudes as complex phenomena. Forecasting audience behavior thus required more sophisticated models that incorporated an understanding of changing attitudes, expectations, and social dynamics. This, too, was part of broader transatlantic exchanges in the social sciences as Viennese émigrés around Paul Lazarsfeld not only offered new survey methodologies to probe motivations. They also contributed to a new understanding of communication flows to consumers, which emphasized the "limited effects" of mass media messages and their social mediation through "opinion leaders" (Lazarsfeld and Katz 1955; Fleck 2011). Lazarsfeld's wartime research research helped him develop these very insights. He served as a consultant to the Research Branch of the U.S. Army's Division of Morale as well as to the OWI's Bureau of Intelligence (and to its predecessor, the Office of Facts and Figures (OFF)). As a group, wartime social researchers advised on survey studies and on forecasting and manipulating civilian morale (Converse 1987, 162–65).

Consumer attitudes and expectations presented a central object of this research on home front morale and behavior (on attitude research: Jahoda and Warren 1966). Katona's studies on inflation dovetailed nicely with the survey work of Paul Lazarsfeld and other scholars studying the U.S. war economy. With its emphasis on "framing" public opinion to influence inflation, *War Without Inflation* immediately caught the attention of Lazarsfeld. Katona's suggestions about survey methodology with regard to attitudes and expectations, he observed in a 1942 memo to OFF staff, "go beyond the things we thought of ourselves" (Lazarsfeld 1942). A couple of years later, Katona, too, moved to Washington to join the Bureau of Agricultural Economics' (BAE) Program Surveys Division, directed by the social psychologists Rensis Likert, which conducted research on consumer attitudes towards household spending and saving and towards food consumption, two core concerns to home-front management efforts.

Predicting consumer behavior became one aim of government survey work that interlinked with broader development in consumer research. Research on the Treasury Department's war bond sales conducted by

Lazarsfeld's Bureau of Applied Social Research at Columbia University, for example, was later used as a model for forecasting buying behavior more generally (Garon 2011, 204–10). Rensis Likert, who had received his Ph.D. in psychology from Columbia University in 1932 for a study on attitude measurements, also came to the BAE with experience in commercial market research (Likert 1932). During the 1930s, he (like Lazarsfeld) had been affiliated with the Psychological Corporation. Indeed, Likert was well acquainted with Lazarsfeld and much of his approach to detailed interviews and open-ended survey questions was developed in exchange with Vienna émigrés (Lazarsfeld 1961). As Likert moved to the BAE in 1939, he pushed for an expansive survey program that soon went beyond strictly agricultural questions. By 1942, his agency conducted thirty-seven "special" studies on a variety of other wartime issues for agencies ranging from the OWI and the Treasury Department, to the War Productions Board and the Office of Price Administration (Likert 1942). Survey topics ranged from "Attitudes toward Buying and Shortages of Consumer Goods" (Program Survey Division 1943) to "What Housewives Eat for Breakfast" (Program Survey Division 1944). Their studies sought to understand the American consumer's views on rationing and shortages, they asked about future buying plans and about assessments of the current situation.

The BAE studies emphasized the importance of attitudes and expectations and the necessity of "understanding" consumer perspectives towards "sacrifice." George Katona initially worked on BAE surveys of the use of wartime incomes, which were conducted at request of the Board of Governors of the Federal Reserve (Campbell and Katona 1946). The household surveys sought to capture both economic and psychological data with a mix of quantitative (statistical area sampling) and qualitative (open interviewing) approaches. Katona's surveys asked how savings habits were acquired and how future spending behavior could be predicted. He emphasized the importance of segmenting consumers, for example, by paying special attention to affluent households. Their attitudes towards saving and spending not only differed from the rest of the population, Katona argued, but they had the most significant impact on the sale of war bonds and on overall domestic economic development during the war (Katona and Likert 1946).

Understanding consumer attitudes could help to predict as well as to shape consumer behavior. Building on the surveys he had conducted in Chicago and at the BAE, Katona theorized about the importance of studying attitudes and expectations for economic policy formation. In contrast to stimulus-response models of mass communication, Katona proposed to involve audiences and consumers in an active learning process. Citing Gestalt psychologists Wertheimer and Koffka, Katona employed their insights on cognitive processes along with Lewin's concept of social frames of reference to understand the formation of consumer expectations and attitudes: "All experience is organized within a framework. A stimulus does not give rise to an isolated experience; the meaning of the stimulus changes according to the greater whole of which it is part" (Katona 1944, 342). Consumer expectations thus crucially depended on the social and cultural contexts in which they arose. What consequences a stimulus (such as e.g. a change in prices or income) would have for consumer actions could differ depending on the circumstances and the way such a stimulus was framed.

For (wartime) consumer research to impact aggregate behavior, Katona believed, the task was to make people think in "appropriate frames," bringing about a genuine understanding of "changed field conditions." Such an "appropriate frame" of reference could be that of a war economy with shortages and a threat of inflation, requiring consumers to limit their spending and to save. In a postwar economy by contrast, Katona believed consumers would need to learn continuous spending to ensure sustained growth: "The task of the teacher and the molder of public opinion is, then, to help the public to gain a general orientation for war and for post-war conditions" (Katona 1944, 346). Katona thus proposed to use the insights of psychology to socially engineer consumer behavior on a macroeconomic level. The analytical and prognostic tools he developed in the context of the war economy would come to full fruition during the era of postwar affluence.

4. Framing the Affluent Society: Consumer Sentiment Surveys as Behavioral Economics

In the context of the postwar consumer society, predicting consumer behavior was first and foremost a tool for increasing sales. Corporate efforts in market and consumer research expanded, building in part on wartime studies. Paul Lazarsfeld stressed the insights of wartime research in a 1952 speech before the American Marketing Association. People were affected by mass media differently depending on the personal environment in which they found themselves, he noted, and they received the content of mass media messages not directly, but rather secondhand through so-called "opinion brokers." Directors of advertising, he warned, were "not sufficiently aware of how greatly people are influenced by the groups in which they live" (Lazarsfeld 1952). By the 1950s, consumer researchers in advertising institutes and corporate marketing departments increasingly sought to forecast consumer decisions and future buying behavior both in terms of social dynamics and of psychological motivations and frames.

Economists and government offices interested in macroeconomic steering and the development of aggregate demand equally furthered their efforts in surveying consumers. George Katona now emerged as a leading expert on consumer sentiment and a champion of psychologically informed "behavioral economics" in the United States. Postwar economic growth, he believed, required a thorough understanding of how changing consumer attitudes impacted macroeconomic trends and growth. Now at the University of Michigan, he refined methods to forecast and predict changes in consumer spending, focusing on the role of expectations, decision-making and the socio-psychological framing that contributed to it. To Katona, consumer sentiment measurements not only presented a way to track consumer attitudes but also to engage prevailing consumer mindsets, adjusting them to, what he believed, would be an era of almost boundless growth and prosperity. Attitudes of optimism, Katona felt, would lead to increased economic confidence and growth, which his surveys were meant to study and foster.

With the end of the war, Katona and many of Likert's former staff moved to the University of Michigan's newly-founded Survey Research Center (SRC). The group brought with them several contracts from Washington, including the Federal Reserve survey on economic behavior and motives. These wartime survey studies provided the organizational and methodological foundation for one of postwar America's most influential centers for empirical social research (Frantilla 1998). In 1949, the SRC was joined with Kurt Lewin's Research MIT Center for Group Dynamics to form the

Institute for Social Research at Michigan (Lewin 1943b). At the university, George Katona held a dual appointment as professor in economics and psychology, and he initiated the "Economic Behavior Program" to pursue a comprehensive set of consumer attitude studies, which included the "Survey of Consumer Finances" (conducted for the Federal Reserve until 1971).

A new, recurring "Survey of Consumer Attitudes" was introduced by the SRC for the Department of Commerce. This study asked representative samples of households about their perceptions and expectations regarding their own finances, the general state of business, and of overall economic development. Initially, the survey was based on personal interviews with respondents selected through random area sampling. By the 1960s, telephone interviews were included and beginning in 1978, the survey was conducted through a random digit dial process. Respondents were part of revolving panels and thus confronted repeatedly with the same qualitative questions about their expectations regarding their own personal finances, their overall economic outlook and their plans for major outlays such as housing, automobiles, major durable purchases (Curtin 1982). Utilizing this data, Katona's team began to calculate an index to predict consumer behavior in the near future. First published as the "Index of Consumer Sentiment" in 1952, it later became part of the Commerce Departments' Leading Indicator composite index.

While Katona and his colleagues touted the reliability of their index to track and predict business cycle swings, the method faced critical scrutiny from the start. In 1955, the Federal Reserve board appointed a committee to assess the quality of the data, which produced a rather skeptical report regarding its predictive qualities (Dominitz and Manki 2004). During the early 1960s, too, several economists cautioned against a heavy reliance on the Michigan index (e.g. Juster 1964). For marketers, the index frequently proved too general to make specific predictions about consumer spending changes with regard to specific markets of products. It contained a seasonal bias (with April and October as recurring high- and low-points of consumer expectations) and did not differentiate between different market segments and target groups within an increasingly differentiated consuming public. Still, many others saw value in the index' seeming ability to forecast recessions or dips in growth about six-months out; and by 1967 the Conference Board's Consumer Confidence Index was established as a second rivalling prognostic tool (Linden 1982). Similar to Katona's survey in its overall approach, the new index asked a bit more concretely about personal purchase intentions and differed slightly in the way the index was calculated.

The basic premise of these consumer confidence indices was the same, however: to gauge attitudinal factors that would help predict consumer ability and willingness to spend. Projections based on income and the ability to spend or extrapolations of past behavior, Katona believed, were not sufficient to forecast consumer spending if they left aside current expectations and attitudes informed by persistent cultural frames as by recent political events (Katona 1975, 61–83). Consumer sentiments, he believed, were highly situational and needed continuous monitoring through surveys. Whether in the context of wartime shortages or under conditions of postwar affluence, the consumer's "frames of reference" needed to be assessed and then adapted whenever necessary. Referencing Kurt Lewin's concept of "life-space," Katona sought to reconstruct consumer perceptions of the present and the past in order to predict future behavior: "The immediate purpose of psychological studies and of economic surveys as well is diagnostic: we want to obtain as complete an account as possible of the current situation, and this account must include people's expectations, aspirations, plans, fears and many other forward-looking (*ex ante*) variables" (Katona 1949). On the macro-level, his interest in forecasting consumer behavior based on psychological data played into the hands of Keynesian economists concerned with steering levels of inflation or aggregate demand. On the micro-level, marketing experts similarly paid attention to Katona's efforts to analyze the psychological dispositions of American consumers. Their attitudes, expectations, and experiences were now seen as relevant variables in understanding purchasing decisions (Pratt 1972).

In many ways, George Katona was an early proponent of behavioral economics, which seeks to bring insights from cognitive psychology to problems of economic decision-making (Hosseini 2011). The conventional "rational actor" models of neoclassical economists, he believed, needed to be augmented with sociological and psychological assumptions about group norms, attitudes and individual motivations (Katona 1947). Much like later behavioral economists, Katona disagreed with the notion of consumers as cost-value optimizers whose behavior could be easily delineated from a simple set of variables such as income and price incentives (Sent 2004; Heukelom 2014). Katona's (1951) *Psychological Analysis of Economic Behavior* argued that attitudes and expectations formed on the basis of an complex interplay of variables rather than mere physical needs or available income became increasingly important in determining household spending patterns as consumers in affluent societies enjoyed more disposable income. Rejecting behaviorist stimulus-response models in favor of Lewin's social psychology (stimulus – organism – response), Katona analyzed decision-making processes which had long been a "black box" to psychologists and economists alike by introducing motivations and attitudes as intervening variables (Katona 1951).

Already in a 1946 article in the *American Economic Review (AER)*, Katona had called on economists to improve their conception of the interplay of experiences and expectations in forecasting economic behavior by integrating social and cognitive psychology findings into their research (Katona 1946). Consumers, he again emphasized drawing on insights from his empirical survey work, were imperfectly informed and partially impulse-driven, mirroring notions of "bounded rationality" which emerged around the same time (Simon 1955; Edwards 1954). Economic theory needed to do justice to the complexity of human decision-making in preparing prognostic models. Consumers were able to learn and to change their behavior and economic modelling had to take account of this in Katona's view: "How can [traditional] theory be improved?" he asked in another *AER* article in 1968, "One possible way is by making the underlying assumptions more realistic. The introduction of principles of social learning and of expectational dynamics into economic theory promises progress in this direction" (Katona 1968a, 19–20; Katona 1968b, 149). While largely ignored by economists at the time, this behavioral perspective increasingly informed marketing scholarship and departments, consumer activists as well as government regulators.

Katona's work on consumer attitude surveys exemplifies what marketing scholar Harold Kassarjian has called a "cognitive revolution" in American consumer research during the postwar decades (Kassarjian 1994). During the 1950s and 1960s, a wealth of publications attested to a broad-based social-scientific interest in consumer behavior, increasingly intertwining social science and marketing research (Festinger and Katz 1953; Lazarsfeld and Rosenberg 1955). Marketing science opened itself up to new behavioral research first in specialized journal articles and, by the 1960s, increasingly in encompassing surveys and edited volumes intended for classroom use (Blankenship 1949; Clawson 1949; Brown 1950; Alderson 1952; Heller 1956; Cox et al. 1964; Newman 1966). European émigrés contributed prominently to this shift. The Gestalt theorists, Kurt Lewin's social psychology and especially George Katona's economic psychology informed a new cohort of consumer researchers in the United States interested in sensory perception as well as in the social fields and cognitive frames of reference within which such perception took place. They brought experimental research designs to the marketing field and combined this approach with mathematical models and statistics (Kassarjian 1994, 271–72; Pietrykowski 2009, 54–78). A massive 1960s anthology of *Consumer Behavior and the Behavioral Sciences*, for example, prominently featured the research of émigré scholars with contributions from George Katona, Paul Lazarsfeld, Kurt Lewin and many others (Britt 1966). Through a wider range of psychological approaches and through a more complex understanding of consumer behavior they fundamentally altered consumer forecasting during the middle of the twentieth century.

5. Framing and Managing Expectations in the Cold War: More Transatlantic Transfers of Consumer Survey Methodology

If consumer confidence was "a key to the economy" as Katona claimed, it was also a fickle friend (Katona 1960). His research cast doubt on exuberant expectations of Keynesian macroeconomic steering that reliable predictions of consumer behavior were possible by simply using a few long-term indicators. The inclusion of rather volatile consumer attitudes in his surveys, he argued, instead allowed his index to out-perform other indicators in times of crisis, e.g. in forecasting the economic recessions of the early 1970s. Yet, consumer confidence was not simply ephemeral in Katona's assessment, but rather based on relatively stable dispositions rooted in the social basis of a society. Thus, Katona, the longstanding analyst of American consumer psychology, also turned to the comparative, transatlantic inquiry of reactions to affluence during the postwar decades. Katona, I argue, regarded his social science methodology as a tool in winning Europeans over to American-style mass consumption, and to manage and adapt consumer expectations during the Cold War.

Promoting mass consumption as a crucial element of the "American Way of Life" was an important focus of the Cold War social sciences (Solovey and Craves 2012). Few scholars were more vocal in their enthusiasm for the American consumer citizen than George Katona (Katona and Mueller 1953; Katona and Mueller 1956; Horowitz 1998). Fostering consumer confidence and its underlying attitudes towards acquiring new goods were vital to consumer capitalism as Katona observed in 1960: "Lasting prosperity calls for sustained high demand [… and for] general striving for higher standards of living […]. Prosperity requires self-reinforcing optimistic attitudes based on sound reasons" (Katona 1960, 173). His attitude research and the work of fellow economic psychologists advanced this agenda: "Consumer psychology, by providing a better understanding of the factors on which consumer demand depends, will contribute to ironing out excessive economic fluctuations and to assuring a greater rate of growth in our economy" (Katona 1961). Consumer research, Katona and many of his colleagues believed, served a larger public purpose.

This broader social impact of his work became especially significant with regard to postwar Europe. Katona returned to Europe several times during the early 1950s as a government advisor for consumer research. He surveyed research institutes at the behest of the American government, helping to assess the state of market and opinion polling in postwar Germany. Because of his prior work in Germany, Katona observed in one report, German people, "usually, talked to me without considering me a representative of the Occupation Authority or a foreigner" (Katona 1950c, 1). Participating in international conferences during the postwar decades, Katona also built up numerous academic connections, including financial economist Günther Schmölders in Cologne who shared his interest in "behavioral economics" and in the psychological determinants of economic development (Schmölders 1971). Translations of several of his major works appeared with the German publisher Econ-Verlag, which also translated books by émigré motivational researcher Ernest Dichter in an effort to make American consumer modernity accessible to German readers (Katona 1962a; Dichter 1964).

Returning émigrés and exiles were particularly influential as facilitators of transatlantic transfers during postwar reconstruction in the early years of the Cold War (Krauss 2001; Krohn and Schildt 2002). Emigration scholars have demonstrated that West-German society was transformed in numerous fields with the help of returning émigrés whose work was frequently tied up within larger American reconstruction and reeducation efforts sponsored by the U.S. State Department or organizations such as the Ford Foundation (Berghahn 2002; Bauerkämper 2005; Hesse 2008). As they returned to postwar Europe, émigré consumer researchers felt they came back with new insights to share, touting the achievements of American scientific marketing, which – with their active involvement – had blossomed over the course of the 1930s and 1940s. Historian Nepomuk Gasteiger finds that returning émigrés were instrumental in disseminating an understanding of consumers as members of discreet sociological market segments whose behavior was influenced by psychological desires and motivations to be explored and exploited by marketing experts (Gasteiger 2010, 19 and 32). Katona in particular helped to bring behavioral approaches back to Europe, familiarizing colleagues on the continent with the marketing applications of Lewinian social psychology (Gasteiger 2010, 142–43). In a keynote address at a 1950 Frankfurt conference on opinion research, Katona discussed recent "American" achievements in the field of opinion research. He stressed the importance of behavioral and attitude research in American consumer studies. Citing Kurt Lewin's insights into group dynamics along with wartime motivation and attitude surveys, Katona offered his German audience the prospect of democratic consumer research contributing to economic growth and a coming age of mass consumption (Katona 1950a).

This was not a simple story of "Americanization," however, as German consumer research dated back to the interwar years and had expanded under the National Socialist regime (Wiesen 2011; Hirt 2013). After the war, these researchers were not always eager to embrace methodological innovations from across the Atlantic. Indeed, Katona encountered resistance to new methodologies perceived as "American" in the social sciences, as he reported to the Allied High Commission. "Germany is, of course, different from the United States," was one objection Katona would hear from his German colleagues who tended to prefer qualitative studies to the more empirical "American" approach he offered (Katona 1950b). When Katona studied German survey research organizations in 1950, he found their number to be "surprisingly large," but most were small, underfunded, and methodologically not quite up-to-date by American standards (Katona 1950c). Still, postwar European consumer research was frequently intertwined with political reconstruction efforts during the Cold War. The well-known Allensbach Institute highlights this intersection of consumer surveys with political attempts to shape a new consuming public (Brückweh 2011; Schwarzkopf 2012).

Consumer confidence and expectations in many European countries, however, appeared to be "lagging behind" in optimism compared to the United States in the eyes of contemporary observers. Katona worried that European consumers had not yet adapted to a mind-set of affluence, which, he feared, could present a major obstacle to continuous growth in Western Europe. In surveys of buying plans, for example, the acquisition of consumer durables was apparently not as important to West German consumers during the postwar decades as to their American counterparts. Indeed, plans to make "major outlays" for consumer durables actually declined among West German households after the late 1950s from 84 % in 1956 and 69 % in 1962 to as low as 54 % in 1967 according to one study. When asked "why not" buy more, more than half of West German consumers (especially middle class households of salaried employees, civil servants and professionals) stated that they "ha[d] everything" while less than 20 % stated lack of money as the reason. In the even more affluent United States, by contrast, cars and new houses topped the Christmas wish lists during the 1950s (Jacobs 2005, 249). Katona wrote drawing on his survey findings that there was "no indication of any increased feeling of saturation on the part of the American people" (Katona, Strumpel and Zahn 1971, 70–72).

George Katona therefore saw it as his mission to persuade Europeans to adopt a frame of reference and attitudes towards consumption, which he considered to be more "appropriate" for affluent societies. In this, changing European attitudes towards consumer credit was a crucial step, as he explained at a 1962 Eurofinas credit conference in Vienna.

Consumer financing, he believed, helped consumers to better budget their finances and to "raise their level of human aspirations" to ensure future prosperity through consumption driven growth (Katona 1962b). In contrast to optimistic Americans striving for more and more goods, Katona found Europeans to still be "maladapted" to modern mass consumption. Psychologically, he noted as late as 1970, Europeans had an "apprehensive" and "defensive" posture towards consumption. The American émigré therefore collaborated with European colleagues to analyze what they saw as a "gap between the reality of a rapidly developing mass-consumption society [in Western Europe] and its perception by the people" (Katona, Strumpel and Zahn 1971, 173–78).

In this context, Katona's index of consumer sentiment ultimately found its way across the Atlantic. During the 1960s, the Gesellschaft für Konsumforschung in Nürnberg (GfK) and the DIVO Institute had already conducted sporadic surveys of consumer sentiment. In 1972, the European Community introduced surveys of consumers in 12 European countries based on the methodology of the Michigan survey. In Germany, the quarterly survey with twelve questions is today still conducted by the GfK, which calculates the so-called Konsumklimaindex based on its results (Caspers 1992). While these consumer attitude surveys were initially less publicly prominent than in the U.S. and some methodological differences remained, their arrival speaks to the way to which Western European societies, too, increasingly began to understand themselves as mass consumer societies by the early 1970s (Fabian 2016; Köhler 2018). Here, too, "the consumer" (and his or her psychological dispositions) now increasingly became a central figure when it came to understanding the economy and predicting its future development. The consumer researcher Katona rejoiced in 1971 that the material conditions had changed tremendously in Western Europe: "Economic development is now much more than before determined by the behavior of consumers [and especially by] their wishes and desires" (Katona, Strumpel and Zahn 1971, 12).

6. Conclusion

Since the 1970s, the prognostic prowess of traditional consumer sentiment measurements has declined somewhat as markets became even more differentiated and more volatile than in the immediate postwar decades. Recently, new tools such as Google trends have outperformed survey-based indicators of consumer behavior in predictive accuracy (Schmidt and Vosen 2009). Still, consumers and their attitudes and expectations remain an important aspect of economic forecasting. The emergence and enduring success of consumer attitude measurements during the second half of the twentieth century, this chapter has suggested, has to be understood within several larger contexts.

First, how and with what indicators economic forecasting was conducted needs to be historicized. In the context of the rise of the mass consumption society, both "the consumer" as an economic actor and disposable household consumption came to play such a significant economic role, that economic forecasting needed to incorporate a gauge of present and future consumer activity. Both corporate and government interests drove the development of consumer research in the United States, which was marked by a mid-century caesura during the 1930s and 1940s. The experience of crisis of the Great Depression as well as the home front needs of World War II spurred on more systematic research into consumer attitudes and expectations. This research came to fruition during the postwar "consumer's republic" when consumer psychology and behavior research informed both corporate marketing and macroeconomic forecasting.

Second, the example of consumer confidence measurements underscores the degree to which economic forecasting was part of an increasing scientization of social and economic process in the mid-century decades of "high modernity" (Brückweh et al. 2012; Logemann, Cross and Köhler 2019). Consumer research promised to provide seemingly predictive and "scientific" data on the development of consumer markets. On the one hand, this was part of a broader search for predictability within corporations and state organizations during these decades. On the other hand, there was a distinctly political and ideological dimension to the rise of consumer confidence measurements. That economic forecasting can be tool for subtly shaping consumer behavior appears obvious in the context of corporate marketing. The case of Katona suggests that forecasting can also be seen as part of more comprehensive efforts in social engineering in the context of economic policy making during World II and the Cold War. Rather than outright manipulation, however, Katona used his consumer attitude surveys in an effort to involve consumers as market participants in an active learning process. By changing their frames of reference he hoped to influence as much as forecast future economic developments. In this, Katona and his fellow consumer researchers engaged in managing expectations in the way recently discussed by economic sociologist Jens Beckert.

Third, the quest to manage markets not only led to the professionalization of consumer research, but also to numerous transnational exchanges that defy simplistic notions of "Americanization." European émigré scholars in psychology, sociology and other behavioral sciences informed the increasingly complex and psychological approach to consumer research of U.S. corporate and government institutions. After the war, they helped transfer new research concepts and methods back to Europe. Katona's contributions to early behavioral economics through insights from social- and Gestalt-psychology speak to this process of transatlantic knowledge exchanges, which was more reciprocal and multifaceted than often assumed.

The development of the consumer sentiment index, finally, is part of a larger story about a changing understanding of the dynamics of markets and the economy. Properly forecasting economic developments, the attitude research suggested, needed to take social and psychological dynamics more comprehensively into account. In this, it went beyond the more mechanistic models of interwar economic forecasting and the simplistic assumptions of early stimulus-response behaviorism. While one should be weary to speak of "scientific progress," consumer research certainly became more rigorous and refined in its methodology e.g. with regard to surveys. Through the work of Katona, Lazarsfeld and many others, the field betrayed a much greater reflexivity and awareness with regard to behavioral factors and social dynamics as they relate to economic and market developments. Through his work on wartime inflation and on postwar buying, George Katona in particular emerged as an early theorist of the interplay of experience and expectations. Building on his empirical research, he sought to bring a more sophisticated understanding of the social and cognitive contexts and of the various intervening psychological stimuli, which informed consumer decision-making, into economic modeling. While he may have not had the impact on economic theory afforded to later behavioral economists, Katona's work can still offer valuable insights on this relationship as it relates to economic forecasting.

References

Alderson, Wroe. 1952. "Psychology for Marketing and Economics." *Journal of Marketing* 17: 119–35.

Bauerkämper, Arnd. 2005. "Americanisation as Globalisation? Remigrés to West Germany after 1945 and Conceptions of Democracy: The Cases of Hans Rothfels, Ernst Fraenkel and Hans Rosenberg." *Leo Baeck Institute Year Book* 49: 153–170.

Beckert, Jens. 2013. "Capitalism as a System of Expectations: Toward a Sociological Microfoundation of Political Economy." *Politics & Society* 41: 323–50.

Benjamin, Ludy. 2004. "Science for Sale: Psychology's Earliest Adventures in American Advertising." In *Diversity in Advertising*, edited by Jerome Williams, 21–39. New York: Psychology Press.

Berghahn, Volker. 2002. *America and the Intellectual Cold Wars in Europe: Shepard Stone between Philanthropy, Academy, and Diplomacy*. Princeton: Princeton University Press.

Berghoff, Hartmut, Jan Logemann and Felix Römer. 2017. *The Consumer on the Home Front*. Oxford: Oxford University Press.

Blankenship, Albert. 1949. "Needed: A Broader Concept of Marketing Research." *Journal of Marketing* 13: 305–10.

Britt, Steuart H. 1966. *Consumer Behavior and the Behavioral Sciences*. New York: Wiley & Sons.

Brown, William. 1950. "The Determination of Factors Influencing Brand Choice." *The Journal of Marketing* 14: 699–706.

Brückweh, Kerstin. 2011. *The Voice of the Citizen Consumer: A History of Market Research, Consumer Movements, and the Political Public Sphere*. New York: Oxford University Press.

Brückweh, Kerstin et al. 2012. *Engineering Society the Role of the Human and Social Sciences in Modern Societies, 1880–1980*. Basingstoke: Palgrave Macmillan.

Campbell, Angus and George Katona. 1946. "A National Survey of Wartime Savings." *Public Opinion Quarterly* 10: 373–81.

Caspers, Wolfagng. 1992. *Das Konsumklima – Indikatorensystem für den privaten Verbrauch*. PhD Diss. Erlangen: University of Nuremberg.

Clawson, Joseph. 1949. "Lewin's Vector Psychology and the Analysis of Motives in Marketing." In *Theory in Marketing*, edited by Reavis Cox and Wroe Alderson, 41–63. Chicago: Richard Irvin.

Clifford, Catherine. 2009. "Consumer Index Sinks to All-Time Low" CNN Money Report, January 27, 2009. https://money.cnn.com/2009/01/27/news/economy/consumer_confidence/?postversion=2009012711 (last access: 1/27/2020).

Cohen, Lizabeth. 2003. *A Consumer's Republic: The Politics of Mass Consumption in Postwar America*. New York: Knopf.

Converse, Jean McDonnell. 1987. *Survey Research in the United States: Roots and Emergence, 1890–1960*. Berkeley: University of California Press.

Cox, Reavis et al. 1964. *Theory in Marketing. Second Series*. Homewood: Irwing.

Croushore, Dean. 2004. "Do Consumer Confidence Indexes Help Forecast Consumer Spending in Real Time?" Studies of the Economic Research Center No. 27.

Curtin, Richard. 1982. "Indicators of Consumer Behavior: The University of Michigan Surveys of Consumers." *Public Opinion Quarterly* 46: 340–52.

Curtin, Richard. 1984. "Curtin on Katona." In *Contemporary Economists in Perspective*, edited by Henry Spiegel and Warren Samuels, 495–522. Greenwich: JAI Press.

Dichter, Ernest. 1964. *Handbuch der Kaufmotive: der Sellingappeal von Waren, Werkstoffen und Dienstleistungen*. Düsseldorf: Econ-Verlag.

Dominitz, Jeff and Charles Manki. 2004. "How Should We Measure Consumer Confidence?" *Journal of Ecnomic Perspectives* 18: 51–66.

Edwards, Ward. 1954. "The Theory of Decision Making." *Psychological Bulletin* 41: 380–417.

Fabian, Sina. 2016. *Boom in der Krise: Konsum, Tourismus, Autofahren in Westdeutschland und Großbritannien 1970–1990*. Göttingen: Wallstein Verlag.

Festinger, Leon and Daniel Katz. 1953. *Research Methods in the Behavioral Sciences*. New York: Holt.

Fleck, Christian. 2011. *A Transatlantic History of the Social Sciences*. New York: Bloomsbury Academic.

Frantilla, Anne. 1998. *Social Science in the Public Interest: A Fiftieth Year History of the Institute for Social Research*. Ann Arbor: University of Michigan.

Freie Universität Berlin. 1982. *Ehrenpromotion von Prof. Dr. George Katona Ann Arbor, Michigan am 15. Juni 1981: Gedenkschrift*. Berlin: Freie Universität.

Fullerton, Ronald. 1990. "The Art of Marketing Research: Selection from Paul F. Lazarsfeld's Shoe Buying in Zurich (1933)." *Journal of the Academy of Marketing Science* 18: 319–27.

Fullerton, Ronald. 2013. "The Birth of Consumer Behavior: Motivation Research in the 1940s and 1950s." *Journal of Historical Research in Marketing* 5: 212–22.

Garon, Sheldon. 2011. *Beyond Our Means: Why America Spends While the World Saves*. Princeton: Princeton University Press.

Gasteiger, Neopmuk. 2010. *Der Konsument: Verbraucherbilder in Werbung, Konsumkritik und Verbraucherschutz*. Frankfurt: Campus.

Glander, Timothy. 2000. *Origins of Mass Communications Research during the American Cold War*. Mahwah: Lawrence Earlbaum.

Heller, Norman. 1956. "An Application of Psychological Learning Theory to Advertising." *Journal of Marketing* 20: 248–54.

Hess, Herbert. 1935. "The New Consumption Era." *American Marketing Journal* 1: 16–25.

Hesse, Jan-Otmar. 2008. „'Ein Wunder der Wirtschaftstheorie': Die 'Amerikanisierung' der Volkswirtschaftslehre in der frühen Bundesrepublik. " *Jahrbuch des Historischen Kollegs* 6: 79–113.

Heukelom, Floris. 2014. *Behavioral Economics: A History*. Cambridge: Cambridge University Press.

Hirt, Gerulf. 2013. *Verkannte Propheten?: Zur "Expertenkultur" (west-)deutscher Werbekommunikatoren bis zur Rezession 1966/67*. Leipzig: Leipziger Univ.-Verlag.

Horowitz, Daniel. 1998. „The Émigré as Celebrant of American Consumer Culture." In *Getting and Spending: European and*

American Consumer Societies in the Twentieth Century, edited by Susan Strasser et al., 149–66. Cambridge: Cambridge University Press.

Hosseini, Hamid. 2011. "George Katona: A Founding Father of Old Behavioral Economics." *Journal of Socio-Economics* 40: 977–84.

Igo, Sarah. 2007. *The Averaged American: Surveys, Citizens, and the Making of a Mass Public*. Cambridge: Harvard University Press.

Jacobs, Meg. 2005. *Pocketbook Politics: Economic Citizenship in Twentieth-Century America*. Princeton: Princeton University Press.

Jahoda, Marie and Neil Warren. 1966. *Attitudes*. Baltimore: Penguin Books.

Jakob, Mark, Alexander Nützenadel and Jochen Streb. 2018. „Erfahrung und Erwartung – eine vernachlässigte wirtschaftshistorische Perspektive?" *Jahrbuch für Wirtschaftsgeschichte* 59/2: 329–42.

Jones, D.G. Brian and Mark Tadajewski. 2011. "Market Research Corporation of America, 1934–1951." *CHARM Proceedings* 15: 232–235.

Juster, Thomas. 1964. *Anticipation and Purchases: An Analysis of Consumer Behavior*. Princeton: Princeton University Press.

Kassarjian, Harold. 1994. "Scholarly Traditions and European Roots of American Consumer Research." In *Research Traditions in Marketing*, edited by Giles Laurent et al., 265–79. Boston: Kluwer.

Katona, George. 1924. *Psychologie der Relationserfassung und des Vergleichens*. Leipzig: Barth.

Katona, George. 1940. *Organizing and Memorizing: Studies in the Psychology of Learning and Teaching* (with a foreword by Max Wertheimer). New York: Hafner.

Katona, George. 1942. *War without Inflation: The Psychological Approach to Problems of War Economy*. New York: Columbia University Press.

Katona, George. 1944. "The Role of Frame of Reference in War and Post-War Economy." *American Journal of Sociology* 49: 340–47.

Katona, George. 1945. *Price Control and Business: Field Studies among Producers and Distributors of Consumer Goods in the Chicago Area, 1942–44*. Bloomington: Principia Press.

Katona, George. 1946. "Psychological Analysis of Business decisions and Expectations." *American Economic Review* 36 (1946): 44–62.

Katona, George. 1947. "Contribution of Psychological Data to Economic Analysis." *Journal of the American Statistical Association* 42: 449–59.

Katona, George. 1949. "Validity of Consumer Expectations," Speech before the American Statistical Association, Dec. 30, 1949. In George Katona Papers, University of Michigan, Bentley Library, Folder 14.

Katona, George. 1950a. „Amerikanische Erfahrungen mit der Untersuchung von Verhalten, Einstellungen und Meinungen." Paper delivered at Frankfurt workshop „Die Erforschung der öffentlichen Meinung," Sept. 16, 1950. In George Katona Papers, University of Michigan, Bentley Library, Folder 16.

Katona, George. 1950b. Report to the HICOG Office of Political Affairs, Oct. 9 1950. In George Katona Papers, University of Michigan, Bentley Library, Folder 17.

Katona, George. 1950c. Report "Brief Resume of My Trip to Germany," Oct. 9 1950. In George Katona Papers, University of Michigan, Bentley Library, Folder 17.

Katona, George. 1951. *The Psychological Analysis of Economic Behavior*. New York: McGraw-Hill.

Katona, George. 1960. *The Powerful Consumer*. New York: McGraw-Hill.

Katona, George. 1961. "Consumer Behavior in our Changing Environment," Speech, Oct. 1961. In George Katona Papers, University of Michigan, Bentley Library, Folder 20.

Katona, George. 1962a. *Die Macht des Verbrauchers*. Düsseldorf: Econ-Verlag.

Katona, George. 1962b. "The Impact of Installment Credit," Eurofinas Association of European Finance Houses, Vienna June 25–26 1962. In George Katona Papers, University of Michigan, Bentley Library, Folder 56.

Katona, George. 1968a. "Consumer Behavior: Theory and Findings on Expectations and Aspirations." *American Economic Review* 58: 19–30.

Katona, George. 1968b. "On the Function of Behavioral Theory and Behavioral Research in Economics." *American Economic Review* 58: 146–49.

Katona, George. 1975. *Psychological Economics*. New York: Elsevier.

Katona, George and Rensis Likert. 1946. "Relationship between Consumer Expenditures and Savings: The Contribution of Savings Research." *Review of Economics and Statistics* 28: 197–99.

Katona, George and Eva Mueller. 1953. *Consumer Attitudes and Demand 1950–1952*. Ann Arbor: Institute for Social Research.

Katona, George and Eva Mueller. 1956. *Consumer Expectations 1953–1956*. Ann Arbor: Institute for Social Research.

Katona, George, Burkhard Strumpel and Ernest Zahn. 1971. *Aspirations and Affluence: Comparative Studies in the United States and Western Europe*. New York: McGraw-Hill.

Köhler, Ingo. 2018. *Auto-Identitäten: Marketing, Konsum und Produktbilder des Automobils nach dem Boom*. Gottingen: Vandenhoeck & Ruprecht.

Krauss, Marita. 2001. *Heimkehr in ein fremdes Land: Geschichte der Remigration nach 1945*. Munich: Beck.

Kreshel, Peggy. 1993. "Advertising Research in the Pre-Depression Years: A Cultural History." *Journal of Current Issues and Research in Advertising* 15: 59–75.

Krohn, Claus-Dieter and Axel Schildt. 2002. *Zwischen den Stühlen? Remigranten und Remigration in der deutschen Medienöffentlichkeit der Nachkriegszeit*. Hamburg: Christians.

Lazarsfeld, Paul. 1942. Memorandum May 25, 1942. In George Katona Papers, University of Michigan, Bentley Library, Folder 11.

Lazarsfeld, Paul. 1952. Speech to the American Marketing Association. December 27, 1952. In Paul Felix Lazarsfeld Archive, University of Vienna, Folder "Rote Mappe: misc. scientific."

Lazarsfeld, Paul. 1961. Interview with Joan Gordon Nov. 29 1961. In Paul Felix Lazarsfeld Archive, University of Vienna, Folder "Columbia Oral History."

Lazarsfeld, Paul and Jehuda Katz. 1955. *Personal Influence: The Part Played by People in the Flow of Mass Communication*. Glencoe: Free Press.

Lazarsfeld, Paul and Morris Rosenberg. 1955. *The Language of Social Research*. Glencoe: Free Press.

Lenel, Laetitia. 2018. "Mapping the Future. Business Forecasting and the Dynamics of Capitalism in the Interwar Period." *Jahrbuch für Wirtschaftsgeschichte* 59/2: 377–413.

Lewin, Kurt. 1943a. "Forces behind Food Habits and Methods of Change." *Bulletin of the National Research Council* 108: 35–65.

Lewin, Kurt. 1943b. Letter to Rensis Likert, Nov. 30, 1943. In Rensis Likert Papers, University of Michigan, Bentley Library, Box 24.

Link, Henry and Irving Lorge. 1935. "The Psychological Sales Barometer." *Harvard Business Review* 14: 193–204.

Likert, Rensis. 1932. *A Technique for the Measurement of Attitudes*. PhD Diss. New York: Columbia University.

Likert, Rensis. n.d. Summary Statement of the Work of the Division of Program Surveys for the Calendar Year 1942. In Rensis Likert Papers, University of Michigan, Bentley Library, Box 1, Folder 3.

Linden, Fabian. 1982. "The Consumer as Forecaster." *Public Opinion Quarterly* 46 (1982): 353–60.

Lockley, Lawrence. 1950. "Notes on the History of Marketing Research." *Journal of Marketing* 14: 733–36.

Logemann, Jan. 2017. "From Wartime Research to Post-War Affluence: European Émigrés and the Engineering of American Wartime Consumption." In *Consumption on the Home Front During the Second World War: A Transnational Perspective*, edited by Hartmut Berghoff, Jan Logemann and Felix Römer, 279–99. Oxford: Oxford University Press.

Logemann, Jan. 2019. *Engineered to Sell: European Émigrés and the Making of Consumer Capitalism*. Chicago: University of Chicago Press.

Logemann, Jan, Gary Cross and Ingo Köhler. 2019. *Consumer Engineering: Marketing between Planning Euphoria and the Limits of Growth, 1930s-1970s*. New York: Palgrave.

Mandler, Jean and George. 1969. "The Diaspora of Experimental Psychology: The Gestaltists and Others." In *The Intellectual Migration*, edited by Bernard Bailyn and Donald Fleming, 371–419. Cambridge: Harvard University Press.

McGarry, Edmund. 1936. "The Importance of Scientific Method in Advertising." *Journal of Marketing* 1: 82–86.

Newman, Joseph. 1966. *On Knowing the Consumer*. New York: Wiley & Sons.

Pietrykowski, Bruce. 2009. *The Political Economy of Consumer Behavior: Contesting Consumption*. London: Routledge.

Pratt, Robert. 1972. "Marketing Applications of Behavioral Economics." In *Human Behavior in Economic Affairs*, edited by Burkhardt Strumpel and Ernst Zahn, 189–212. Amsterdam: Elsevier.

Program Survey Division (Bureau of Agricultural Economics). 1943. "An Exploratory Study of Attitudes toward Buying and Shortages of Consumer Goods." March 5, 1943. In Rensis Likert Papers, University of Michigan, Bentley Library, Box 2, Folder 3.

Program Survey Division (Bureau of Agricultural Economics). 1944. "What Housewives Eat for Breakfast," Oct. 16, 1944, In Rensis Likert Papers, University of Michigan, Bentley Library, Box 3, Folder 15.

Robinson, Daniel. 1999. *The Measure of Democracy: Polling, Market Research and Public Life, 1930–1945*. Toronto: University of Toronto Press.

Root, Alfred and Alfred Welch. 1942. "The Continuing Consumer Study: A Basic Method for the Engineering of Advertising." *Journal of Marketing* 7: 3–21.

Samuel, Lawrence. 2010. *Freud on Madison Avenue: Motivation Research and Subliminal Advertising in America*. Philadelphia: University of Pennsylvania Press.

Schmidt, Torsten and Simeon Vosen. 2009. "Forecasting Private Consumption: Survey-Based indicators vs. Google Trends." *Ruhr Economic Paper* 155.

Schmölders, Günther. 1971. Letter to Katona, 31. Jan. 1971. In George Katona Papers, University of Michigan, Bentley Library, Folder 3.

Schwarzkopf, Stefan. 2012. "Markets, Consumers, and the State: The Uses of Market Research in Government and Public Sector in Britain, 1925–1955." In *The Rise of Marketing and Market Research*, edited by Hartmut Berghoff, Phillip Scranton and Uwe Spiekermann, 171–91. New York: Palgrave Macmillan.

Schwarzkopf, Stefan. 2016. "In Search of the Consumer: The History of Market Research from 1890 to 1960." In *The Routledge Companion to Marketing History*, edited by D.G. Brian Jones and Mark Tadajewski, 61–84. London: Routledge.

Sent, Esther-Mirjam. 2004. "Behavioral Economics: How Psychology Made Its (Limited) Way Back Into Economics." *History of Political Economy* 36: 735–60.

Simon, Herbert. 1955. "A Behavioral Model of Rational Choice." *Quarterly Journal of Economics* 69: 99–118.

Solovey, Mark and Hamilton Cravens. 2012. *Cold War Social Science: Knowledge Production, Liberal Democracy, and Human Nature*. New York: Palgrave Macmillan.

Strumpel, Burkhard et al. 1972. *Human Behavior in Economic Affairs: Essays in Honor of George Katona*. Amsterdam: Elsevier.

Sudman, Seymore and Norman Bradburn. 1987. "Organizational Growth of Public Opinion Research in the United States." *Public Opinion Quarterly* 51: 67–78.

Taylor, Malcolm. 1936. "Progress in Marketing Research." *Journal of Marketing* 1: 56–64.

Usui, Kazuo. 2008. *The Development of Marketing Management, the Case of the USA, c. 1910–1940*. Farnham: Ashgate.

Ward, Douglas. 2009. "Capitalism, Early Market Research, and the Creation of the American Consumer." *Journal of Historical Research in Marketing* 1: 200–23.

Wheeler, Ferdinand. 1937. *The Technique of Marketing Research*. New York: McGraw-Hill.

Wiesen, Jonathan. 2011. *Creating the Nazi Marketplace: Commerce and Consumption in the Third Reich*. Cambridge: Cambridge University Press.

Marion Ronca (Universität Zürich)

The Economist as Futurologist: The Making and the Public Reception of the *Perspektivstudien* in Switzerland, 1964–1975

Abstract: In the 1960s, long-term studies of the future that forecasted the development of a country became fashionable in the Western world. Whereas certain countries prioritized a multidisciplinary approach, in which both economic development and social change were taken into account, others only considered the development of economic variables and in particular economic growth. The *Perspektivstudien*, which projected the future of Switzerland 30 years ahead, focused solely on the economic development of the country, implicating that political events had no impact on economic development in the long run. This contribution traces back the conceptualization of the economy as a separated sphere that was inherent to the *Perspektivstudien* and investigates the historical context in which they were created. This chapter shows that to understand the emergence of those studies, Keynesianism has to be taken into account as a governmentality in which the idea of a macroeconomic controllability prevailed. Furthermore, the contribution suggests to conceptualize those long-term forecasts not as mere descriptions of possible outcomes, but as performative economic knowledge that invented an a-historical future.

Keywords: Long-term studies, Swiss economy, history of economic thought, performativity of economic knowledge

In 1968, the Swiss government assigned the economist Francesco Kneschaurek to analyze and forecast the economic development of Switzerland up to the year 2000.[1] This assignment laid the basis for the *Perspektivstudien*, which asked for a study group to investigate the "ideal and long-term" development of Switzerland. The motion also pointed to the necessity of a general planning of the country, but it remained ambivalent whether the requested studies should forecast or suggest concrete goals for planning the country's future.[2]

---

1 Pressemitteilung der Schweizerischen Bundeskanzlei vom 21. Februar 1968, BAR E1010B#1986/151#181#.

2 Motion Borel (97170), vom 18. Dezember 1964, BAR, E1070#1974/32#1080*.

In an international context, neither the mandate nor the ambivalence of the request were exceptional. In the course of the reconstruction of Europe after World War II and the rise of macroeconomic governance, planning and forecasting became intertwined and widely accepted practices of economic policy[3] (Laak van 2010, 4). At the same time, futurology as an interdisciplinary approach to investigate the future gained momentum at the end of the 1950s, which caused a growing interest in long-term studies of social and economic development (Seefried 2015). Despite the fact that futurology had its origins in the humanities, a strong connection between economic planning and futurology became apparent at the beginning of the 1960s. This was most notably in the case of France, where economic planning had been known since the end of World War II. In 1962, the Commissariat du Plan asked the "Groupe 1985," which included experts from distinct fields such as economics, medicine, agriculture, business and construction, to determine the most important features of the French economy and society by the year 1985 (La Documentation française 1964). Under the impression of lasting economic growth, the French planning horizon was pushed from five years up to twenty years. Moreover, by commissioning an interdisciplinary group to investigate the future of the country, the Commissariat du Plan considered planning no longer only as a means to achieve macroeconomic goals. Instead, it was also envisioned to anticipate the challenges of social change[4] (Quinet 1990, 44–46).

In the case of the United States, in the "Commission on the Year 2000" presided by the sociologist Daniel Bell, the interest in economic development was less pronounced. The study group rather focused on long-range social questions and possible shifts of values (American Academy of Arts and Sciences 1968). Other countries such as the Netherlands, Germany, and Switzerland, however, strongly prioritized the long-term economic

---

3 According to Dirk van Laak, the idea of planning as a state practice appeared in the context of the authoritarian High Modernism, that is from the beginning of the 20th century to the end of World War II, encompassing both world wars and the great depression and spread after 1945 in the context of the reconstruction.

4 Whereas the first plan contained no macroeconomic goal, the plans from 1954 to 1957, 1957 to 1961 and 1962 to 1965 asked for economic growth amongst others.

and demographic development[5] (Steinmüller 2000, 41–42; Seefried 2015, 313–24). As those studies had a long-term perspective they were– despite their economic focus – forced to make assumptions about the overall development of the country. They had thus to consider also the possible change of non-economic factors or to conceptualize social change as the result of economic development. In Switzerland, Francesco Kneschaurek, who was mandated with the long-term study to the year 2000, chose the second option. This decision was not only motivated by the final parliamentary request, which asked for prioritization of the economic development, but was also in line with Kneschaurek's professional convictions. He relied on Neoclassical theory to make assumptions about the future, which traditionally conceptualizes non-economic factors either as constant or as exogenous[6] (Persky 1990). In both cases, the economy is treated as a separate sphere that is supposed to evolve following inherent principles and is only sparsely affected by socio-political events.

The *Perspektivstudien* are a suitable research topic to historicize the emergence of long-term forecasts in the 1960s that focused primarily on the development of the economy. They enable historians to problematize the neoclassical concept as a general framework in long-term studies and to analyze its implications regarding processes of self-reflexivity in modern societies. Accordingly, this contribution traces the origins of the conceptualization of the economy as a separated sphere and shows its crucial role in the design of the Swiss *Perspektivstudien*. Furthermore, this chapter investigates the historical context in which the *Perspektivstudien* were created, the political setting and the processes that led to the mandate and the

5 In the Netherlands, the economist Jan Tinbergen directed the Centraal Planbureau and started in 1955 to realize future studies. The German government mandated the private company Prognos that was specialized in economic forecasting for studies about the development of the German population and economy.

6 Classical economists adopted the term "ceteris paribus" first used by William Petty in the 17th century to make clear that they assumed "all other things" that is non-economic factors that account for social change to be constant. It was then spread by Alfred Marshall in his Principles of Economics. Correspondingly Robert Solow conceptualized technological progress in his neoclassical growth model as exogenous to avoid formalizing it in purely economic terms.

publication of the studies. By this means, the article aims to provide a better understanding of the overall emergence of long-term studies in the 1960s. Finally, the contribution explores the impact of the *Perspektivstudien* shortly before and during the recession of 1975 in order to explain the effect of this specific type of economic knowledge in the 1970s.

1. The Economy as a Separated Sphere

The conceptualization of the economy as a separate sphere is of vital importance to understand the emergence of long-term studies focusing on the macroeconomic development in the 1960s[7] (Morgan 1990; Armatte 1992; Tooze 2001; Friedman 2014). Whereas it contributed to a specific understanding of social change during the 20th century, in which the idea of a development towards modernity was emphasized,[8] the conceptualization of the economy as a distinct sphere was itself the consequence of a momentous socio-political change: the rise of capitalism. As Ellen Meiksins Wood argues in her seminal essay "The separation of the 'economic' and the 'political' in capitalism," classical economics emphasized the economic aspects of capitalism over the social aspects, thereby "emptying capitalism of its social and political content" as it dealt with society in the abstract (Meiksins Wood 1995, 19, 22). Karl Marx, by contrast, considered the economy as a set of social relations and accordingly the mechanism of surplus value as a particular social relation between "appropriator and producer" (Meiksins Wood 1995, 21, 24). As Meiksins Wood argues, Marx' conception of the economy did not deny that the rise of capitalism was accompanied by a process of differentiation of the economic sphere, in which production and distribution increasingly assumed an 'economic form' that Karl Polanyi later on qualified as disembedded

7 In contrast with long-term studies, short-run economic forecasts go back at least to the 1920s when numerous business cycle institutes and economic services released forecasts on a regular basis.

8 This idea of an overall development of mankind towards modernity appears particularly clearly in Walt Rostow's "The stages of economic growth" in which the author conceptualizes social change as a mutual reinforcement of technological progress and increased economic output leading to new social forms (Rostow 1960).

from social structures. However, Marx regarded this process as a historically specific development that could only be understood by considering its social meaning (Meiksins Wood 1995, 25, 28).

Whereas classical economics mainly relied on the idea that the economy could be differentiated from the social sphere as a means to understand the functioning of markets, this conceptualization was put to a next level with the emergence of marginalist and neoclassical economics, in which the economy became further formalized strengthening the idea of economic laws[9] (Taylor 1929, 4–8; Hodgson 2013, 30–31). The idea of a universally valid description of market mechanisms remained, however, contested, as the *Methodenstreit* between Gustav Schmoller und Carl Menger in the 1880s and 1890s showed. Whereas the former argued that the economy generally takes a specific historical form reflecting power relations and institutions, the latter claimed the existence of universal economic laws. The *Methodenstreit* addressed the question whether empirical or deductive methods are better suited to describe the economy, but pointed also to the role of history in the development of economy. The prevalence of the deductive approach, as it finally materialized in modern mainstream economics, strengthened the belief in universal economic laws and led, as Geoffrey Hogdson argues, to the spread of the conviction that markets and the economy as a whole can be explained without taking historical or cultural specificities into account (Hodgson 2001).

It can be assumed that the conception of a separated economic sphere was originally methodically motivated by the notion of the historical specificity of economic development and the interdependence, respectively the distinction of social and economic factors, which appeared as far too complex to be taken into account. As institutions and the political balance of power could be considered as stable in the short-run, this heuristic was helpful to understand the functioning of markets and methodically acceptable as a simplification. Applied in the long-run however,[10] as can be

9 Whereas the idea that economic actions are ruled by "natural laws" can be traced back to antiquity but remained implicit in the classical writings, it became explicit by the marginalist and neoclassical endeavor to formalize economic behavior such as scientific laws.

10 A long-run economic development is considered as a period of one or several decades.

found in growth models after 1945[11] (Solow 1956; 1957), the conceptualization of the economy was no longer a simple heuristic but became a deterministic assumption about economic development and gained thus a strong ideological component. It is no coincidence that those growth models, whether they were Keynesian or neoclassical, emerged in the context of Keynesianism, that is an era, in which the idea of a controllability of the economy spread and economic interventionism became generally accepted[12] (Hall 1989; Schanetzky 2007, 87, 169; Schmelzer 2016). As growth models reduced long-term growth to the outcome of economic variables, they did not only perpetuate the conception of the economy as a separated sphere but became part of the Keynesian governmentality (Foucault und Lemke 2005, 1759:171–72).[13]

With the rise of Keynesiansim, the general understanding of the function of economic knowledge changed (Mitchell 2008).[14] It was no longer

11 Whereas the Harrod-Domar model treated long-term growth as the outcome of investment and capital stock, the Solow-Swan growth model added technical change as explanatory variable to the Harrod-Domar model. But Solow treated technical change as a residual and did not further conceptualize it or investigate its origin. The model remained thus stuck in the general framework of a separated economic sphere.

12 Many Western countries applied Keynesian principles of anticyclical demand management to different degrees and at different points in time depending on their institutional setting, their political agenda and not last the status and influence of economic experts. However, as a significant number of countries adhered somehow to policies inspired by Keynesian theory and identified with the growth policy of the OECD that presupposed the possibility of growth planning, a general belief in the controllability of the economy can be assumed for the three decades after 1945.

13 The term governmentality refers here to the Foucauldian concept of an ensemble of institutions, procedures, analyses and ideas that secure and perpetuate an economic order and legitimize specific policies. Whereas Foucault spoke of a governmentality of neoliberalism to point in particular to the aspect of the individual internalization of neoliberal values, I argue that Keynesianism, too, can be considered as a governmentality in the Foucauldian sense, since the prevalence of Keynesian policies cannot be explained only by Keynes' theoretical concepts. However, it also has to be understood as the convergence of different ideas, values, and technologies of the nation state that gained momentum after World War II such as national accounting, unemployment assurance, economic planning etc.

14 According to Timothy Mitchell "the economy" was invented as an object only mid-20th century. Although this article doesn't follow Mitchell's claim of the

perceived solely as academic descriptions and explanations of markets, but became increasingly understood as a strategic means to improve the functioning of the economy at a national scale.[15] This new understanding augmented the «performative» power of economic knowledge, that is its ability to influence the way the economy and more generally reality was perceived (Callon 2006, 7, 8, 21).[16] In this new understanding and by the increased application in politics economic knowledge became popularized. However, beyond academia economic knowledge circulated in a reduced form. In particular, the methodological considerations and restrictions that a had led to a conditional acceptance of the conceptualization of the economy as a separated sphere were no longer explicit. Thus, the idea that the economy could be understood in itself without considering social forces and historical processes became increasingly taken for a fact rather than a contestable methodological position.

The spread of the concept of the economy as a separated sphere during Keynesianism affected not only how the economy was perceived, but also the general understanding of the future, changing its meaning from an uncertain horizon to a projection screen. As such it altered also the meaning of history. Since the future was no longer uncertain, history as an unpredictable event became associated with the idea of a planning error, that is an outcome that could have been avoided. In 1970, the Swiss philologist Karl Schmid argued along those lines when he stated: "Geschichte erscheint nun beinahe als eine illegitime Kategorie, die durch planendes Denken eliminiert werden sollte. Ausdrücke wie 'Macht des Schicksals', 'Gesetz der Geschichte' und ähnliche sind heute kaum mehr angängig.

late invention of "the economy," it shares its understanding of the increased meaning of economic knowledge in the context of Keynesinism when it became increasingly used in a strategic way and in the believe that the economy could be managed in the way of a company.

15 The idea that economic knowledge could be used a strategic means emerged with early concepts of scientific management already at the beginning of the 20th century. With Keynesianism the concept that economic knowledge could be used to regulate and plan the economy spread at a national level.

16 According to Michel Callon's concept of performativity economic concepts should be understood as programs altering the way how reality is perceived and thus changing the way actors behave.

Geschichte war einmal; was vor uns liegt, soll nicht Geschichte sein, deren Objekt wir wären – man will die Zukunft in den Griff bekommen und steuern können" (Schmid 1971, 707).

2. Future Perspectives for an Economically Underexplored Country

For Switzerland, the Motion Borel that requested long-term planning of Switzerland's future and led to the subsequent Perspektivstudien, was a novelty in many ways. Up to the end of the 1960s, neither economics nor future studies had played a major role in the guidance of Swiss economic policy. Switzerland had not developed explicitly interventionist economic policies up to this point. Due to its corporatist and federalist form of government applying the principle of subsidiarity, the Swiss Federal state developed political instruments for demand management only slowly, and with a considerable lag, in comparison to other European countries. Up to the end of the 1970s, the competences of the state regarding the organization of the economy remained limited to the prevention of economic downturns and the fight of already on-going recessions (Prader 1981).

The constitution of the Swiss federal state and its limited economic competences explain largely why Switzerland had not founded a federal institute for economic observation before the 1930s. The 1932 established commission for economic observation (*Kommission für Konjunkturbeobachtung KfK*) worked only part-time and was essentially trying to find an agreement amongst its very different members that ranged from officials from different departments to representatives from trade associations and unions. Economists from academia were underrepresented during in the first two decades, not at last because there was – due to the restricted interventionist competences of the government – only little use for economic expertise. Furthermore, the lack of economic statistics made it very difficult for the KfK to keep pace with the economic observation as it was practiced on an international level.

Especially the absence of production statistics, which were not introduced in Switzerland before the 1980s, made it almost impossible for economists to get a real-time sense of the "pulse" of the Swiss economy. And it prevented the implementation of national accounts according to the international standard System of National Accounts that provided an internationally standardized template for national accounts and the calculation of the Gross Domestic Product (GDP) for decades. The absence of production statistics was less due to a lack of demand, but the result of a political power struggle between representatives of the state administration (especially of the Bundesamt für Statistik) and members of trade associations that had fought it very successfully since the 1920s. Thanks to their traditionally strong position in politics that eventually granted them a voice in legislative affairs, trade associations repeatedly managed to prevent the introduction of productions statistics (Ronca 2020).

Finally, another factor contributed to the fact that economic observation and forecasting developed with a considerable lag in Switzerland. Because of its marginal position and the lack of relevant statistics, economic observation remained a small academic niche with very little competition among economists. For decades, a single name dominated Swiss economic observation: Eugen Böhler. The economist at the Federal Institute for technology in Zurich (ETH) was a distinguished expert for economic policy and in particular for economic observation. Böhler, who was member and later on president of the KfK, founded a center for economic observation at the ETH in 1938 that rapidly took over the economic observation that formerly had been supplied by the KfK. Being member of almost all federal commissions concerned with economic policy, Böhler had a strong influence on the Swiss government and on the perception of the business cycle from the 1940s up to the end of the 1950s (Prader 1981, 189). Böhler started his career with a strong disposition towards theory and scientific progress. Throughout the 1950s, he continued to expect an imminent economic downturn[17] (Kommission für Konjunkturbeobachtung 1957; Prader 1981, 189–92). Due to his influence inside the state administration, Böhler's belief in the imminent return of the economic crisis of the 1930s

17 Böhler was among the first Swiss economists to embrace John Maynard Keynes' General Theory and to promote keynesianism within the KfK. Although Böhler made hardly no original contribution to economic theory he kept up with the development of economics, taking up new economic theories and methodologies. This became amongst others apparent in his text book he continuously revised.

contributed strongly to a political culture of crisis expectation. For a long time, this culture prevented the perception of the economic expansion of the post-war era[18] („Bericht des Schweizerischen Bundesrats über seine Geschäftsführung im Jahr 1965“ 1965, 232, 239, 287).

The misinterpretation of economic expansion as a short-term boom that was supposed to last only for a couple of years became apparent only at the beginning of the 1960s. Estimations of the state department of public finances showed that state income and state expenditure had repeatedly and systematically been underestimated due to the expectation of an economic downturn or at least a "normalization"[19] (Jöhr 1966, 11–12; Kleps 1967, 7, 31; Eisinger 1998, 72–73). Moreover, the existing infrastructure of the country proved to be less and less adapted to meet the needs of a growing population and the expanding business activity. This situation explains why no less than three parliamentary requests submitted in 1964 were concerned with the long-time consideration of the country's economic future. While the "Interpellation Schürmann" suggested a long-term finance policy, the "Motion Heil" requested a long-term economic policy. The "Motion Borel," finally, called for a study group to investigate the long-term problems of the country.[20]

The coincidence of the three parliamentary requests could be explained by a late and somehow brutal awakening of the country from its post-Great Depression trauma to face the challenges of growth. This interpretation, however, would not sufficiently take into account that the demand for "long-term" forecasting emerged internationally almost at the same point

18 This culture of crisis expectation appeared distinctly in the figure of the deputy of work provision. This role had been institutionalized during the great depression, but remained in place up to the mid-1960s when it finally became converted into a deputy for economic fluctuation since the lasting economic growth made the role of a deputy for work provision appear superfluous.

19 This misperception of the economic development became particularly apparent when the state department of public finances underestimated repeatedly state income as expenditure.

20 Interpellation Schürmann vom 23. September 1964, Nationalrat Herbstsession 1964, BAR E6100B-01#1980/#198*, Nationalrat. Herbstsession. Motion Heil. Langfristige Konjunkturpolitik, in: Amtliches Bulletin der Bundesversammlung, 1964, 406, Motion Borel vom 18. Dezember 1964, BAR E1070#1974/32#1080*.

of time.[21] Because of the lack of forecasting and planning in Switzerland up to this point, the *Perspektivstudien*, which emanated from the "Motion Borel" could not rely on pre-existing practices. This permits to analyze the emergence of these long-term studies as a specific historical moment when the development of the economy was established internationally as a leading variable for the overall future of the country.

3. The Motion Borel: Between Planning and Forecasting

While the "Interpellation Schürmann" and the "Motion Heil" had a clear economic focus, the "Motion Borel" as it was submitted to the Ständerat[22] a couple of months later in 1964, was not restricted to economic questions. In his request to the Council of States, Alfred Borel rather emphasized the general difficulty of the country to meet the different political, economic and social challenges of the present and the future. He highlighted the need for important investments to improve the country's infrastructure, its educational system, water protection as well as the development of nuclear energy. To determine the order of priority, the motion asked for a study group that should investigate the broad lines of an optimal long-term development.

The request did not explicitly mention future or prospective studies, as they were called in France since the end of the 1950s to distinguish them from short-term and extrapolative forecasts (Steinmüller 2000, 41). The wording of the request, however, suggests that Borel had the academic work of the French futurologists Betrand de Jouvenel and Gaston Berger in mind, whose work he cited in a newspaper article from 1967 (Borel 1967). As the request brought up issues from different political fields, it was at first not clear which department of the federal administration had to answer it. It was eventually passed to the Finance and Customs department of the federal administration since it emphasized the importance of future investments.[23]

21 See introduction and footnote 8.

22 The Ständerat is the upper house of the Federal Assembly of Switzerland.

23 Stellungnahme des Finanz- und Zolldepartements zur Motion Borel betreffend die Schaffung einer Arbeitsgruppe zum Studium der langfristigen Landesprobleme, 23.01.1967, BAR E1070#1974/32#1080*.

When the request was discussed in the Ständerat, it became clear that Borel had an almost exclusively economic focus in mind, which he had missed to make clear in the text of the motion. In his introduction to the Ständerat debate, Borel not only enumerated many examples of countries already practicing economic planning, but also harshly criticized the Swiss government for its reluctance to pass laws to fight the overheated economy.[24] Borel made clear that the overall goal of his request was to determine a long-term policy of growth. He asked for an improvement of economic statistics, a determination of measures for economic planning, and an appropriate economic policy.[25] This was surprising, as it did not correspond with the original motion and overlapped with the Motion Heil that had asked for a long-term economic policy. Moreover, as Borel did not communicate the focus of his request to the head of the finance department, this led to an incongruity between his introductory remarks and the statement of the finance department which essentially focused on financial planning. Nevertheless, the Ständerat accepted the request and passed it to the Nationalrat,[26] which also accepted it but did not take Borel's focus on economic development into account. The Nationalrat did, however, emphasize the necessity of studies considering the overall development of the country.[27]

After the Nationalrat had accepted the request, it was – despite its disputed focus – passed to the deputy for economic questions, Hugo Allemann.[28] Allemann, an economist himself, argued that the mandate,

---

24 Ständerat Wintersession 1965. Auszug aus dem stenographischen Protokoll der Sitzung vom 30. November 1965. 9170 Motion Borel. Arbeitsgruppe zum Studium der langfristigen Landesprobleme. BAR E1070#1974/32#1080*.

25 Ständerat. Wintersession. Auszug aus dem stenographischen Protokoll der Sitzung vom 30. November 1965, S. 5, BAR E1070#1974/32#1080#, p. 4.

26 The Nationalrat is the lower house of the Federal Assembly of Switzerland. Together with the Ständerat, they form the Swiss legislative.

27 Kommission des Nationalrates für die Behandlung der Motion Borel – Arbeitsgruppe zum Studium der langfristigen Landesprobleme, Protokoll der Sitzung vom 1. Februar 1967, S. 5, 7, BAR E1070#1974/32#1080*.

28 Schreiben des Vorstehers des Finanz- und Zolldepartements Roger Bonvin an den Vorsteher des Volkswirtschaftsdepartements Hans Schaffner vom 19. April 1967 betreffend die Motion Borel; Arbeitsgruppe zum Studium der langfristigen Landesprobleme, BAR E6100B-01#1980/150#198*.

should it lead to useful results within reasonable time, had to be limited to the economy. Allemann's request implied an implicit assumption of a separated economic sphere that could be studied independently. This assumption became explicit in Allemann's recommendation that the study group should consider non-economic factors such as technical progress or the structure of society only insofar as they had an actual influence on economic development.

Allemann did not make clear in which case non-economic factors had an influence on the economy and how this influence could be assessed. Instead, he merely argued that the general objective of the motion, the determination of the long-term development, could only be achieved by limiting the scope of the request.[29] It is unclear whether Allemann made this suggestion for the sake of the feasibility of the request or because he was convinced that the Swiss future could be forecasted by only considering the economic development. The fact, however, that Allemann justified this decision by merely pointing to its feasibility suggests that the implicit conceptualization of the economy as a separated sphere was not controversial and that there was a consensus within the Federal Administration regarding the economic development as driving force of the society.

Focussing mainly on economic growth, Allemann proposed to mandate the professor for economics from the University of St. Gallen, Francesco Kneschaurek, who had distinguished himself as an expert for economic growth and forecasting as well as for future studies.[30] In 1968, Kneschaurek had founded an institute for future studies at the university of St. Gallen and considered himself a futurologist and founded in 1968 the St. Galler Zentrum für Zukunftsforschung at the University of St. Gallen (Reyhl 1976). Kneschaurek remained true to his conviction that the future was overall projectable – even when future studies went out of fashion after the 1970s[31] (*Neue Zürcher Zeitung* 1990). Already in the

29 Notiz für Herrn Dr. K. Huber, Generalsekretär des Eidg. Volkswirtschaftsdepartements vom 27.9.1967, BAR E7296A#1994/333#431*.

30 Bericht und Antrag über das weitere Vorgehen i. S, Motion Borel von Hugo Allemann an den Bundesrat vom 29. Dezember 1967, S.5, BAR E4110B#1986/81#248*.

31 In his valedictory lecture "Der Griff nach der Zukunft" of 1990, which Kneschaurek titled after the German futurologist Robert Jungk's writing, he

1950s, Kneschaurek was publicly known for advocating a perception of the economic boom as a growth process, that was quite different from Böhler's pessimistic outlooks (Kneschaurek 1956; 1962; Kneschaurek, Kaufmann, und Geiger 1964).

The Bundesrat[32] as well as the different state departments accepted Allemann's proposition to study mainly the long-term development of the economy without major modifications. Only the department of finance requested that the study group should not include merely "theorists" but also welcome "realists," indicating thereby a certain reservation towards growth theorists.[33] Francesco Kneschaurek became the director of the study group that was composed of economists from his chair. Collaboration with exponents from other disciplines only took place in smaller ad-hoc working groups.[34]

4. The Perspektivstudien and the Swiss Economy as a Separated Sphere

The reports of Kneschaurek´s study group were called "*Perspektivstudien*." The first edition of the *Perspektivstudien* appeared in eight parts between 1969 and 1972, a revised version was published between 1972 and 1973. The final report and summary followed in 1974.[35] A second edition of the

tried again to promote the importance of future studies and to defend it against wide spread objections.

32 The Bundesrat is the Swiss executive.

33 Bericht und Antrag über das weitere Vorgehen i. S. Motion Borel, Mitbericht des Eidg. Finanz- und Zolldepartements zum Antrag des Eidg. Volkswirtschaftsdepartements vom 29. Dezember 1967, BAR E 7001C#1982/118#1626*.

34 Beschluss des Bundesrates bezüglich des Expertenauftrag an Prof. Rotach vom 22. März 1968, BAR E7001C#1982/118#1626*, Schreiben der Schweizerischen Bundeskanzlei an die Departemente und Abteilungen vom 7. Mai 1968, BAR E7296A#1994/333#431*.

35 The first report focused on the development of the population and the workforce, the second on the development of the economy, the third on the sectoral development of the industry and the last five reports respectively on the development of the agriculture, the education, transportation, energy and construction (Kneschaurek 1980, 39).

Perspektivstudien appeared in 1978, but was much less publicized than the former edition (Kneschaurek 1980, 46). Originally, the studies were supposed to be published as a final report at the end of the investigation, in order to test the coherence of its different parts. Kneschaurek and the federal authorities agreed, however, that it was preferable to publish the results of the different parts right away as they thought that the studies could benefit from discussions and critical comments (Arbeitsgruppe Perspektivstudien 1970, 1).

The *Perspektivstudien* attracted much attention from the media, but were also harshly criticized (Kneschaurek 1980, 46). Because of the negative publicity of the *Perspektivstudien*, the Federal council abstained from holding a press conference to present the results of the second edition, as it had been done for the first edition in the early 1970s. Kneschaurek himself was ambivalent towards the critique. While he acknowledged the importance of a public feedback and a critical discussion of the results, he hardly took the critique into account. Notably, he at first ignored the harsh but well-grounded critique of his colleague, the economist Walter Wittmann, and attacked him personally, calling his critique dilettantish and contradictory, without addressing the different points in question in detail (Kneschaurek 1972).

The conception of the economy as a separate sphere appeared in the *Perspektivstudien* in different ways. In accordance with Allemann's request, the *Perspektivstudien* only considered economic factors: the development of the population and workforce, overall productivity, different economic sectors, the educational system and agriculture. Non-economic factors such as shifts in values or new demographic or educational trends were assumed to be constant. This became obvious in Kneschaurek's understanding of the so-called "Leitbilder" (overall concepts that are supposed to guide an entity). As he explained, he based his forecasts on the currently existing economic and socio-political "Leitbilder" of Switzerland. Kneschaurek's use of the expression "Leitbilder" was unfortunate, since Borel's request had asked precisely for developing new "Leitbilder" with the help of the studies. Moreover, no such official «Leitbilder» existed in Switzerland, or at least many of them were competing with another, as Walter Wittmann observed in his critique of the *Perspektivstudien* (Wittmann 1972, 1).

By using the term "Leitbilder," Kneschaurek wanted to make clear that he relied on the ceteris paribus principle. He assumed the social sphere to be constant and had not the intention to investigate social change. This decision was at least questionable with regard to the Swiss immigration policy, since an intense discussion about the limitation of immigration took place at this very moment in Switzerland. A popular petition issued at the beginning of the 1970s asked to limit the quota of foreigners to maximum 10 percent. If the initiative would have been accepted in the referendum, it would have led to the expulsion of hundreds of thousands of non-Swiss residents and would have strongly influenced the demographic development. The close run of the referendum with 46 percent yes-votes against 54 no-votes demonstrated that there was no "Leitbild" regarding immigration in Switzerland that could be assumed to be constant at that time (Maiolino 2011).

Though Kneschaurek acknowledged that it was not possible to make forecasts of the development of the non-Swiss population by considering past development patterns, he did not abstain from forecasting the development of the foreign population in Switzerland, as other studies did. Instead, Kneschaurek simply assumed that the number of foreigners would stabilize in the long run (Arbeitsgruppe Perspektivstudien 1969, 41–42). For the development of the Swiss population, Kneschaurek relied on models of democratic transition which predicted a continuous decline of the birth rate for industrial nations. Doing so, Kneschaurek neither took the ongoing value change of 1968 into account nor possible variations of the birth rate in relation to the growing female workforce participation (Arbeitsgruppe Perspektivstudien 1969, 17). Overall, Kneschaurek expected the Swiss population to grow from 5.9 million in the year 1965 to 7.5 million by the year 2000 (Arbeitsgruppe Perspektivstudien 1969, 59).

Retrospectively, this forecast proved to be accurate since the overall population of Switzerland counted 7.164 million inhabitants in the year 2000. This accuracy was, however, less the result of a correct population model rather than of Kneschaureks conviction that the number of non-Swiss residents and the overall situation would stabilize in the long-run. Retrospectively, this is surprising given the context of the cold war as well as of the experience of major global conflicts in the first half of the 20th century.

That Kneschaurek based his forecasts on an implicit concept of economic development rather than on the assessment of individual economic and non-economic factors, became especially clear in his second report on the development Swiss economy. Kneschaurek had previously been criticized for not taking political factors into account[36] (Arbeitsgruppe Perspektivstudien 1970, 13). So he decided to make explicit why he shared the conviction that the impact of non-economic factors could be ignored. In a first step, Kneschaurek acknowledged that non-economic factors such as political events had had an effect on the development of the economy during the last 25 years. In a second step, however, he argued that those events counterbalanced in the long-run so that it was not necessary to take them into account (Arbeitsgruppe Perspektivstudien 1970, 13). To illustrate his assertion, Kneschaurek added a graphic to the second volume of his study that showed the development of the Swiss GDP starting from 1946 to 1968 and amended what he called the most important events of global relevance. With an additional dotted-line, Kneschaurek traced the general trend of the Swiss economy, showing that the non-economic factors overall counterbalanced each other.

As Kneschaurek stated, it was remarkable that those numerous global events had in sum almost no influence on the Swiss economy (Arbeitsgruppe Perspektivstudien 1970, 22). It seems obvious that the graphic served primarily as a justification for his methodology. It started precisely in the year 1947, when the Swiss economy had recovered from World War II, and was moving on a remarkably steady growth path. This had not been the case in the first half of the century, as Kneschaurek knew from his doctoral thesis on the Swiss business cycle from 1929 to 1939 (Kneschaurek 1952). Kneschaurek did not explain by which criteria he had selected the "most important events" of global relevance and how he assessed and isolated their assumed effects on the economy.

Kneschaurek did not explain his methodology in detail, but he reacted strongly regarding the critique that he had merely extrapolated historical trends. As he objected, the forecasts of the Swiss economy were not based on statistical extrapolations but resulted from international

36 Kneschaurek was accused of assuming a standstill of the political discussions or a neutralization of all non-economic factors.

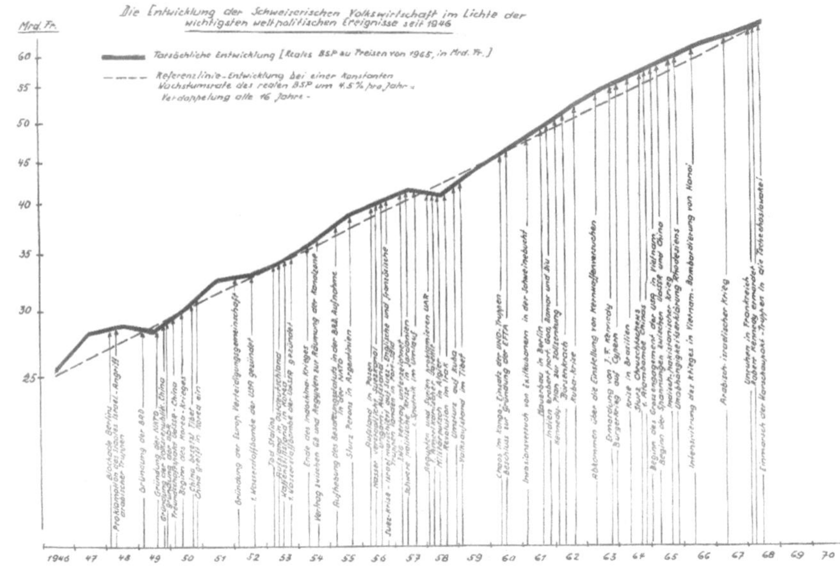

Fig. 1: "The Development of the Swiss Economy in the Light of the Most Important International Events since 1946."
Source: Arbeitsgruppe Perspektivstudien (1970), 24.

comparisons[37] (*Schaffhauser Nachrichten* 1972; Wittmann 1972, 1). Kneschaurek used many graphs to demonstrate historical trends in his reports, but it seems nevertheless probable that he used historical data and trend extrapolation to historicize the economy and to assess possible developments. To forecast the Swiss GDP up to the year 2000, Kneschaurek could, however, not use trend extrapolation since there were no data series for the national production available. Kneschaurek instead used a simple production function which derived economic growth from the increasing employment rate and increasing productivity (Arbeitsgruppe Perspektivstudien 1970, 31). To determine the future productivity of Switzerland, Kneschaurek took the past productivity

37 It was mainly the economist Walter Wittmann who accused Francesco Kneschaurek of using only extrapolation of time series and of not considering the accelerated change.

development of the USA, which he implicitly perceived as the highest developed country. He assumed, that Switzerland would follow the economic development path of the US with a time lag, disregarding the individual features of the Swiss economy.[38] (Arbeitsgruppe Perspektivstudien 1970, 40)

Kneschaurek thus had – whether consciously or unconsciously – a "modern" conception of economic development, in which the United States were considered the highest developed country and a model for reaching modernity other countries such as Switzerland should follow (Wehler 1975, 12). Using past productivity records of the U.S., Kneschaurek expected the Swiss productivity to slow down as it had happened in the United States. Accordingly, he forecasted that Switzerland's annual growth rate would drop from 4.6 percent to 3 to 3.5 percent in average (Arbeitsgruppe Perspektivstudien 1970, 21, 37–38, 43).

5. A Switzerland of 10 Million Inhabitants

Kneschaurek and the federal administration wanted to initiate a discussion about the future of Switzerland by publishing the results of the different reports right away. By doing so, they acknowledged that the forecasts of the *Perspektivstudien* could have an effect on the development of the country. They expected, however, that this effect would primarily materialize in political debates on future planning. The media coverage was accordingly of great relevance for the overall debate of the projects results (Arbeitsgruppe Perspektivstudien 1970, 3–4). The *Perspektivstudien* received a lot of media attention, as they were the first Swiss studies forecasting the future over a period of thirty years. Furthermore, the repeated publication of the reports from 1969 to 1974 and the set of press

---

38 With regard to the USA, Kneschaurek wrote: „Die USA werden doch im allgemeinen als das Land mit dem fortgeschrittensten Stand der Technik und der ausgeprägtesten Unternehmerdynamik bezeichnet, in welchem die Rationalisierung, Standardisierung und neuerdings Automatisierung besonders grossgeschrieben werden. Es kommt nicht von ungefähr, dass man selbst von einem 'technological gap' oder von einem 'managereal gap' zwischen den USA und den industriell am weitesten fortgeschrittenen Industrieländern Westeuropas spricht."

conferences that emphasized the importance of the results contributed to the fact that the *Perspektivstudien* remained a talking point for years (Weber 1970). When Francesco Kneschaurek became the new deputy for economic questions (Delegierter für Konjunkturfragen) in 1973, replacing Hugo Allemann, the *Perspektivstudien* got even more publicity. This was especially the case because Kneschaurek's double function as forecaster and top-ranking official for economic policy was controversial (*Basler Nachrichten* 1973).

As Kneschaurek noted in his second report about the development of the Swiss economy, most newspapers gave a correct account of the published reports. In some cases, however, some of the results were incorrectly reproduced or falsely interpreted. The decreasing growth rate of economic wealth, for instance, was taken as evidence of generally decreasing wealth. This reactivated the fear of an economic downturn (Arbeitsgruppe Perspektivstudien 1970, 3). Generally, the newspapers interpreted the results of the study as alarming, even those which reproduced Kneschaurek´s forecasts correctly. The *Neue Zürcher Zeitung* worried about the slowing growth rate of the Swiss wealth (*Neue Zürcher Zeitung* 1970). The *Basler Nachrichten* qualified Kneschaurek's forecast of the development of population and employment as indicating a "catastrophic labor shortage" (*Basler Nachrichten* 1970). The *Aargauer Tagblatt* started their article with Kneschaurek's own words of a "keineswegs ermutigende Prognose" (*Aargauer Tagblatt* 1970).

These reactions were not only expected by Kneschaurek and Allemann, but intended. They inaugurated the first press conference with the confession that they had intentionally tried to shock the audience by presenting forecasts in an alarming way and that they wanted to wake the Swiss people from their lethargy (*Berner Tagwacht* 1970). Kneschaurek and Allemann thus communicated their forecasts as worst-case scenarios to prevent undesirable developments. This, however, contradicted Kneschaurek's implicit development model, which promulgated an evolutionary process towards modernity supposedly valid for all countries. Moreover, in Kneschaurek's and Allemann's dystopic conceptions, the ambivalent character of the original mandate between planning and prediction became again apparent. The forecasts were presented both as a future to come and as a future that should be prevented by planning it.

In 1974, the public perception of the *Perspektivstudien* started to change. Firstly, newspapers did not comment on the expected slowdown of the economic growth rate anymore, although Kneschaurek expected an even smaller growth of rate of 2.6 to 3.2 percent for the Swiss economy by the year 2000 in his revised report of January 1974 (Arbeitsgruppe Perspektivstudien 1974, 77). This can possibly be explained by the fact that the revised report did not get the same attention as the first one. The final report that followed a couple of months later contained hardly any numerical forecasts anymore, but focused on the description of the expected structural problems of the Swiss economy. Accordingly, the newspapers summarized the main statements without taking up particular aspects. Only a few articles honored Kneschaurek's work that now came to an end (Böckli 1974; Keller 1974; Stauffer 1974). Others, however, questioned the general usefulness of the Perspektivstudien in the light of imminent problems such as inflation or the oil crisis (Meyer 1974). The public, it seems, had grown tired of the Perspektivstudien when the final report was released in August 1974.

At the end of the year 1974, however, when a severe economic recession hit Switzerland, Kneschaurek and his *Perspektivstudien* received again a lot of media attention. The rapidly worsening economic situation triggered a discussion about the "culprit" of the crisis. The building industry was hit particularly hard by the recession and experienced a dramatic downturn of demand that resulted in a fall in employment of 40 percent. Kneschaurek, who had been appointed Deputy for economic questions in 1973, attributed this overcapacity to a poor planning by industry. He explained that constructors had made the mistake to extrapolate the growth rate of demand of the last couple of years. As he argued, there was no possibility to get back to the pre-crisis equilibrium. The building industry had therefore no other option than to adjust their supply to a realistic amount (*Basler Nachrichten* 1975).

The problem was, however, that Kneschaurek had never – neither in his forecasts nor in his role as Deputy for economic questions – pointed to the possibility of an imminent recession that would force the building industry to reduce their supply dramatically. Therefore, exponents of the industry refused to be blamed for their situation and stroke back by accusing Kneschaurek for having forecasted a population of 10 million inhabitants in Switzerland by the year 2000. Among Kneschaurek's harshest critics was the building contractor and national councilor Karl Flubacher, who expressed his deep contempt towards the economists who advised the Bundesrat in a talk at the annual conference of the association of the master carpenters in 1975:

> „Der Schaden, der durch wirtschaftsfremde Theoretiker angerichtet wurde, ist wesentlich grösser als der Erfolg (…). Allzulange hat sich der Bundesrat bei seinen Entscheidungen auf den Rat wirtschaftspolitischer Technokraten verlassen. Während die Propheten die These von 10 Millionen Einwohnern im Jahr 2000 verkündeten und sich heute davon absetzen, macht man uns den Vorwurf, wir hätten zu vielen Wohnungen gebaut. (…) Viele wurden durch die falschen Bevölkerungsprognosen zu Fehlinvestitionen verleitet. Die Warnungen unsererseits, dass der Wohnungsmangel – aus politischen Gründen – stark übertrieben wurde, verhallten ungehört. Erst als man in den städtischen Agglomerationen Tausende von Leerwohnungen feststellte, zog man die Alarmglocken und suchte prompt Sündenböcke, aber am falschen Ort. Sie wurden nämlich von jenen Leuten gesucht, die selbst für die Misere verantwortlich sind" („Die Widerwärtigkeiten der heutigen Zeit" 1975, 643).

Flubacher did not name the *Perspektivstudien* and Kneschaurek personally, but pointed to the general practice of economic advising and forecasting, which he made responsible for decisions that went against the market expertise of the building industry. Flubacher's critique shows that not the individual results of the *Perspektivstudien*, but the general practice of forecasting had contributed to the idea that the post-war prosperity would last forever. This became particularly clear in the case of the figure of 10 million inhabitants, which did not stem from the *Perspektivstudien*. The 10 million inhabitants represented precisely the idea that the population growth rate of the 1960s would persist and with it the high demand for apartments and consumption goods that that had boosted the Swiss economy. The figure of 10 million inhabitants was thus a metaphor for a stable growth path, in which the future became stabilized as a prolongation of the present state.

The practice of long-term forecasting relying only on the development of economic variables such as productivity and the workforce created thus a reality, in which institutions, political power relations as well as the conditions of world markets were assumed to be stable, thus discarding social change as a driving force. Since this projected reality inspired investment decisions, it became performative, changing the overall orientation of economic actors towards the future, and thus their decisions and actions. Their disappointment vis-à-vis the outburst of the crisis, in turn, cast doubt on the expertise of economists and the government and thus affected the political power relations in place.

Although the figure of 10 million inhabitants did not appear in the *Perspektivstudien*, the accusation that Kneschaurek had put it in circulation was taken over by newspapers and spread quickly (*Walliser Volksfreund* 1975, 13). The *Perspektivstudien* also came under attack politically by a parliamentary request that questioned their usefulness, alluding to the fact that the forecasts had to be readjusted repeatedly. Kneschaurek asked the Chancellor of the Confederation for an official clarification.[39] In his cover letter that accompanied his request for clarification, Kneschaurek noted that neither he nor his team had ever forecasted a population of 10 million inhabitants.[40] In a session of the parliament, the Federal Councillor and head of the economic department of the state, Ernst Brugger, declared accordingly that Kneschaurek never had forecasted a population of 10 million for Switzerland for the year 2000 (Brugger 1975, 656). Unfortunately, it turned out that Kneschaurek had once referred to the possibility of a Switzerland with 10 million inhabitants in a paper of 1962 (*Die Tat* 1975, 1).

The somehow odd recurrence of the figure of a Switzerland of 10 million inhabitants shows that economic long-term forecasts of the 1960s and 1970s cannot be conceptualized as mere descriptions or projections of an actual state of the economy that help political elites to anticipate unwanted developments. Instead, they have to be considered as performative, as they contributed to an overall idea that the future state of the economy could be projected and that its development was solely relevant to foresee the future of the overall society. Economic knowledge that relies on the conceptualization of the economy as a separated sphere to predict the long-term future of societies constructed a deterministic, a-historical

39 Einfache Anfrage Ganz vom 30. Januar 1975, Frühjahrssession des Nationalrates, Amtliches Bulletin der Bundesversammlung, Bd. II, 1975, p. 589.

40 Notiz von Francesco Kneschaurek an den Bundeskanzler vom 19.02.1975, BAR E1010C#2009/102#53*.

reality that disconnected actors from short-run events and changes. The readiness to accept those studies and their methodical assumptions must be seen in the context of Keynesianism, in which after the experience of the Great Depression the idea that the economy could be controlled by demand management prevailed.

To understand the emergence of long-term studies and their temporary spread, Keynesianism has to be understood as a governmentality in which not only Keynes' macroeconomic concepts, but also practices and institutions of the post-1945 nation-states supported and idealized the undertaking of a macroeconomic management that led eventually to a belief in the controllability and therefore predictability of the economy. The focus on the economic development, however, cannot be explained only by the emergence of Keynesianism. The Cold War and in particular the growing competition between capitalist and socialist countries, too, contributed to a prioritization of economic development and led to an obsession with economic growth rates and a neglect of the role history. It has thus a certain irony that the a-historical conceptualization of the economy as a separated sphere that reached an ideological summit with the emergence of long-term economic forecasts turned them into history with the outbreak of the economic crisis of the 1970s.

References

Aargauer Tagblatt. 1970. „Abflauender Wohlstand des Schweizers?", March 25, 1970.

American Academy of Arts and Sciences, Commission on the Year 2000. 1968. *Der Weg ins Jahr 2000: Perspektiven, Prognosen, Modelle; Bericht der „Kommission für das Jahr 2000"*. Modelle für eine neue Welt. München: Desch.

Arbeitsgruppe Perspektivstudien. 1969. *Bevölkerung und Erwerbstätigkeit. Teil I*. Entwicklungsperspektiven der Schweizerischen Volkswirtschaft bis zum Jahre 2000. St. Gallen: Arbeitsgruppe Perspektivstudien.

Arbeitsgruppe Perspektivstudien. 1970. *Gesamtwirtschaftliche Entwicklungsperspektiven. Teil II*. Entwicklungsperspektiven der Schweizerischen Volkswirtschaft bis zum Jahre 2000. St. Gallen: Arbeitsgruppe Perspektivstudien.

Arbeitsgruppe Perspektivstudien. 1974. *Gesamtwirtschaftliche Entwicklungsperspektiven. Teill II*. 2., überarbeitete Auflage. Entwicklungsperspektiven der Schweizerischen Volkswirtschaft bis zum Jahre 2000. St. Gallen: Arbeitsgruppe Perspektivstudien.

Armatte, Michel. 1992. „Conjonctions, conjonctures et conjectures. Les baromètres économiques (1885–1930)". *Histoire & Mesure* VII (1/2): 99–150.

Basler Nachrichten. „Dräuendes Gewölk am Wirtschafts-Horizont. Die Schweizer Wirtschaft bis zum Jahr 2000", April 4, 1970.

Basler Nachrichten. „Professor Kneschaurek wird neuer Konjunkturdelegierter des Bundesrates", August 30, 1973.

Basler Nachrichten. „Bauwirtschaft soll gesundschrumpfen", February 14, 1975.

„Bericht des Schweizerischen Bundesrats über seine Geschäftsführung im Jahr 1965". 1965. *Geschäftsberichte des Bundesrates*, 109: 1–416.

Berner Tagwacht. 1970. „Düstere Zukunft der Schweiz? Ungünstige Prognosen für das Jahr 2000", March 24, 1970.

Böckli, Hans-Rudolf. 1974. „Bewundernswert". *St. Galler Tagblatt*, June 15, 1974.

Borel, Alfred. 1967. „Du devoir de prévision". *Journal de Genève*, October 19, 1967.

Brugger, Ernst. 1975. „Zur aktuellen konjunkturellen Lage, insbesondere auf dem Bausektor". *Schweizerische Bauzeitung* 93 (42): 654–58.

Callon, Michel. 2006. "What Does It Mean to Say that Economics Is Performative?" https://halshs.archives-ouvertes.fr/halshs-00091596 (last access 2/5/2020).

Die Tat. 1975. „Finderlohn für den Zürcher «Stapi». Professor Kneschaurek und das Schweizer 10-Millionen-Volk", June 30, 1975.

„Die Widerwärtigkeiten der heutigen Zeit". 1975. *Hoch + Tiefbau* 74 (47): 642–44.

Eisinger, Angelus. 1998. „Die Rolle des Föderalismus und der Referendumsdemokratie in den Debatten um die Bundesfinanzordnung zwischen 1948 und 1970". *Dynamisierung und Umbau. Die Schweiz in den 60er und 70erJahren*, edited by Mario König, Georg Kreis, Franziska Meister, and Gaetano Romano. Zurich: Chronos.

Foucault, Michel, und Thomas Lemke. 2005. *Analytik der Macht*,. Frankfurt am Main: Suhrkamp.

Friedman, Walter A. 2014. *Fortune Tellers. The Story of America's First Economic Forecasters*. Princeton: Princeton University Press.

Hall, Peter A. 1989. *The Political Power of Economic Ideas : Keynesianism across Nations*. Princeton: Princeton University Press.

Hodgson, Geoffrey M. 2001. *How Economics Forgot History: The Problem of Historical Specificity in Social Science (Economics As Social Theory)*. London: Routledge.

Hodgson, Geoffrey M. 2013. "On the Complexity of Economic Reality and the History of the use of Mathematics in Economics". *Filosofía de la Economía* 1 (1): 25–45.

Jöhr, Adolf. 1966. *Schätzung der Einnahmen und Ausgaben des Bundes 1966–1974 : Grundlagen einer langfristigen Finanzplanung des Bundes: Bericht der Eidgenössischen Expertenkommission zur Bearbeitung von Problemen einer langfristigen Finanzplanung im Bunde*. St. Gallen: n. p.

Keller, Jakob. 1974. „Plädoyer für Kneschaurek". *Tagesanzeiger, Zurich*, June 15 1974.

Kleps, Karlheinz. 1967. *Langfristige Finanzplanung der öffentlichen Hand*. Zeitfragen der schweizerischen Wirtschaft und Politik 90. Zurich: Redressement National.

Kneschaurek, Francesco. 1952. *Der schweizerische Konjunkturverlauf und seine Bestimmungsfaktoren: dargestellt auf Grund der Periode 1929 bis 1939*. Zurich: Polygraphischer Verlag.

Kneschaurek, Francesco. 1956. „Langfristige Wirtschaftsentwicklung und Konjunkturentwicklung". *Gotthard-Brief* 16 (January-February): 1–7.

Kneschaurek, Francesco. 1962. "National Product Forecasts in Switzerland". In *Europe's Future in Figures*, edited by R. C. Geary, 184–90. Amsterdam: North-Holland.

Kneschaurek, Francesco. 1972. „Schade um die Zeit". *Schweizerische Finanzzeitung*, April 26, 1972.

Kneschaurek, Francesco. 1980. *Der „Trendbruch" der siebziger Jahre und seine wirtschaftlichen Konsequenzen*. Diessenhofen: Rüegger.

Kneschaurek, Francesco, O. K. Kaufmann, and W. Geiger, eds. 1964. „Konjunktur- und wachstumsgerechte Wirtschaftspolitik. Ein Programm für die Schweiz“. *Wirtschaft und Recht* 16 (3): 148–271.

Kommission für Konjunkturbeobachtung. 1957. „Konjunkturentwicklung und Teuerungsbekämpfung“. *Mitteilungen der Kommission für Konjunkturbeobachtung*, Beilage zu «Die Volkswirtschaft», 127 (May).

La Documentation française. 1964. *Réflexions pour 1985*. Bd. 5. Travaux pour le plan. Paris: La Documentation Française.

Laak van, Dirk. 2010. „Planung, Planbarkeit und Planungseuphorie“. *Docupedia-Zeitgeschichte* 1.0 (February). http://dx.doi.org/10.14765/zzf.dok.2.577.v1.

Maiolino, Angelo. 2011. *Als die Italiener noch Tschinggen waren. Der Widerstand gegen die Schwarzenbach-Initiative*. Zurich: Rotpunktverlag.

Meiksins Wood, Ellen. 1995. *Democracy against Capitalism. Renewing Historical Materialism*. Cambridge: Cambridge University Press.

Meyer, Werner. 1974. „Schicksal oder machbare Welt? Anmerkungen zum Schlussbericht über die Perspektiven der schweizerischen Volkswirtschaft“. *Neue Bündner Zeitung*, July 9, 1974.

Mitchell, Timothy. 2008. “Rethinking Economy”. *Geoforum* 39: 1116–21.

Morgan, Mary S. 1990. *The History of Econometric Ideas*. Cambridge: Cambridge University Press.

Neue Zürcher Zeitung. 1970. „Kneschaureks Wachstumsprognose – eine Warnung“, April 5, 1970.

Neue Zürcher Zeitung. 1990. „Der Griff nach der Zukunft. Emeritierung von Prof. Kneschaurek“, February 6, 1990.

Persky, Joseph. 1990. “Retrospectives: Ceteris Paribus”. *The Journal of Economic Perspectives* 4 (2): 87–193.

Prader, Gaudenz. 1981. *50 Jahre schweizerische Stabilisierungspolitik. Lernprozesse in Theorie und Politik am Beispiel der Finanz- und Beschäftigungspolitik des Bundes*. Zurich: Schulthess.

Quinet, Emile. 1990. *La planification française*. Que sais-je? : le point des connaissances actuelles. Paris: Presses universitaires de France.

Reyhl, Erich. 1976. „Futurologen haben es nicht leicht". *National-Zeitung*, October 7, 1976.

Ronca, Marion. 2020. „Die unsichtbare Volkswirtschaft. Die Verhandlungen um eine Schweizer Produktionsstatistik 1920–1982". In *Wissensökonomie und Digitalisierung. Geschichte und Perspektiven der wissensbasierten Wirtschaft*, edited by Yaman Kouli, Peter Pawlowsky, and Markus Hertwig. Berlin: Springer.

Rostow, Walt Whitman. 1960. *The Stages of Economic Growth: A Non-Communist Manifesto*. Cambridge: Cambridge University Press.

Schaffhauser Nachrichten. 1972. „Eine tiefe Furche in die Zukunft ziehen. Gespräch mit Prof. Francesco Kneschaurek", May 26, 1972.

Schanetzky, Tim. 2007. *Die grosse Ernüchterung: Wirtschaftspolitik, Expertise und Gesellschaft in der Bundesrepublik 1966 bis 1982*. Berlin: Akademie Verlag.

Schmelzer, Matthias. 2016. *The Hegemony of Growth: The OECD and the Making of the Economic Growth Paradigm*. Cambridge: Cambridge University Press.

Schmid, Karl. 1971. „Gedanken über die Planung der Zukunft. Festvortrag vor der 72. Generalversammlung des SIA, gehalten am 3. Juli 1971 im Opernhaus Zürich". *Schweizerische Bauzeitung* 89 (28): 707–11.

Seefried, Elke. 2015. *Zukünfte. Aufstieg und Krise der Zukunftsforschung 1945–1980*. Berlin; Boston: De Gruyter Oldenbourg.

Solow, Robert Merton. 1956. "A Contribution to the Theory of Economic Growth". *The Quarterly Journal of Economics* 70 (1): 65–94.

Solow, Robert Merton. 1957. "Technical Change and the Aggregate Production Function". *The Review of Economics and Statistics* 39 (3): 312–20.

Stauffer, Pierre-André. 1974. „Quel visage se composera la Suisse de l'an 2000?" *Journal de Genève*, June 15, 1974.

Steinmüller, Karlheinz. 2000. „Zukunftsforschung in Europa. Ein Abriss der Geschichte". In *Zukunftsforschung in Europa. Ergebnisse und Perspektiven*, edited by Karlheinz Steinmüller, Rolf Kreibich, and Christoph Zöpel. Baden-Baden: Nomos.

Taylor, Overton Hume. 1929. "Economics and the Idea of Natural Laws". *The Quarterly Journal of Economics* 44 (1): 1–39.

Tooze, Adam. 2001. *Statistics and the German State, 1900–1945. The Making of Economic Knowledge*. Cambridge: Cambridge University Press.

Walliser Volksfreund. 1975. „Zu viel Bern – zu viel Verwaltung", March 6, 1975.

Weber, Max. 1970. „Ernst oder Spielerei". *Berner Tagwacht*, April 2, 1970.

Wehler, Hans-Ulrich. 1975. *Modernisierungstheorie und Geschichte*. Göttingen: Vandenhoeck & Ruprecht.

Wittmann, Walter. 1972. *Zukunftsperspektiven der Schweiz. Auseinandersetzung mit der Kneschaurek-Studie*. Separatdruck aus der National-Zeitung. Basel: n. p.

Timo Walter (University of Edinburgh)

The Janus Face of Inflation Targeting: How Governing Market Expectations of the Future Imprisons Monetary Policy in a Normalized Present

Abstract: Modern 'inflation targeting' is widely praised as having achieved a level of technical sophistication and efficacy unprecedented by previous modes of monetary policy. Building on the Rational Expectation Hypothesis, it is premised on the idea that it is possible to influence *future* outcomes (inflation) by shaping and conducting economic expectations in the *present*. Monetary authorities thus rely on the structure of market expectations as the *medium* that transmits their intended policy into the future, allowing them to focus on fine-tuning the 'communicability' (credibility and transparency) of their *signals*. However, even among practitioners the precise nature and functioning of this inter-temporal link remains contested, despite its seeming effectiveness and the lack of a practical alternative. In this chapter, I want to deploy some concepts and analytics from a recent literature in sociology and anthropology on the coordination of social futures to query the link between present and future on which inflation targeting is premised. My objective is to uncover the social and organizational preconditions of this form of economic temporality, in order to better understand what limitations they place on central banks' ability to 'govern the future'. To this end, I look at the so-called Volcker experiment in which the fundamental procedures for governing the future were developed – although their significance only became clear later. The gist of my argument is that the consensus view of 'modern' monetary policy insufficiently distinguishes between the *present future* (the future as it is imagined and projected from the present) and the *future present* (as it materializes at a later point in time). Inflation targeting rests on procedures which set up what, sociologically speaking, amounts to a tightly integrated and formalized 'interaction order' between central bank and financial markets. This interaction order enables a fine-tuning of expectational reactions by markets to policy signals – but at the price of decoupling monetary policy from the economic structures required for securing a congruence between present future and future present.

Keywords: Central banks, monetary policy, expectations, futurity, economic coordination, indicators, inflation targeting

1. Introduction: Monetary Policy and the Problems of 'Knowing the Future'

Over the decade starting in the mid-1980s, central banking underwent a "Quiet Revolution" and "went modern" (Blinder 2004). By the mid-1990s, ongoing changes cohered enough to begin giving them a more formal codification and a name: *inflation targeting* had been born (Bernanke and Mishkin 1997; Bernanke and Woodford 2006; Cobham 2010). Where the 'old' view of monetary policy (implementation) attempted to shift the hydraulics of macroeconomic aggregates (commonly, by seeking to control various *monetary* aggregates), the 'new' view's "key proposition ... is that the appropriate operational target of monetary policy implementation is the short-term interest rate, and that this is the case independently of the characteristics of financial markets and independently of the monetary policy strategy" (Bindseil 2004, 5). Inspired by the "Rational Expectations Revolution" (Muth 1961; Lucas 1972; Sargent and Wallace 1976; Phelbs and Taylor 1977; see also Miller 1994), central banks worldwide have stopped attempting to push policy signals heavy-handedly through the cumbrous hydraulic machinery of monetary quantities and macroeconomic variables of yore. Instead, they have shifted towards attempting to *directly* 'conduct the conduct' (Foucault et al. 1991, 48) of market actors "whose activities propel the transmission mechanism of monetary policy" (Braun 2015, 369).

Since then, it has become conventional wisdom that this new channel of policy transmission by *directly* influencing the structures of expectations of economic actors greatly improves monetary policy's efficacy in achieving its primary objective of controlling inflation. By disentangling the technical procedures of monetary policy *implementation* from the problem of the transmission or propagation of the signals thus generated, central banks are capable of signaling their policy stance far more clearly than in the 'old' system, when the causalities on which implementation relied were tightly entwined with macroeconomic aggregates and dynamics. Thanks to this improvement in the *communicability* (Stinchcombe 2001, chap. 2) of its intended purposes, monetary policy can now shape inflation expectations (more or less) *directly* through alterations in its key policy instrument, the short-term interest rate, in such a way that they materialize into the desired inflation rate (of course, with a lag).

Modern monetary policy thus is *performative* in the sense developed by a growing literature in the field of economic sociology and the so-called 'Social studies of finance' (Callon 2007; MacKenzie, Muniesa, and Siu 2007). As Mann (2018, 18) has put it, "if [monetary policy] is believable enough to shape (rational) expectations, it will work itself out like a self-fulfilling prophecy" –at least, that is, "to the extent that economic actors adjust their practices to fit the narrative" (Beckert 2016, 116) or state of the (economic) world that the policy intended. This also means that monetary policy has become inherently *forward-looking*, as it seeks to govern (through) the future, or more accurately: govern the future *in* the present *through expectations about* the future. To ensure that policy signals emitted in the present indeed produce their desired effects in the future, central banks have heavily invested in their forecasting apparatus. This has allowed them to focus their operating procedures on keeping track of the (shifting) *expectations about the future* held by the actors "whose activities propel the transmission mechanism of monetary policy" (Braun 2015, 369). Investments in central banks' economic modeling capacities have helped improve the sophistication of their forecasts, which have been integrated more tightly with the decision-making process (see, e.g. Smart 2006). Better forecasting then allows for more fine-tuned policy signals, as well as increasing the transparency of those signals to the observers whose behavior and calculations it is meant to influence, especially when the reasons for the policy stance are openly communicated (Guthrie and Wright 2000; Geraats 2002; Issing 2005; Demertzis and Hughes Hallett 2007).

By making such "investments in forms" (Thévenot 1984), which help in mapping (market) expectations, and tracking the effects of their policy interventions, central banks thus have been able to construct highly standardized and formalized shared "frames," creating "an expectations environment that can be managed" (Morgan 2013, 744 – cited in Braun 2015). Within such a joint(ly generated) *frame*, the signals sent through central banks' manipulation of the *short-term interest rate* are translated into *long-term interest rate(s) and asset prices*, providing monetary policy with control over shaping the trajectory of inflation over time (cf. the account given by Braun 2015).

Practitioners take immense pride in this technical arrangement, a view often shared not only by academic economists but also adopted by many observers in the social sciences who have studied this 'communicative turn' in monetary policy as an exemplar of a more general trend towards "future-oriented" or anticipatory modes of social coordination and governance (Holmes 2014; Braun 2015; on the sociology of the future, see Tavory and Eliasoph 2013; Beckert 2016). There is, however, astonishingly little sustained reflection within expert circles (both practitioners and their academic observers and interlocutors) about the forms of temporality that underpin this technical arrangement, or about the tricky epistemological and theoretical problems involved in, first, *knowing the future* and, second, of using it as an instrument for shaping expectations. Beckert has put the problem in a nutshell when he points out that (present) expectations are necessarily (only) "*pretended* representations of a future state of affairs" (Beckert 2013, 226). Whether these representations turn out to be true, and thus whether the expectations based on them turn out to have been "fictional" or "rational", will only be revealed in the future once it arrives.

The importance that contemporary accounts of monetary policy attach to the somewhat elusive concept of its *credibility* illustrates this problem. Credibility necessarily lies in the eye of the beholder: for monetary policy signals to be *credible* to (present) market actors, they need to align with these actors' *present* "pretended representations of a future state of affairs" (long) *before* it can be decided whether they were, in fact, true. Whether credibility in terms of a two-way alignment between intended signals and expectations *in the present* actually extends to a three-way alignment *with the future* is a question that has received (too) little systematic attention. In aligning its signals to the structure of those beliefs about a "fictive" (Beckert 2016) imagined future, can monetary policy also be assumed to be influencing *that* future which eventually becomes real, and in terms of which the initial expectations will have been proven "rational"[1]? Indeed, it seems that "there is no consensus on why the framework is successful,

1 A problem solved by modern microfoundations economics *by assumption*: namely, the assumption of an a-priori congruence of structures of expectations with economic structures with only the probabilities of different possible states of the world being 'unknown' (Beckert and Bronk 2018, 8).

why and how expectations become anchored by virtue of these targeting protocols" (Blinder 2004, 74 ff.; Holmes 2009, 403).

A number of well-placed and knowledgeable observers have raised serious issues with assuming a smooth transition of policy intentions through expectations that are isomorphic with (and based on perfect knowledge of) the true structure of the economy, to the economy's future state(s). For instance, Orphanides has shown in a series of publications (Orphanides 2001, 2002, 2003; Orphanides and Williams 2007) that considerable gaps (may) exist between the (imperfect) knowledge actors can form in real-time about the economy and its structures as revealed in ex-post data, leading to considerable misfires of (intended) policy signals. Alan Blinder (2004, 67 ff.) has pointed out how, in attempting to align their policy (implementation) to market expectations, central banks may actually end up simply "following the market" rather than shaping its expectations to the futures they hope to enact. More troubling still, serious doubts exist about the mechanisms by which policy signals (by varying the short-term interest rate) become translated over longer terms into real economic prices, thus eventually shaping inflation. The standard linkage or transmission channel is, of course, provided by the so-called expectations theory of the term structure, roughly suggesting that longer-term interest rates should be the average of short-term rates expected over the longer-term. Not only does this relationship fail to hold consistently, but more worryingly still, "the implied interest rate forecasts (expectations) that can be deduced from the yield curve bear little resemblance to what future interest rates actually turn out to be" (Blinder 2004, 77). Despite the fact that "the abject empirical failure of the expectations theory of the term structure of interest rates is a well-established fact" (ibid.), central banks continue to use the yield curve to "read the future" (Zaloom 2009; Christophers 2017) from the market expectations it (supposedly) captures– as well as assuming market actors to translate their (short-term) policy signals into longer-term price signals along its lines.

In this chapter, I want to draw on insights that have been developed in fields *outside* economics for understanding how future-oriented, forward-looking and expectations-based modes of coordination function – in particular a recent and growing literature in the fields of sociology (and anthropology) (Mische 2009; Esposito 2011; Mallard and Lakoff 2011;

Tavory and Eliasoph 2013; Beckert 2016). The goal is not, as has become something of a fashion among social scientists, to provide an external critique of economic theories and methods as "undersocialized" (Barber 1995; Beckert 2003) – a critique that comes lightly to disciplines whose bread and butter *is* "the social." Rather, my objective is to investigate in what ways the insights gained in these literatures can help us understand better *how and why* it is possible for central banks to "govern the future" by managing expectations. This will then allow us to develop a finer understanding of the conditions on which this ability depends, and what limitations these conditions imply.

To this end, I will be looking at a historical episode that has been crucial to the development of some of the key technical procedures and infrastructure on which inflation targeting relies, as well as having been formative to many of the theoretical debates and practical reflections that still shape our understanding of this form of monetary policy today. I will be looking at the policy experiments of the (early) Volcker years (approximately 1979 to the mid-1980s). This "Monetarist Experiment" was aimed at breaking the so-called "Great Inflation" of the 1960s and 1970s by restoring effective control over the money supply. While the experiment failed to achieve the latter, it produced a number of technical innovations which subsequently became the technical basis for modern, independent monetary policy seeking to control inflation through the manipulation of market expectations. I will historically contextualize these innovations, which today form a naturalized platform for inflation targeting, by showing how they respond to historically specific *problems* and, as a consequence, how the *solutions* on which modern monetary policy is premised still contain the traces of this origin, and are in important ways limited by this path-dependency.

2. The Temporalities of Modern Central Banking: Using the Future to Escape the Fetters of the Present

The sociologist Niklas Luhmann (1976), based on discussions with historian Reinhart Koselleck (2002), developed a fundamental distinction that provides much analytical leverage for our problem. He distinguished the *future present,* the future that will be an *actual* present at a future point in time, from the *present future*, that is the *possible* future(s) projected in the present on the basis of various "instruments of imagination" (Beckert 2016). While this is often used simply as a terminological distinction allowing us to designate two temporally differentiated meanings of the word "future," it opens up a much deeper theoretical problem: namely, *how* do expectations about *imagined* futures link (action in) the present to the *actually realized future(s)*? As we have seen, monetary policy theory assumes such a link to exist *if* only signals shape expectations appropriately *in the present*, and are credible.

However, a closer inspection of the *origins* of this mode of monetary policy might give us some pause. The later development of full-fledged interest rate targeting as the standard for monetary policy worldwide is commonly portrayed as something of an unintended consequence of the so-called Volcker experiment (or Monetarist Experiment). The experiment initially tried, and failed, to develop procedures that would allow a firmer and more effective control over the money supply. Attempting to avoid the disruptions resulting from a too rigid and mechanical pursuit of money supply targets, experimentation led the Fed towards a strategy of interest rate targeting. Initially, by attempting to manage non-borrowed reserves (through what today is called open-market operations) to achieve a particular interest rate, the Fed sought to indirectly control the path of borrowed (at the discount window) reserves, understood as a proxy for the overall money supply. In time, as market reactions to these interest rate signals remained stable despite the volatility of the money supply, this ability to shape market reactions through those signals became the linchpin of both practical monetary policy implementation and theoretical reflexion about it. Today, *forward-looking monetary policy that operates by manipulating expectations of future inflation in the present* has become naturalized as a trans-historical technical benchmark for good central banking (see Bindseil 2004 for an explicit argument to this effect).

In this paper, my goal is not to challenge the existing, well-founded scholarship and historical accounts of the Volcker experiment. Rather, I want to question the eagerness with which the set of procedures that emerged from it has since been naturalized as the irreducible technical basis for monetary policy. Instead of taking for granted that central banks actually exercise effective control over the future by shaping market expectations,

I want to apply some sociological concepts that allow us to better describe the temporal and social relations involved in this form of governing. My goal is twofold. First, I want to show how its technical procedures remain bound to an original historical context of tools and institutions, problems and institutions. Second and based on this, I will suggest that the technical logic of 'modern' central banking is not as transcendental and timeless as it likes to pretend – and that looking at the traces left by its origins may well help explain some of the difficulties it has been experiencing over the last decade.

The *technical* problems that many central banks faced in controlling inflation in the 1960s and 1970s are commonly seen to be tightly related to the question of central bank independence. At the time, the Fed was in many ways entangled with diverse societal interests – not simply by being subject to scrutiny by political authorities, but more importantly because of the very mechanisms though which it pursued and implemented monetary policy. Krippner (2011) has provided a detailed account of how the Fed, over the course of the 1980s, struggled to extricate its fight against inflation and the operative procedures on which it relied from social struggles about the distribution of income and credit, and the inevitable contestations of each of its policy measures this entailed. Her account favours a political-economy perspective, emphasizing how loosening the control over international capital flows and inter-bank lending and endogenous credit-creation allowed the Fed to avoid making hard choices. Seen from this angle, the shift to forward-looking monetary policy quite logically appears as a de-politicizing strategy, intended to deflect responsibility for (macroeconomic) outcomes by "letting the market show through" in the determination of the interest rate, rather than depicting the longer-term interest rate as an instrument fully under control of the central bank (Krippner 2011, 120).

Where sociologists and political-economists are wont to emphasizing the social and political struggles that shaped the transformation of central banking during this time, economists and central bankers are more prone to looking at it as a process of technical evolution and improvement. Beyond the question of how political dependence reduced the Fed's overall *effectiveness*, they are also interested in how these problems manifested themselves at the level of *technical efficiency*. From this perspective, US monetary policy in the 1960s and 1970s was clearly deficient: it consistently failed to convey a transparent and credible policy stance, with each failure further undercutting its ability to achieve its policy objectives. As *hydraulic* monetary policy incurred considerable lags as it waited for its policy signals to work their way through the system of macroeconomic variables, both market observers and the Fed itself struggled to obtain timely feedback information about the effects and effectiveness of its policies (Orphanides 2002). In this context, ideas such as Friedman's "adaptive expectations," arguing that the ambiguity and lags in monetary policy encouraged a cumulative build-up of inflationary expectations (1968), became increasingly influential: as he pointed out, economic agents *adapted* their expectations *upwards* each time monetary policy failed to clearly and unambiguously achieve its declared inflation target – which it rarely did, given the difficulties just discussed.

Over almost two decades, the Fed struggled to find solutions to these problems, seeking in particular new ways of technically improving the credibility and reducing the ambiguity of its policy signals due to lags and interaction effects. However, improving the clarity of policy signals *within* the hydraulic monetary policy system proved challenging: it would mean avoiding, in particular, overly powerful policy interventions that would trigger sharper reactions than intended, which then required further (confounding) sterilizing actions on its part and further muddied the waters. The devious results are known under the twin terms of *interest rate smoothing* and a resultant *base drift*. Fear of political repercussions as well as technical considerations prevented the Fed from moving the interest rate sufficiently strongly and anti-cyclically to control inflation, with the resultant lags generally reinforcing subsequent cyclical countermovements and allowing the monetary base (thought to be directly correlated with inflation) to grow in an uncontrolled fashion (Axilrod and Lindsey 1981; Meltzer 1991, 39; 43).

Going through the *economics* literature on this period, one encounters a shared narrative that suggests political interference and entanglements prevented the Fed (and other central banks) from developing and adopting technically superior instruments and solutions for achieving its primary objective, price stability. In contrast to such "Whiggish" storylines built around histories of technical progress being held back (temporarily) by political and social entanglements, sociological and political-economy perspectives refuse to conceive of the field(s) of possible technical solutions as given (more or less) 'a priori.' Instead, they seek to "open the black boxes" (MacKenzie 2005) of technical arrangements to analyse how the ways in which they are assembled reflect competing social interests and the struggles through which they find (political, and eventually technical) expression. In particular the field of Science and Technology Studies (STS) has argued very forcefully (e.g. Pickering 1995) that technical problems and solutions are never given *a priori* – as much as it will look that way in retrospect, once a new "paradigm" has emerged from a scientific or technical revolution (Kuhn 1996). The technical solutions that prevail (and in retrospect always appear inevitable and rational) are thus contingent upon wider fields and contexts of social interests (Habermas 1969; Bloor 1991; Barnes 2015), path-dependent on a "seamless web" of available technical elements from which they are assembled (Hughes 1986) as well as on the scientific knowledge(s) providing the "instruction sheets" (Blyth 2003) for developing them.

As David Stark (2009; and others, e.g. Callon 1998) has shown, economic domains are indeed rarely, if ever, fully subsumable to the formal-technical accounts deployed by economists and central banks alike. These accounts and models depict fields of interdependent economic actions which are given descriptions as coherent (collective) calculative problems, which in turn makes them amenable to being governed as unambiguous *technical* problems. As Stark points out, however, in reality economic domains are marked by what he calls competing "accounts of worth," that is, (collective or shared) projects of assigning economic value (and resources) to competing social purposes or activities. The technical coherence of economic policies and regulations is thus the result of what Kallinikos (2014, 9) calls a (working) *functional simplification*, that is, "the demarcation of an operational domain within which the complexity of the world is reconstructed as a simplified set of tight cause-and-effect couplings." A functional simplification establishes robust technical 'means-ends' control relations by demarcating and insulating procedures of intervention from interference by 'external' causal sequences or influences (Kallinikos 2006, 32 ff.).

Monetary policy *prior* to the transformations it underwent in the 1980s provides a perfect illustration of the *failure* to demarcate and insulate a technical domain in which coherent and stringent interventions can occur. The Fed, by the 1970s, had integrated various competing accounts of worth, and as a consequence heterogeneous conceptions of and operative strategies for controlling inflation, into rather ambiguous and heterogeneous policy procedures. Different theoretical conceptions of the causal mechanism(s) driving inflation co-existed uneasily within its operative paradigm. Most famously, the so-called notion of "cost-push inflation" led the Fed into various attempts to target the credit extended to particular economic sectors and considered to be driving general inflation, and into attempts to control wage dynamics. The real bills doctrine (see Glasner 1992) with its notion that productive credit could never be inflationary long persisted within the Fed, so that targeting *free reserves* (reserves not backing productive credit) was seen as a way to combat speculative pressures that could lead to asset and, through it, generalized inflation. Such partially incoherent *substantive* theories of inflation and the operative mechanisms they implied uneasily coexisted within the Fed's monetary policy. Its multifaceted conception of inflation also entailed a complex apparatus of technologies such as regulations of interest rates, relative (credit) prices and the allocation of money to different sectors of the economy (Konings 2011, 106 ff.). Through this, monetary policy became drawn into and contested over an entire spectrum of competing accounts of social worth – with a little artistic license, whether to fund schools or missiles, homeownership or poor relief. And, confronted with multiple, (partly) contradictory policy signals, market actors found it difficult to form clear-cut expectations about the Fed's policy stance and actions.

As the Fed pursued multiple (intermediate and ultimate) objectives simultaneously, implementing them through various (and frequently incompatible and interacting) channels of transmission, all conceived in terms of the interactions of a growing number of policy-variables, confusion crept in. Expert debates at the time revolved around the problems of demarcating an operational domain for monetary policy in such a way that (i) it achieved "tight cause-and-effect couplings," and would (ii) be able to send unambiguous, transparent and credible policy signals. These debates were cast in terms of the so-called *Instrument-Target Problem* (Poole 1970; Bindseil 2004, 29 ff.). While conducted in a highly technical jargon hard to decipher for posterity, the Instrument-Target Problem essentially revolved around the endogeneity problems facing monetary policy due to the lags observed between (a growing number of) operative and target variables (organized in multiple, mutually overlapping and interacting transmission sequences), and the resulting instabilities of the functional relations between variables.

This discussion is directly analogous to a widely debated issue in organizational sociology and organization studies, namely the problem of "tight" vs. "loose coupling" of an organization to its relevant environment (Orton and Weick 1990). A *tight coupling* in this context refers to a situation in which *too many* variables from the environment appear in the instrumental sequences and procedures by which the organization seeks to "represent and intervene" (Hacking 1983) in its environment. The tighter the coupling between an organization and its environment, the more difficult it becomes (ceteris paribus) for the organization to achieve a working functional simplification. A functional simplification isolates tight cause-effect couplings *between variables in the domain in which it means to intervene*, by shutting out other *lateral* couplings that dilute the intended control relation. A tight coupling can make achieving such a simplification more difficult, by inscribing the inherent contradictions present (to varying degrees) in all domains of social practices inside the organization's operative procedures. Rational organizations attempt to organize their procedures for intervention in a way that guarantees robust and iterable *means-ends-relations* (Stinchcombe 2001; Kallinikos 2004), and secures technical rationality for these interventions. If incompatible interests, institutional logics, or practical rationalities present *within* a domain manifest themselves as contradictory logics and imperatives within the policies and its instruments of an organization, both the effectiveness and legitimacy of the organization is threatened (see e.g. Meyer and Rowan 1977), as we have seen was the case for the Fed in the 1960s and 1970s.

In contrast, if an organization's ways of representing and intervening are more "loosely coupled" to its environment, it becomes easier for it to focus on specific functional relationships (effectively). A loose coupling thus means that an organization must deliberately bracket or black-box many of the causal and functional interdependencies between relevant variables (Orton and Weick 1990, 203). This bracketing allows it, however, to focus its attention and available instruments on means-ends-relations that align well with its (main, central) objective or mission, and can be seen as a reliable and robust technical foundation for pursuing substantive policy goals.

To central banks in the late 1970s and early 1980s, the vocabulary and theorems of (Rational) Expectations provided just such an idiom which promised a plausible "loose coupling" and functional simplification around which a more effective monetary policy could be constructed. In particular, it suggested a way of short-circuiting the complex morass of entangled instrument- and (direct, intermediate, and ultimate) target-variables and cross-cutting transmission channels, by shaping economic agents' *expectations* about inflation directly. The outcome, of course, is well-known: by "decoupling" its manipulation of the *short-term interest rate* from the movements of other (lateral) variables, the Fed gained additional degrees of freedom allowing it to move this "policy rate" as required for signaling its (longer-term) policy stance. Due to the higher transparency and credibility this permitted, its signals would be transmitted through the expectations of economic actors to the price system of the economy, giving the Fed more effective control over the evolution of the general price level.

In this way, the Fed demarcated and insulated *policy implementation* from the problem of monetary policy strategy and transmission. By improving its ability to control a *particular* (tightly coupled) cause-effect coupling, monetary policy thus has vastly increased the "communicability" (Stinchcombe) of its policy intentions: reactivity between policy signals and (presently observable) market expectations have greatly improved under the inflation targeting operational paradigm. However, these improvements in communicability were achieved by black-boxing the wider domain of causal pathways and functional relationships which link the (imagined) *present futures* monetary policy shapes to the *future present* it seeks to influence. This raises the obvious question: (how) is the undeniably high reactivity between monetary policy signals and observed expectations *in the present* transmitted to macroeconomic outcomes *in the future*?

In the next section, we therefore will have a closer look at how the Fed tried to develop novel means for ensuring the adequacy of the *present futures* it generates and manages through is functional simplification and policy implementation, to the *future presents* as they unfold in time. If we do not simply assume that (all) agents' expectations are a priori commensurable (by virtue of partaking in the same 'true model' of the economy), what secures the commensurability of agents' expectations and their continuity through time? Can they serve as an unproblematic transmission mechanism if the techniques of implementing monetary policy are decoupled from the macroeconomic structures through which it is to be transmitted to the future? How does the Fed (try to) observe and ensure its signals elicit the intended outcomes in the 'moving target' of the *future present*?

3. What 'Futures' Does Future-Oriented Monetary Policy Govern – and How?

Against the backdrop of today's almost common-sensical operative and conceptual separation of monetary policy *implementation* and *strategy/transmission*, the notion that central banks would target inflation through (market) expectations appears like a straightforward technical implication and application of the Rational Expectations hypothesis. And yet, all insights gained by Science and Technology Studies since it emerged as a discipline in its own right in the 1970s caution against such "Whiggish" narratives. What in retrospect appears as logical and effective solution to a scientific or practical problem, on closer inspection usually involves significant experimentation and "heterogeneous engineering" (Law 2012). By "drawing things together" (Latour 1990) into novel configurations, old tools and instruments can be reconstructed and deployed as part of a new functional simplification for governing a particular social domain or field. The seemingly natural identity of a scientific idea or technological concept with its practical implementation thus is "socio-technical artefact" (Kallinikos 2014) obscuring the contingency of each such translation between theory and practice.

For the case at hand, this suggests that we need to have a closer look at the processes of *abstraction* (Stinchcombe 2001), of reconfiguring the ways of "representing and intervening" (Hacking 1983) on which central banking rests, from which inflation targeting emerged as a possibility. What we need to understand is how it became plausible to conceive of shaping and governing inflation expectations in abstraction from how monetary policy is transmitted (to the future) through concrete causal pathways (in terms of macroeconomic and monetary aggregate variables). How did it become possible and plausible for monetary policy to focus (almost) exclusively on the communicability of its policy signals? To explain this rather remarkable outcome, we need to track how the Fed "black-boxed" how the present futures generated by shaping expectations are transformed into the eventual future presents of which targeted future inflation rates are a part.

As we have seen, before the Volcker experiment, the Fed as an organizational actor[2] faced a fundamental problem of how to improve the transparency and credibility of its policy signals, which was greatly impeded by the tight coupling of monetary policy's representations and mode of intervention *to* its target-domain. This tight coupling meant that interest rate signals were not unambiguously read by markets as a clue to the Fed's longer-term policy stance, but primarily considered as affecting short-run refinancing costs, and as responses to the business cycle. This left the Fed with two options: amplify its signals, which however also amplified the business cycle rather than tighten the Fed's control over it – or try to "smoothen" and steady the interest rate signals, which entailed a persistent "base drift" and further undercut the Fed's anti-inflation credibility with financial markets.

---

2 While it is uncommon in disciplines such as anthropology or history to think of organizational forms as coherent actors in their own right, it is common practice in other disciplines. In the following, I adopt the (primarily sociological) conception of organizational agency as a function of the existence of institutionalized scripts (consisting of formal knowledges, technologies, and procedures) which govern its interaction with an equally rationalized environment (Meyer and Rowan 1977; Meyer and Bromley 2013). Within rationalized social environments, the existence of such scripts thus is the basis for assigning organizations 'actorhood' (accountability, goal-directedness) in social practice (ibid.), so that individual agents (both within and outside the organizations) stand in relation of "structural equivalence" (Lorrain and White 1971) to it. My research interest lies precisely in the historical evolution of such 'scripts' of interaction between two highly rationalized organizational forms, the Federal Reserve (and, through the global diffusion of this script, eventually shared by central banks worldwide) and financial markets. Therefore, for the sake of brevity, I adopt the sociological usage of treating organizations as actors in their own right for this limited purpose.

At first, the Fed did not attempt to decouple its interest rate signals from monetary aggregates at all – but instead sought to enhance the *reactivity* between its signals and financial market reactions, by *binding* them to a system of feedback mechanisms. These feedback mechanisms would then effectively chart a longer-term *nominal anchor in terms of monetary aggregates* for expectations about inflation, communicating the Fed's intended outcomes as well as its credibility in pursuing them. The first attempt at installing such a mechanism became known as *non-borrowed reserve targeting*. By observing the divergence of past volumes of borrowed reserves from the projection a desired overall money growth path, the Fed would target the short- and medium-term growth of non-borrowed reserves through open-market operations, to restore it to the desired growth path of the money supply. Making banks bid for this pre-set volume allowed market expectations of the appropriate interest rate to 'show through' (Krippner 2011, p. 121 ff.). The discount window provided a security value and upper bound, avoiding the problems the Fed had experienced when implementing too biting constraints. In this way, both the Fed and the markets could gauge whether the volumes realized matched the Fed's desired outcomes. Observing the movements of the interest rates and the eventual volume of discount borrowing allowed both to adjust their expectations on a convergent path (Walter and Wansleben 2019, 11).

In this way, the Fed hoped to avoid the lags between the *sending of its* policy signals and the *materialization* of their effects in the inflation rate (the "ultimate target variable") that previously had created considerable noise and information deficits in its attempts to combat inflation (cf. Orphanides 2003). Thanks to these feedback loops and the (more) direct reactivity relation they generated, financial institutions' plans (or 'expectations') were not only revealed to the Fed, but it allowed the Fed to signal whether it considered these plans well-aligned to its own. The (tight) coupling of this mechanism to (indicators of) monetary aggregates worked, at least in theory, as a common benchmark or frame securing the commensurability of expectations between the Fed and the markets. In binding expectations to a structural background (i.e. the intended trajectory of monetary growth), it established a congruence and a substantive linkage between *present future* and *future present*.

This system also entailed a number of problems, however. Most fundamentally, the stability of this frame (and thus of this entire mode of conducting monetary policy, and the link between present and future) depended on the stability of the functional relationship between the Fed's interest rate signals, monetary growth rates and inflation. As markets initially failed to read Fed policy effectively (Cukierman and Meltzer 1986, 69; Feinman and Poole 1989), the Fed's attempts to signal a tougher policy stance induced precisely the types of overshoots and credit crunches the Fed had sought to avoid by this mechanism (Rosenblum and Strongin 1983; Meltzer 1991, 40). Unfortunately for the Fed, as the financial system relied more and more on *market-based liquidity*, credit expansion became increasingly erratic. Overall growth of endogenous credit-money accelerated significantly while inflation rates decreased – as the Fed's tougher stance induced a series of recessions and pushed credit from the real economy into financial circulation.[3]

At the same time as this structural background of functional relationships which the Volcker reforms had relied on as a frame for governing (through) expectations dissolved, the Fed noticed something else: the reactivity between its policy signals (sent by manipulating the short-term interest rate) and market pricing of the assets through which the Fed conducted its money market operations (basically, US treasuries) persisted and even *improved*. Pragmatically, over the course of the 1980s, the Fed reacted to this novel situation by cutting out the middleman: it simply black-boxed the initial functional relationships that involved monetary aggregates, and focused on honing the direct reactivity relation it had observed between its policy signals and what, in time, came to be labeled 'market expectations'. However, this functional simplification *also* meant that the structural background which had made expectations legible, and which had provided a durable, structural link between the *present futures* manufactured by the Fed and the *future presents* in which inflation was to be shaped, had been suppressed.

---

3 On the positive side, though, the credit crunches and extremely high interest rates that resulted from this served the Fed as "credibility tests," which established its credentials as being tough on inflation (Goodfriend 2007, 51).

As a substitute, the Fed proceeded to construct an alternative frame in terms of which the impact of its policy interventions on their intended target (*future* inflation) could be made legible. To forge such a link, the Fed since this time has relied on what Beckert has called "instruments of imagination," and what Mallard and Lakoff (2011, 341) more tellingly call "techniques of prospection with a constitutive purpose." Specifically, the Fed has developed increasingly sophisticated models for *forecasting* inflation (Brayton et al. 1997), and learned to use the expectations theory of the term structure for making legible the structure of market expectations (Johnson 1988; Frankel and Lown 1994). Through these instruments, "expectations in the economy are... anchored in prevailing cognitive models, which function as instruments for the construction of imagined futures" (Beckert 2016, 89). More specifically, monetary policy makes 'constitutive use' of the future by constructing *present futures* in terms of which expectations can be coordinated *in the present.* Using imagined futures as constitutive frame for coordinating (actions or expectations) in the present is doubtlessly *future-oriented* – but whether this coordination ultimately produces *future presents* commensurate with these projections is an open question.

Through these (and other) "techniques of prospection with a constitutive purpose" (Mallard and Lakoff 2011, 341), the Fed thus is able to construct a frame (Braun 2015) or 'present future' in terms of which it can coordinate expectations. The idea, supported theoretically by the Rational Expectations Hypothesis, is of course that expectations themselves constitute a bridge between present and future. This means that through expectations, the effects that policy interventions will have in a *future present* to come would become *legible in the present.* Observing the effects of its policy signals in and through these present futures (and assuming policy credibility) a central bank would then be able to fine-tune its signals until the desired effects manifest themselves.

However, there is considerable play between present future and future present built constitutively into this new mode of monetary policy. Indeed, in order to avoid problems with information lags that had crippled previous modes of monetary policy, inflation *targeting* in practice becomes *inflation forecast targeting.* As Svensson has pointed out, "inflation targeting implies inflation forecast targeting: The central bank's inflation forecast becomes an intermediate target (Svensson 1997, 1113). Targeting *present* inflation forecasts rather than *future* inflation is expressly motivated by the desire to improve the legibility of policy effects, and thus the *communicability* of policy signals:

> "The central bank's inflation forecast is indeed an ideal intermediate target: it is by definition the current variable that is most correlated with the goal, it is more controllable than the goal, and it can be made more observable than the goal. It can also be made very transparent, and may therefore facilitate the central bank's communication with the public, and the public's understanding of monetary policy" (Svensson 1997, 1114).

While this procedure has vastly increased the communicability of monetary policy signals, it effectively means that these signals are now tailored to *second-order expectations* about the effects of those signals (ibid., 1119). This is a sharp departure from previous practice, where they were aimed at the actual manifestation of effects in terms of the trajectory of monetary aggregates as concrete, first-order economic variables. The congruence of the present futures governed by the central bank with the future present that constitutes its ultimate target is condensed to a single, derivative indicator – but whether forecast and inflation turn out the same is only revealed in retrospect (and the reasons for correspondence, or lack thereof, remain external to this metric itself). Due to this time lag, the best operative procedure available is to try and achieve convergence of inflation target and forecast. Ex post divergence can be explained (and: explained away) by forecast and control error, often due to disturbances occurring within the control lag. The competence of a central bank then depends crucially on the quality of its forecasts. Assuming it uses the best forecasts available, its accountability does not extend to the actual correspondence of inflation target and outcome, *but only to* the convergence of target and forecast (Svensson 1997, 1120)!

As the goal of the exercise is to shape market expectations, the Fed (and other central banks) rely on a second instrument to achieve a "reflexive modeling" (Beunza and Stark 2012) of market expectations in relation to its policy signals. In order to achieve a (near-)real-time feedback on whether policy signals will have the desired effect, it is necessary to make legible its impact on (present) *expectations*, which are the moving forces supposed to transmit the policy signal through the economy. For this, the

Fed relies on a device that we have already briefly touched upon above – namely, the so-called *term structure of the interest rate* (see Goodfriend 1998). By focusing on the yield curve of the asset categories through which money market operations for implementing monetary policy are conducted, central banks thus seek to make the effects of their policy signals on expectations visible *in the present* (Blinder 2004, 67; Mann 2018, 12). These observed (changes in) expectations then provide the parameters that can be fed into the forecasting models in order to project the effects of policy signals.

To see what might be problematic with this (at first sight, seemingly rather sensible) procedure, it is useful to have a closer look at the *previous* uses made of this same device for contrast. The term structure had been used as a prism for reading the market within the Fed since since the 1920s. Before its new use for the reflexive modeling of expectations was discovered, however, it was used in line with the free-reserves doctrine to detect whether idle reserves were producing speculative distortions in the structure of asset prices. This would then allow the Fed to sterilize these anomalies (by mopping up idle reserves) and restore normalcy to the structure of expectations (see Mehrling 2011, 47 ff.) – and, in doing so, remove local expectation dynamics that could interfere with the global, normal transition path from the present to the future.

The new use that has developed since the 1980s constitutes a complete reversal of this causality. The yield curve makes expectations legible by relating yields at different points in time into an overall curve, whose shape can then be "read" as a summary of market expectations relevant for monetary policy (Christophers 2017), but also investment decisions (Zaloom 2009):

> "Central banks typically estimate both nominal and real yield curves for government debt instruments, and are able to extract from the combination and comparison of these what is referred to as the 'inflation term structure' or 'implied inflation curve' - in other words, the rates of inflation expected by the market at different points in time" (Christophers 2017, 66).

This constitutive use of the term structure of expectations creates a *present future* which can be taken to indicate substantive facts about the *future present*. One can "look first to the interest rate itself as a clue to underlying conditions... allowing the interest rate to speak not only about the contemporary financial order but also about the impact that current events may have on future economic conditions" (Zaloom 2009, 253). As the Fed always sets the short-end of the yield curve directly through its policy actions, the form of the curve can be read as an indicator of market expectations as to future policy measures (Christophers 2017, 65). It thus provides the Fed with a ready measure of the credibility and projected effects of its policy signals in a however *imagined* future constituted wholly in the present.

While this game of expectations is thus played out entirely within a *present future* constituted and disciplined by instruments of imagination, theoretically this current use entails that the term structure represents substantive facts about the *future present* – so that in shaping expectations as read through the term structure, one is also substantively (re-) shaping decisions in the *future present,* re-constituting causal pathways into the future. Christopher summarizes this shared belief when he writes that "monetary policy fashions the economy through the yield curve; the economy reacts back on monetary policy through the yield curve" (Christophers 2017, 68). However, this expectations game does not actually involve "the economy," strictly speaking. What happens is that markets and the central bank are calibrating their respective *present futures* wholly endogenously within a jointly produced frame and "interaction order" (cf. MacKenzie 2019). As expectations are coordinated around a single metric (expectations of future interest rates as summarized in the yield curve), this game can proceed largely decoupled from the specific, substantive content of the *future presents* projected. As Zaloom (2009, 253) points out, "the interest rate as a number disconnected from a specific time and place provided a powerful argument... to look first to the interest rate itself as a clue to underlying conditions. The number could be interpreted without initial reference to the specifics of time and place." And indeed, as markets have come in turn to use the yield curve for predicting central banks' presumed policy stance (Christophers 2017, 66), there has been a marked tendency for them to simply converge on central banks' published (and intended) projections of inflation, without much attention being paid to the specific reasons underlying these projections (Braun 2015, 379).

4. Conclusion: Why Standardizing the Future Increases Uncertainties

Is there reason to worry about the disconnect between the *present futures* of policy implementation, and the *future presents* that central banks seek to influence? From the perspective of most practitioners and academic economists, the answer is quite certainly a resounding 'no:' not only for them, there can be few if any doubts about the downsides of the old "tightly coupled" mode of conducting monetary policy. On top of this, the record of inflation targeting up until the 2007–2008 financial crisis seems rather impressive, although somewhat qualified by its heavy emphasis on price stability at the expense of considerable blind spots regarding financial stability (e.g. Fligstein, Stuart Brundage, and Schultz 2017). Additionally, as in fact every social action and practice is future-oriented (Tavory and Eliasoph 2013), it would appear only natural that central banks attempt to exploit this fact to direct present actions in a way to bring about desired outcomes in the future.

In contrast, the argument advanced here, while suggestive rather than conclusive, entails that we should think again, and more carefully, about the conditions under which monetary policy as it is still currently practiced[4] is actually in a position to "govern the future" (Braun 2015). As we have seen, looser forms of coupling an organization's operations to their target-domain often are a precondition for governing effectively – but they also transform what is being governed, and how. The specific arrangement of procedures and instruments on which modern inflation targeting rests not only *decouples* its implementation from the lagged structural background movements of monetary aggregates – but it *quite tightly re-couples it* to endogenously shifting market expectations within a joint and significantly "functionally simplified" frame.

With a little 'sociological imagination' (Mills 2000), the concerns raised by practitioners and observers about (i) whether policy signals are effectively translated to the *future present* (or remain contained in the *present*

4 The recent period of "unconventional monetary policy" (Bowdler and Radia 2012; Braun 2018) indeed attempts to restore the conditions for inflation targeting rather than constituting (conceptually) a departure from it.

future), as well as (ii) about the possibility that monetary policy might be forced into "following the market" as it seeks to govern through the market's expectations, reveal themselves as quite natural results of such a tightly coupled interaction order. As we have seen, inflation targeting is centered, above all, upon the strong reactivity relation between *numeric* policy signals and *numeric* inflation expectations.

In sociological terms, this interaction order thus functions analogously to how *standards* organize social interaction(s) (cf. Brunsson, Rasche, and Seidl 2012). It provides a common (numeric) benchmark around which the present futures of the central banks and market actors can be coordinated. Just like a standard, it "simplifies in two ways: by making irrelevant vast amounts of information, and by imposing on what remains the same form—a shared metric" (Espeland and Sauder 2007, 17). Additional information matters to coordination through standards only insofar as it facilitates convergence *within* the interaction order. Very much like in the case of *rankings* (a special case of a social standard), performance becomes measured exclusively in terms of the common metric: what matters is whether the measures taken in the multiple dimensions this metric summarizes achieve the desired outcomes in terms of the ranking – not whether these measures achieve any substantively rational (in terms of the dimensions) objectives[5] (Espeland and Sauder 2007). As Espeland and Sauder (2007, 17) point out, "commensuration as a mechanism of sense making is notable for how rigorously it simplifies information and for how thoroughly it decontextualizes knowledge." Successful coordination in terms of the standard or disentangled frame thus can become radically decoupled from actual, successful interventions in the wider context which the standard allegedly "measures" if and when the standard becomes the main or only criterion of success (Espeland and Sauder 2007; Tavory and Eliasoph 2013, 925). Translated to monetary policy, this suggests that improving the ability to fine-tune policy signals *within the interaction order* comes at a steep price. Increasing the credibility of policy action and thus its efficiency in influencing market expectations,

---

5 What matters is one's place *in relation to the others being ranked* – not whether there is any substantive improvement in performance in any of the dimensions summarized by the ranking.

reduces the *effective* control over the substantive shape and content of the *future present*. Indeed, as Stinchcombe (2001) demonstrates, a high(ly efficient) *communicability* of such signals does not entail their substantive effectiveness – which depends on the *adequacy and alignment* of the functional simplification with the wider context(s) in terms of which substantive effectiveness is defined. Proceduralization thus essentially entails that *efficiency* in terms of the procedure does not (automatically) entail *effectiveness* in terms of achieving the broader, more substantive set of (societal) objectives which the procedure was meant to realize: "as long as the procedure is followed, the result obtained belongs to a sphere that is neither that which is true or just, but the unfalsifiable" (Salais 2016, 121 ff.). Proceduralization, in this as in other cases, entails that the immediate reactivity and appropriateness to the other's (re-)action overrides the longer-term, "projective" significance of what is being done (see Tavory and Eliasoph 2013, 924).

The "intensive discursive exchanges within the epistemic community and 'the economy'" (Beckert 2016, 260; see also Holmes 2009, 392) typical of modern central banking are considered key to its newfound effectiveness not only by central bankers and academic economist, but also by many external observers from the social sciences (see Holmes 2014). However, as a number of observers and practitioners have pointed out, the pragmatic problem of converging on a number ends up consistently trumping the question of what this number "means" in terms of wider economic structures: in particular during the "Great Moderation," market actors have taken to simply adopting without question the projections of future inflation rates, even irrespective of their own private forecasts (Braun 2015, 379). Substantive questions about whether this mechanism actually covered all relevant dimensions of its 'target problem' of inflation, such as in particular the problem of asset inflation that helped push the global financial system into utter chaos in 2007–2009, could thus all the more easily be rationalized away (see, e.g. Bernanke and Gertler 2001; Raines, McLeod, and Leathers 2007), as they were 'black-boxed' from the technical and operative core of monetary policy.

Discursive interactions thus have become subordinate to the "interactive nature of the 'signaling process' between the central bank and those economic actors whose activities propel the transmission" (Braun 2015, 369), locking central banks into a shadow play with financial markets.

The de-contextualization involved in functional abstraction and proceduralization thus loosens the coupling of monetary policy to its target-domain, providing it with additional degrees of freedom with regard to the 'accounts of worth' and social interests inscribed in the structures of this domain. At the same time, it constrains central banks' abilities for organizational learning, which requires "an abstraction system ... to have a *trajectory of improvement* so that it can track changes in the world, increase its scope, and correct its errors" (Stinchcombe 2001, 10).

This line of argument suggests that the blind spots and failures to "see" problematic developments within the economic system are, at least in part, endemic to modern monetary policy. In contrast to much of recent scholarship (both among economists and observers from other disciplines), which has put the problem down to faulty models and groupthink (see Fligstein, Stuart Brundage, and Schultz 2017), it suggests that these problems were not accidents befalling an otherwise sound and technically flawless mode of conducting monetary policy. Rather, the very functional simplification and proceduralization on which inflation targeting is built might be in for a rethink.

References

Axilrod, Stephen H., and David E. Lindsey. 1981. "Federal Reserve System Implementation of Monetary Policy: Analytical Foundations of the New Approach." *American Economic Association* 71 (2): 246–52.

Barber, Bernard. 1995. "All Economies Are 'Embedded': The Career of a Concept, and Beyond." *Social Research* 62 (2): 387–413.

Barnes, Barry. 2015. *Interests and the Growth of Knowledge*. Abingdon: Routledge.

Beckert, Jens. 2003. "Economic Sociology and Embeddedness: How Shall We Conceptualize Economic Action?" *Journal of Economic Issues* 37 (3): 769–87.

Beckert, Jens. 2013. "Imagined Futures: Fictional Expectations in the Economy." *Theory and Society* 42 (March): 219–40. https://doi.org/10.1007/s11186-013-9191-2.

Beckert, Jens. 2016. *Imagined Futures: Fictional Expectations and Capitalist Dynamics*. Cambridge, MA: Harvard University Press.

Beckert, Jens, and Richard Bronk. 2018. "An Introduction to Uncertain Futures." In *Uncertain Futures: Imaginaries, Narratives, and Calculation in the Economy*, edited by Jens Beckert and Richard Bronk, Vol. 1, 1–38. Oxford: Oxford University Press. https://doi.org/10.1093/oso/9780198820802.003.0001.

Bernanke, Ben, and Mark Gertler. 2001. "Should Central Banks Respond to Movements in Asset Prices?" *The American Economic Review* 91 (2): 253–57.

Bernanke, Ben, and Frederic S. Mishkin. 1997. *Inflation Targeting: A New Framework for Monetary Policy?* 5893. NBER Working Paper. Cambridge, MA: National Bureau of Economic Research.

Bernanke, Ben, and Michael Woodford, eds. 2006. *The Inflation-Targeting Debate*. Paperback ed. National Bureau of Economic Research Studies in Business Cycles 32. Chicago, IL: Univ. of Chicago Press.

Beunza, Daniel, and David Stark. 2012. "From Dissonance to Resonance: Cognitive Interdependence in Quantitative Finance." *Economy and Society* 41 (3): 383–417. https://doi.org/10.1080/03085147.2011.638155.

Bindseil, Ulrich. 2004. *Monetary Policy Implementation*. Oxford; New York: Oxford University Press.

Blinder, Alan. 2004. *The Quiet Revolution : Central Banking Goes Modern*. New Haven, CT: Yale University Press.

Bloor, David. 1991. *Knowledge and Social Imagery*. 2nd ed. Chicago, IL: University of Chicago Press.

Blyth, Mark. 2003. "Structure Do Not Come with an Instruction Sheet: Interests, Ideas and Progress in Political Science." *Perspectives on Politics* 1 (4): 695–706.

Bowdler, Christopher, and Amar Radia. 2012. "Unconventional Monetary Policy: The Assessment." *Oxford Review of Economic Policy* 28 (4): 603–21. https://doi.org/10.1093/oxrep/grs037.

Braun, Benjamin. 2015. "Governing the Future: The European Central Bank's Expectation Management during the Great Moderation." *Economy and Society* 44 (3): 367–91. https://doi.org/10.1080/03085147.2015.1049447.

Braun, Benjamin. 2018. "Central Bank Planning? Unconventional Monetary Policy and the Price of Bending the Yield Curve." In *Uncertain Futures: Imaginaries, Narratives, and Calculation in the Economy*, edited by Jens Beckert and Richard Bronk, 31–37. Oxford: Oxford University Press.

Brayton, Flint, Andrew Levin, Ralph Lyon, and John C. Williams. 1997. "The Evolution of Macro Models at the Federal Reserve Board." *Carnegie-Rochester Conference Series on Public Policy* 47 (December): 43–81. https://doi.org/10.1016/S0167-2231(98)00004-9.

Brunsson, Nils, Andreas Rasche, and David Seidl. 2012. "The Dynamics of Standardization: Three Perspectives on Standards in Organization Studies." *Organization Studies* 33 (5–6): 613–32. https://doi.org/10.1177/0170840612450120.

Callon, Michel. 1998. "An Essay on Framing and Overflowing: Economic Externalities Revisited by Sociology." *The Sociological Review* 46 (S1): 244–69. https://doi.org/10.1111/j.1467-954X.1998.tb03477.x.

Callon, Michel. 2007. "What Does It Mean to Say that Economics Is Performative?" In *Do Economists Make Markets?: On the Performativity of Economics*, edited by Donald MacKenzie, Fabian Muniesa, and Lucia Siu, 311–57. Princeton, NJ: Princeton University Press.

Christophers, Brett. 2017. "The Performativity of the Yield Curve." *Journal of Cultural Economy* 10 (1): 63–80. https://doi.org/10.1080/17530350.2016.1236031.

Cobham, David P., ed. 2010. *Twenty Years of Inflation Targeting: Lessons Learned and Future Prospects*. New York, NY: Cambridge University Press.

Cukierman, Alex, and Allan H. Meltzer. 1986. "A Theory of Ambiguity, Credibility, and Inflation under Discretion and Asymmetric Information." *Econometrica* 54 (5): 1099. https://doi.org/10.2307/1912324.

Demertzis, Maria, and Andrew Hughes Hallett. 2007. "Central Bank Transparency in Theory and Practice." *Journal of Macroeconomics* 29 (4): 760–89. https://doi.org/10.1016/j.jmacro.2005.06.002.

Espeland, Wendy Nelson, and Michael Sauder. 2007. "Rankings and Reactivity: How Public Measures Recreate Social Worlds." *American Journal of Sociology* 113 (1): 1–40.

Esposito, Elena. 2011. *The Future of Futures: The Time of Money in Financing and Society*. Cheltenham; Northampton, MA: Edward Elgar.

Feinman, Joshua, and William Poole. 1989. "Federal Reserve Policymaking: An Overview and Analysis of the Policy Process: A Comment." *Carnegie-Rochester Conference Series on Public Policy* 30 (March): 63–74. https://doi.org/10.1016/0167-2231(89)90020-1.

Fligstein, Neil, Jonah Stuart Brundage, and Michael Schultz. 2017. "Seeing Like the Fed: Culture, Cognition, and Framing in the Failure to Anticipate the Financial Crisis of 2008." *American Sociological Review* 82 (5): 879–909. https://doi.org/10.1177/0003122417728240.

Foucault, Michel, Graham Burchell, Colin Gordon, and Peter Miller, eds. 1991. *The Foucault Effect: Studies in Governmentality: With Two Lectures by and an Interview with Michel Foucault*. Chicago, IL: University of Chicago Press.

Frankel, Jeffrey A., and Cara S. Lown. 1994. "An Indicator of Future Inflation Extracted from the Steepness of the Interest Rate Yield Curve Along Its Entire Length." *The Quarterly Journal of Economics* 109 (2): 517–30. https://doi.org/10.2307/2118472.

Friedman, Milton. 1968. "The Role of Monetary Policy." *The American Economic Review* 58 (1): 1–17.

Geraats, Petra M. 2002. "Central Bank Transparency*." *The Economic Journal* 112 (483): F532–65. https://doi.org/10.1111/1468-0297.00082.

Glasner, David. 1992. "The Real-Bills Doctrine in the Light of the Law of Reflux." *History of Political Economy* 24 (4): 867–94.

Goodfriend, Marvin. 1998. "Using the Term Structure of Interest Rates for Monetary Policy." *Federal Reserve Bank of Richmond Economic Quarterly* 84 (3): 13–28.

Goodfriend, Marvin. 2007. *How the World Achieved Consensus on Monetary Policy*. 13580. NBER Working Paper Series. Cambridge, MA: National Bureau of Economic Research.

Guthrie, Graeme, and Julian Wright. 2000. "Open Mouth Operations." *Journal of Monetary Economics* 46 (2): 489–516. https://doi.org/10.1016/S0304-3932(00)00035-0.

Habermas, Jürgen. 1969. *Technik Und Wissenschaft Als "Ideologie."* Edition Suhrkamp. Frankfurt am Main: Suhrkamp Verlag.

Hacking, Ian. 1983. *Representing and Intervening: Introductory Topics in the Philosophy of Natural Science*. Cambridge; New York: Cambridge University Press.

Holmes, Douglas R. 2009. "Economy of Words." *Cultural Anthropology* 24 (3): 381–419. https://doi.org/10.1111/j.1548-1360.2009.01034.x.

Holmes, Douglas R. 2014. *Economy of Words: Communicative Imperatives in Central Banks*. Chicago, IL; London: The University of Chicago Press.

Hughes, Thomas P. 1986. "The Seamless Web: Technology, Science, Etcetera, Etcetera." *Social Studies of Science* 16 (2): 281–92. https://doi.org/10.1177/030631286016002004.

Issing, Otmar. 2005. "Communication, Transparency, Accountability: Monetary Policy in the Twenty-First Century." *Federal Reserve Bank of St. Louis Review* 87 (2): 65–83.

Johnson, Manuel. 1988. "Current Perspectives on Monetary Policy." *Cato Journal* viii: 253–60.

Kallinikos, Jannis. 2004. "The Social Foundations of the Bureaucratic Order." *Organization* 11 (1): 13–36. https://doi.org/10.1177/1350508404039657.

Kallinikos, Jannis. 2006. *The Consequences of Information: Institutional Implications of Technological Change*. Cheltenham: Edward Elgar.

Kallinikos, Jannis. 2014. *Governing through Technology: Information Artefacts and Social Practice*. Basingstoke: Palgrave Macmillan.

Konings, Martijn. 2011. *The Development of American Finance*. New York, NY: Cambridge University Press.

Koselleck, Reinhart. 2002. *The Practice of Conceptual History : Timing History, Spacing Concepts*. Translated by Todd Samuel Presner. Stanford, CA: Stanford University Press.

Krippner, Greta. 2011. *Capitalizing on Crisis : The Political Origins of the Rise of Finance*. Cambridge, MA: Harvard University Press.

Kuhn, Thomas. 1996. *The Structure of Scientific Revolution*. 3rd ed. Chicago, IL: University of Chicago Press.

Latour, Bruno. 1990. "Drawing Things Together." In *Representation in Scientific Practice*, edited by Michael Lynch. and Steve Woolgar. Cambridge, MA: MIT Press.

Law, John. 2012. "Technology and Heterogeneous Engineering: The Case of Portuguese Expansion." In *The Social Construction of Technological Systems. New Directions in the Sociology and History of Technology*, edited by Wiebe E. Bijker, Thomas P. Hughes, and Trevor Pinch, 105–28. Cambridge, MA: The MIT Press.

Lorrain, François, and Harrison C. White. 1971. "Structural Equivalence of Individuals in Social Networks." *The Journal of Mathematical Sociology* 1 (1): 49–80. https://doi.org/10.1080/0022250X.1971.9989788.

Lucas, Robert E. 1972. "Expectations and the Neutrality of Money." *Journal of Economic Theory* 4 (2): 103–24. https://doi.org/10.1016/0022-0531(72)90142-1.

Luhmann, Niklas. 1976. "The Future Cannot Begin: Temporal Structures in Modern Society." *Social Research* 43 (1): 130–52.

MacKenzie, Donald. 2005. "Opening the Black Boxes of Global Finance." *Review of International Political Economy* 12 (4): 555–76.

MacKenzie, Donald. 2019. "How Algorithms Interact: Goffman's 'Interaction Order' in Automated Trading." *Theory, Culture & Society* 36 (2): 39–59.

MacKenzie, Donald, Fabian Muniesa, and Lucia Siu, eds. 2007. *Do Economists Make Markets?: On the Performativity of Economics*. Princeton, NJ: Princeton University Press.

Mallard, Grégoire, and Andrew Lakoff. 2011. "How Claims to Know the Future Are Used to Understand the Present: Techniques of Prospection in the Field of National Security." In *Social Knowledge in the Making*, edited by Charles Camic, Neil Gross, and Michèle Lamont, 339–78. Chicago, IL: The University of Chicago Press.

Mann, Geoff. 2018. "Equation and Adequation: The World Traced by the Phillips Curve: Equation and Adequation." *Antipode* 50 (1): 1–28. https://doi.org/10.1111/anti.12321.

Mehrling, Perry. 2011. *The New Lombard Street : How the Fed Became the Dealer of Last Resort*. Princeton, NJ: Princeton University Press.

Meltzer, Allan H. 1991. "The Fed at Seventy Five." In *Monetary Policy on the 75th Anniversary of the Federal Reserve System*, edited by Michael T. Belongia, 3–65. Dordrecht: Springer Netherlands.

Meyer, John W., and Patricia Bromley. 2013. "The Worldwide Expansion of 'Organization.'" *Sociological Theory* 31 (4): 366–89. https://doi.org/10.1177/0735275113513264.

Meyer, John W., and Brian Rowan. 1977. "Institutionalized Organizations: Formal Structure as Myth and Ceremony." *The American Journal of Sociology* 83 (2): 340–63.

Miller, Preston J., ed. 1994. *The Rational Expectations Revolution: Readings from the Front Line*. Cambridge, MA: MIT Press.

Mills, C. Wright. 2000. *The Sociological Imagination*. Oxford; New York: Oxford University Press.

Mische, Ann. 2009. "Projects and Possibilities: Researching Futures in Action." *Sociological Forum* 24 (3): 694–704. https://doi.org/10.1111/j.1573-7861.2009.01127.x.

Morgan, Jamie. 2013. "Forward-Looking Contrast Explanation, Illustrated Using the Great Moderation." *Cambridge Journal of Economics* 37 (4): 737–58. https://doi.org/10.1093/cje/bes069.

Muth, John F. 1961. "Rational Expectations and the Theory of Price Movements." *Econometrica* 29 (3): 315–35.

Orphanides, Athanasios. 2001. "Monetary Policy Rules Based on Real-Time Data." *The American Economic Review* 91 (4): 964–85.

Orphanides, Athanasios. 2002. "Monetary-Policy Rules and the Great Inflation." *The American Economic Review* 92 (2): 115–20.

Orphanides, Athanasios. 2003. "Monetary Policy Evaluation with Noisy Information." *Journal of Monetary Economics* 50 (3): 605–31. https://doi.org/10.1016/S0304-3932(03)00027-8.

Orphanides, Athanasios, and John C. Williams. 2007. "Robust Monetary Policy with Imperfect Knowledge." *Journal of Monetary Economics* 54 (5): 1406–35. https://doi.org/10.1016/j.jmoneco.2007.06.005.

Orton, J. Douglas, and Karl E. Weick. 1990. "Loosely Coupled Systems: A Reconceptualization." *Academy of Management Review* 15 (2): 203–23. https://doi.org/10.5465/AMR.1990.4308154.

Phelbs, Edmund S., and John B. Taylor. 1977. "Stabilizing Powers of Monetary Policy under Rational Expectations." *Journal of Political Economy* 85 (1): 163–90.

Pickering, Andrew. 1995. *The Mangle of Practice: Time, Agency, and Science*. Chicago, IL: University of Chicago Press.

Poole, William. 1970. "Optimal Choice of Monetary Policy Instruments in a Simple Stochastic Macro Model." *The Quarterly Journal of Economics* 84 (2): 197–216.

Raines, J. Patrick, J. Ashley McLeod, and Charles Leathers. 2007. "Theories of Stock Prices and the Greenspan – Bernanke Doctrine on Stock Market Bubbles." *Journal of Post Keynesian Economics* 29 (3): 393–408. https://doi.org/10.2753/PKE0160-3477290302.

Rosenblum, Harvey, and Steven Strongin. 1983. "Interest Rate Volatility in Historical Perspective." *Economic Perspectives* 7 (1): 10–19.

Salais, Robert. 2016. "Quantification and Objectivity. From Statistical Conventions to Social Conventions." *Historical Social Research / Historische Sozialforschung* 41 (2): 118–34. https://doi.org/10.12759/hsr.41.2016.2.118-134.

Sargent, Thomas J., and Neil Wallace. 1976. "Rational Expectations and the Theory of Economic Policy." *Journal of Monetary Economics* 2 (2): 169–83. https://doi.org/10.1016/0304-3932(76)90032-5.

Smart, Graham. 2006. *Writing the Economy: Activity, Genre, and Technology in the World of Banking*. Studies in Language and Communication. London; Oakville, CT: Equinox.

Stark, David. 2009. *The Sense of Dissonance: Accounts of Worth in Economic Life*. Princeton, NJ: Princeton University Press.

Stinchcombe, Arthur L. 2001. *When Formality Works: Authority and Abstraction in Law and Organizations*. Chicago, IL: University of Chicago Press.

Svensson, Lars E.O. 1997. "Inflation Forecast Targeting: Implementing and Monitoring Inflation Targets." *European Economic Review* 41 (6): 1111–46. https://doi.org/10.1016/S0014-2921(96)00055-4.

Tavory, Iddo, and Nina Eliasoph. 2013. "Coordinating Futures: Toward a Theory of Anticipation." *American Journal of Sociology* 118 (4): 908–42. https://doi.org/10.1086/668646.

Thévenot, Laurent. 1984. "Rules and Implements: Investment in Forms." *Social Science Information* 23 (1): 1–45. https://doi.org/10.1177/053901884023001001.

Walter, Timo, and Leon Wansleben. 2019. "How Central Bankers Learned to Love Financialization: The Fed, the Bank, and the Enlisting of Unfettered Markets in the Conduct of Monetary Policy." *Socio-Economic Review*, March. https://doi.org/10.1093/ser/mwz011.

Zaloom, Caitlin. 2009. "How to Read the Future: The Yield Curve, Affect, and Financial Prediction." *Public Culture* 21 (2): 245–68. https://doi.org/10.1215/08992363-2008-028.

Werner Reichmann (Universität Konstanz)

Social Interaction, Emotion, and Economic Forecasting

Abstract: From the perspective of traditional philosophies of science, economic forecasts may be perceived as the results of purely rational reasoning, applying scientific theories, and econometric modeling. Yet, a sociological view on economic forecasting shows that economic forecasts mobilize more than these conventional epistemic resources. First, economic forecasters are embedded in a huge interaction network including different kinds of economists, policy makers, and representatives of the economy. In the epistemic process of economic forecasting, this network actively helps improve the forecasts in (at least) three ways: it helps forecasters to produce new imaginaries of the economic future and to discover emerging developments, it increases the forecasts' social legitimacy, and it produces a common view on the economic future that helps to decrease uncertainty in markets. Second, economic forecasters mobilize emotions that help them to overcome the shortcomings of quantitative data, statistics, and econometric modeling: they develop a feeling for numbers – and numbers support them in developing a feeling for the economy – they have to control their emotions to keep cool when the economy or politics confronts them with increasing dynamics, and they are impassioned about their work. Drawing on data gathered in numerous economic forecasting institutes in Germany, Austria, and Switzerland, I argue that the main resources in producing credible and accurate economic forecasts consist of various forms of social interaction and the mobilization of emotion.

Keywords: Economic forecasting, economics, emotion, interaction, social network

1. Introduction

Modern capitalistic economies are future-oriented. To be successful in such an economy, economic actors manufacture knowledge about possible futures of the economy, and they aim at bringing their plans, strategies, and actions in line with this knowledge. The main challenge in this endeavor lies in the future in general (including the economic future) being open. Thus, producing scientific knowledge about the future is a radically uncertain process. This chapter asks how one specific kind of actor – the scientific economic forecaster – resolves this challenge and forms legitimate knowledge about the economic future, how this actor builds expectations and produces economic forecasts.

This chapter argues that there are two epistemic resources helping economic forecasters bridge the gap between present and future. First, drawing on the notion of "epistemic participation" (Reichmann 2013), I argue that interaction between economic actors, economists, and policymakers compensates for the radical uncertainty of the future. And second, I introduce emotion as another epistemic resource. Both notions, interaction and emotion, underline how the formation of economic expectations – even scientific ones – unfolds in a social environment.

Using interaction and emotion when producing economic forecasts has some main advantages. First, embedding the production of economic forecasts in social networks sharpens economic forecasts in three ways: it brings to light *novel imaginaries* about the economic future, it ensures the forecasts' social *legitimacy*, and it *stabilizes the view of the future*. Emotion is also being used as an epistemic resource. As data, models, and econometrics are not as unequivocal as some may hope, forecasters have to "add" something; they supplement them with different kinds of feelings, coolness, and passion.

The paper's arguments are illustrated by using empirical data from a case study involving economic forecasters in German-speaking countries. Their forecasts are a special case of expectations about the economic future: the forecasts are made under the constraints of (and in alignment with the rules and methods of) scientific work; they are expectations based on theoretical approaches and methods from economics.

Two assumptions underlie this chapter. First, we cannot predict the economic future. Whereas some elements of the economy count as ergodic and are governed by causal mechanisms and stable regularities, other parts of the economy are non-ergodic, transmutable, and undetermined (Davidson 1996). To date, no scientific discipline has developed a method, an apparatus, or an experimental arrangement to access these non-ergodic, and hence unknowable, elements of the future. The second assumption is that – irrespective of assumption one – economic agents (have to) predict the future. This chapter asks how economic forecasters handle the gap between these two assumptions and what they do to compensate and supplement for the implications of the economy's non-ergodic side. I argue that this gap is bridged by interaction and emotion.

1.1. The Field: Economic Forecasters in German-Speaking Countries

Before I present my results, I have to clarify which empirical field I am talking about. Nowadays, numerous organizations publish economic forecasts: banks, financial institutes, rating agencies, academic research units, etc. The institutes examined in my research share at least four common characteristics. First, they earn their money exclusively by producing economic expertise (for example, forecasts) and do not use forecasts to sell something else. Thus, as an example, banks are excluded because they use their forecasts to sell other services or use them as part of their customer relationship management. Second, the institutes are called "semi-official": their work is partly financed by the government, and it is institutionalized within the policy-making process (Reichmann 2009). Third, they are "independent" in a specific way: they do not belong to any political movement, to a company, an interest group, or a political party and have neither commercial nor political aims. And fourth, the forecasting institutes' members consider themselves to be part of academia: they have an identity as academic scholars and do things only scholars do (for example, giving courses at universities, earning their *Habilitation*, and so on) and their practices stick to the rules of economics' methodology (Evans 1997, 408). However, despite their academic identity, the vast majority of the forecasting institutes analyzed in this paper are organized outside universities.

Another important clarification is that, in German-speaking countries, the growth rate of the Gross Domestic Product (GDP) stands at the center of every economic forecast, and, especially in public discussions, it is what economic forecasts are often reduced to. The forecasts under research are very different. Most of them contain about one hundred pages. Others are part of reports of about 700 pages. Forecasts are summarized in short press releases showing the main economic indicators and a few points outlining the main messages. The institutes publish economic forecasts two to four times a year, and most of them present their forecasts to the public at press conferences.[1]

The article is divided into two parts. The first one shows how different kinds of social interaction enable forecasters to produce knowledge about the economic future. In the second one, I analyze how they mobilize emotion as an epistemic resource. It starts by presenting two theoretical concepts that help in understanding how actors use interaction to produce expectations and assumptions about the future. Then I describe and analyze the social conditions of the epistemic process in the field of economic forecasting and examine the two dimensions of "epistemic participation" in detail. In a final section, I take a closer look at the role emotion plays in producing economic forecasts.

2. Interaction and the Future

In his classic definition, Erving Goffman states that "[s]ocial interaction can be identified narrowly as that which uniquely transpires in social situations, that is, environments in which two or more individuals are physically in one another's response presence" (Goffman 1983, 2). In the 21st century, Goffman's "body to body starting point" (Goffman 1983, 2) of interaction must be reformulated because new technologies enable humans to interact and form social situations without being bodily co-present. Nevertheless, Goffman's main point remains useful: interaction is a reciprocal social action of two or more individuals. Each interaction partner orients his or her actions towards the past, present, or future actions of the other partner(s). In Goffman's understanding, interaction does not have to be reduced to oral speech; although speaking is a common element

1 The data used in this paper were collected starting in 2004 and (at the time of writing this paper) consist of 42 qualitative interviews (30–100 minutes) with economists directly engaged in producing the forecasts, which are used by national, regional, and local governments, special interest groups, and labor unions. In addition, I spent some time at different forecasting institutes taking notes and have collected a large volume of documents from all forecasting institutes in the German-speaking countries. The interviews were conducted in German and translated by the author. Quotes from the interviews are marked "Interview," followed by the number of the interview and a time stamp.

of interaction, it is not a prerequisite. However, human interaction does include a consensus on a common immediate goal of action, a common definition and understanding of the situation, and it is embedded in a complex interaction order. It also plays a significant role in the process of producing expectations about possible futures.

In the following sections, this paper briefly introduces two theoretical concepts – "mental time traveling" and "foretalk" – that stem from different scientific fields but come to a common result. These concepts help us to understand how actors produce assumptions about the future by emphasizing the underlying interactional element of forecasting.

2.1. Mental Time Traveling and Foretalk

Thomas Suddendorf's work on the development of mental capacities in young children and animals provides an interesting view on how humans interact to imagine the future. Initially, his approach may seem to be slightly a-sociological, but, on closer inspection, it acquires an interactional element.

Suddendorf focuses on the question "What makes humans unique?". In his book *The Gap* (Suddendorf 2013), he identifies eight main differences between humans and animals: one of them is that humans are able to do what he calls "mental time traveling," that is, mentally form expectations and stories about the future. It is one of the fundamental human capabilities to imagine the future; and no other being in the world is able to "recall past episodes and imagine future events, including entirely fictional scenarios (such as the invention of an actual time machine)" (Suddendorf 2013, 89).[2]

Suddendorf argues that "mental time travel into the past and mental time travel into the future are two aspects of the same faculty" (Suddendorf 2013, 90). He refers to brain imaging studies that "have found that when participants are asked to recall past events and imagine future situations, the same areas of the brain [...] are involved" (Suddendorf 2013, 94). In a second step, he argues that the human imaginative capacity, no matter

2 The claim that only humans have the preconditions for "mental time traveling" is challenged by biologists and animal researchers such as Clayton et al. (2008).

whether about past or future events, is divided into three systems: a memory for how to do things (procedural memory), a memory for facts (semantic memory), and a memory for events (episodic memory).

Episodic memory is not just responsible for us remembering past experiences, it also produces and imagines futures (Suddendorf 2013, 91). Humans use episodic memory in several ways to produce imaginaries. Of course, they use experiences from the past to construct futures. However, they are also able to imagine situations they have never experienced before. There is almost no limit to possible situations humans can imagine and, interestingly enough, humans can even evaluate these fictional situations (Suddendorf 2013, 95).

The problem is that episodic memory is well-known to be error-prone, no matter whether we use it oriented towards the past or the future (Suddendorf 2013, 98 ff.). But – and this is the more sociological aspect of Suddendorf's argument – humans have developed a unique technique to increase the quality of their episodic memory and their "mental time travels," namely interaction. As Suddendorf states, "we have radically improved our chances of getting it right through a wonderfully effective trick: we share our plans and predictions with others [and] we have an extraordinarily effective way of exchanging our mind travels through language [...]." Suddendorf argues that, by "exchanging our experiences, plans, and advice, we have vastly increased our capacity for accurate prediction" (Suddendorf 2013, 99).

Suddendorf is an evolutionary psychologist. As such, he argues that both the ability to mind-travel and the ability to share real and fictitious stories about the past and the future with others interactionally increase the chance of survival. For him, it is an advantage in evolutionary competition to be able to create mental images for possible futures and thereby control the future better (Suddendorf 2013, 101–3).

David Gibson (2011b, 2012) also emphasizes the interactional element of imagining the future, and, by asking how this interaction is shaped in microsociological and conversational detail, he comes to two conclusions that enrich Suddendorf's argumentation. He refers to interaction about possible futures using the term "foretalk" – a combination of forecasting and talk (Gibson 2012). He focuses on conversation and decision-making under extreme circumstances; in other words, on "talk at the brink." As an example, he analyses the process of decision-making during the Cuban Missile Crisis in 1962, when President Kennedy and his top advisers had to decide within a couple of hours how to react to the Soviet Union's installation of nuclear missiles on the island of Cuba (Gibson 2011a). In such extreme situations, people create possible future scenarios together by "foretalking" (Gibson 2011a). This group "foretalk" shapes decisions through two mechanisms. First, "foretalk" brings to light possible futures that might not otherwise have been imagined. Thus, "foretalk" is an epistemic resource that enables us to produce new imaginaries of the future. Second, decision-makers anticipate the need to legitimate their decisions afterwards. The "foretalk" helps to justify decisions and improves their legitimacy.

Both Suddendorf and Gibson emphasize the interactional basis of producing knowledge about the future. They show that the production of possible futures, for example, about economic development, does not take place in a social vacuum – it is not a purely mind-centered skill. It follows that concepts such as fantasy, creativity, mathematics, or cognition alone are not enough to provide an understanding of how fictional expectations are constructed. There are social and interactional aspects of producing economic futures that go beyond the "reserve stock of knowledge" (Schutz 1967, 77) that individual people have accumulated and can access. Economic forecasts are based on an interactional process.

3. Interaction and Economic Forecasting

The ways in which economic forecasters generate a common view by constantly negotiating their views with each other and with external groups – how they "foretalk" and how they exchange ideas from their "mental time travels" – can be elucidated empirically. Economic forecasters produce their forecasts using several channels of interaction as part of their epistemic process. To avoid misunderstandings, it is important to emphasize that this paper focuses on forecasting institutes in German-speaking countries, which operate quite differently from, for example, forecasting institutes in the United States or in the UK. There are national differences between forecasting systems and the political uses of the forecasts, especially between the United States and Europe (Campbell and Pedersen

2014). In general, one could say that American forecasters are more commercially oriented whereas European forecasters operate closer to the state (Friedman 2009, 2014).

3.1. Interaction and Econometrics

Textbooks show different ways of producing economic forecasts (e.g., Döhrn 2014; Tichy 1994). They differ mainly in terms of whether forecasters have more trust in numbers, quantitative data, mathematics, and econometric models or whether they rely more on qualitative data gathered from representatives of the economy (Evans 1997; McNees 1990).

In practice, forecasters never rely solely on calculation. Econometric models are used merely as a starting point. And these models are increasingly taking a back seat in the process of manufacturing a forecast. In fact, econometric models play a fairly minor role in producing economic forecasts, and the interviewees for this study agreed with Evans's claim that "macroeconomic models support forecasting activity, but do not actually produce forecasts" (Evans 1997, 426).

Instead of econometrics, the more important parts of the forecasting process consist of various forms of interaction with various interaction partners. Interaction can be either informal or more institutionalized (see also Reichmann 2013, 861–67), and the interaction includes both internal partners (such as colleagues from the same institute) and external ones (such as academic economists and representatives of "the economy"). Forecasters have developed numerous formal and informal interaction channels and a permanent communication flow enabling them to contact those who represent, in one way or another, "the economy." They build formal and informal platforms where they meet these representatives to gather data and information and thus jointly produce an image of the economic future. Economic forecasters supplement the human capacity for "mental time traveling" to imagine possible futures using the "trick" (Suddendorf 2013) of sharing their predictions with others to obtain information about their respective views of and alternative perspectives on the future. Furthermore, forecasters "foretalk" (Gibson 2011b) with selected interaction partners in several ways, thereby ensuring that economic forecasting does not take place in a social vacuum.

This paper emphasizes three reasons why forecasters engage in foretalking with various representatives of economics and the economy: novelty, legitimacy, and stability. First, foretalking enables forecasters to entertain possible futures and spot emerging developments they would have missed without the foretalk. They use interaction as a resource for novel imaginaries. Second, foretalk increases the social legitimacy of the forecasts in the sense that they are more likely to be believed. As Holmes (2013) shows, central bankers also develop strategies to increase their legitimacy by intensive communication with the public and the economy. Holmes' argument is parallel to the way in which forecasters increase the legitimacy of their forecasts by involving those who use forecasts in the process of producing them. Users become co-producers of forecasts and thereby have less reason to reject them. Third, foretalk improves the stability of the view of the future. Foretalk helps to bridge the gap between the knowable and unknowable elements of economic futures by providing (highly) unstandardized data, including judgments that econometric models could not process. This comprehensive interaction process may not make economic forecasts more accurate in a numerical sense. Nevertheless, it increases the range of knowledge about the intentions and assumptions of economic and political actors and therefore builds a more reliable basis for creating forecasts.

3.2. Patterns of External Interaction

The forecasters are embedded in a network that includes several groups of interaction partners, such as other economists from universities, entrepreneurs, policymakers, and members of the government and the state administrations. This interaction network is a constitutive part of the epistemic process of economic forecasting. The members of this network are transformed from ordinary interaction partners into co-producers of the economic forecasts. This network is called here an "epistemic network" because it is an active part of the forecasters' epistemic processes. The forecasters do not just interview, survey, or observe the others in the network; they want them to actively co-produce the forecasts. In this sense, forecasters give them the opportunity to participate in the epistemic process of forecasting – this is why I call it "epistemic participation" (Reichmann 2013).

This epistemic network includes a lively interaction between economic forecasters from different institutions. The forecasting institutes may follow conflicting scientific paradigms and they compete for funding; nevertheless, they frequently interact and cooperate, both formally and informally. On the more formal side, the institutes' members attend meetings and workshops to discuss economic topics; they talk in advance about their views on current economic development; they meet at conferences, political hearings, and public discussions. On the more informal side, the forecasters know each other from a variety of activities and relationships developed outside their formal work, whether from their time together as university students or from previous cooperations, co-authoring articles, or spending leisure time together. Within the forecaster community, all forecasters have individually formed networks of "foretalkers" (Gibson 2011b) and personal sources of information. Furthermore, economic forecasters are part of a network of scholars working at academic institutions: they hold lectures and seminars at universities, they work on common research projects, and they co-author papers and books with researchers from universities. These close ties to universities not only sustain the forecasters' identities as scientists (Evans 1997, 408) but also give them the chance to exchange ideas, share new insights and discuss problems, or, in Gibson's (2011b) words, to "foretalk" with academic economists. As Evans (2007, 691) argues, these "professional networks" are the source of certain types of expertise that help overcome the uncertainties of econometric models and allow judgment between models.

Exchanging ideas with colleagues is something familiar to most scientists. But the forecasters' epistemic networks include not just other economists who have more or less similar knowledge they can bring into the "foretalk." In particular, their external networks include policymakers and business representatives. The policymakers with whom they interact – for example, members of government units, federal banks, interest groups, lobby organizations, labor unions, and social partners, etc. – provide a different stock of knowledge and a fresh view on "the economy." This part of the external interaction network enables forecasters to interact with "the economy" to gather information about "the economy's" plans. In practice, forecasters are able to interact only with a limited number of representatives of "the economy." Still, for the forecasters, their interaction partners are like intermediaries for "the economy." When forecasters talk about their network, they rhetorically reify "the economy" and utter sentences such as: "It is really important to speak to the economy." Of course, they are aware that they cannot really speak to "the economy" as such, but they interpret their intermediaries as windows on it.

Forecasters describe this part of their network as the most important one. Indeed, they say it is more important than econometric models or academic conferences. It is a place where those who forecast economic developments meet to "foretalk" with those who create economic policy, shape the economic policy frame, and actually make economic decisions. And it is a place where two quite different groups of "mental time travelers" exchange their imagined futures.

The business representatives in their networks (such as CEOs, businessmen, and industrial lobbyists) consider forecasters to be scientific consultants conducting studies to answer their questions. But forecasters also give informal advice that helps the business representatives get an idea of what others think about recent economic developments and of the expectations in other economic sectors. Forecasters allow them to leave the "fog of uncertainty" (Interview 10, 00:36:45) and get a "bird's eye view" (Gilbert and Jaszi 1944) on the economy. For that purpose, several economic forecasting institutes conduct regular panel studies. To obtain information about business representatives' views of the economic future, they gather data from certain groups – for example, financial experts, CEOs, purchasing managers, port executives, and so on – at specific time intervals using standardized questionnaires. This process can also be conceptualized as one part of an ongoing (standardized) interaction between various groups of "mental time travelers."

The integration of this external group works in many ways. During the forecasting process, the forecasting institutes first autonomously produce a forecast, which is called a "draft forecast" (field term). This first step is dominated by applying econometric models, which are analyzed by Evans (1997, 1999) in detail. After that, the continuous formal and informal discussions with the groups start. With an eye to recent problems on the political agenda, forecasters contact specialized policymakers to discuss the draft forecast, exchange views regarding ongoing economic developments, and explore the perceptions of the members of the policymaker network.

This process is generally not standardized, and it is permanently ongoing. As one member of a special interest group puts it:

> "There are consultations; there are even continuous consultations between us and these forecasting institutes. Of course, we do not influence the results; they are their own. But within this process of consultation, actually we are not the only ones participating in this process: the collective bargaining partners and the most important ministries are involved. In most cases, this is an ongoing process, but one that practically comes to a head when the forecasts are actually produced. In fact, they ask us to give input, to make them more true. Actually, our insights, those of the economic chambers, and those of the Treasury, Federal Reserve Bank, perhaps the Ministry of Economic Affairs are extremely highly valued by the forecasters. Not to say that the insight of the others is less valued, labor unions and so on, but we do indeed have our own data, and we are very liberal with this information, and we give it to the forecasters, and when they see that our insights are contrary to their forecast or their capital-investment tests, they have to think of a response. Well, this is how it works. It is an ongoing process that obviously comes together four times a year. But I think that the real value lies in the ongoing consultations. In the official meeting, to be honest, they tell us the forecast, and those of us who already know it and were somehow consulted during the preparations nod and the others watch, that's it." (Interview 17, 00:27:50)

Before the forecasts are presented to the public, several meetings take place. They are formal in comparison to the more informal talks previously described in this section. At these meetings, the final draft forecasts are discussed with a group of policymakers. Normally, those who participate in these meetings are also involved in the prior talks. A forecast takes about two to three weeks to prepare completely, but the interaction and the "foretalk" take place continuously. The "mental time travelers" keep in permanent contact and ensure that information on economic policy plans, on the political climate, and even on shifts in the economic paradigm are exchanged continuously.

We should not misinterpret this dense epistemic interaction network of forecasters and policymakers as purely a question of political power. Although the interests of particular groups and organizations may influence forecasts in the process of epistemic participation, there is no evidence that ideologically suitable forecasts can be simply ordered by policymakers. What is more important for the question of how forecasts for the uncertain (and non-ergodic) parts of the economy are made is that it is really the economic forecasters who benefit most from being in a process of epistemic networking with policy makers. The impact of these contacts with political actors on the epistemic process of economic forecasting cannot be overstated: they bring to light new imaginaries about the future, they socially legitimate the forecasts, and they help to base the forecasts on better information and more diverse perspectives.

3.3. Patterns of Internal Interaction

Another part of the epistemic process is much more closed and takes place inside the forecasting institutes. This process of internal interaction enables different forecasters to harmonize and stabilize their "mental time travels" and involves another type of "foretalk."

There are five discrete internal roles the forecasters have to play.[3] Each role is responsible for a specific part of what they call "the economy." One examines public finance and the government's budget; another focuses on the labor market; a third looks at fiscal policy and inflation; and a fourth studies foreign trade. The fifth role is to integrate the data, the arguments, and the information collected by the other economists: the economist concerned is the one responsible for the national economy and is the "single person" also found in a group of econometric modelers – the one who "integrate[s] the disparate inputs and make[s] judgments about the wide range of factors that have impacts on the national and international economy" (Evans 2007, 688).

At the outset, each of the five economists playing those roles individually produces a forecast on their respective topics using both quantitative models and additional information gathered during the external interaction described in the previous section (Patterns of External Interaction). Each of them produces calculations, creates interpretations, and thinks about the assumptions underlying these results. In this part of the forecasting process, each forecaster tries to "*get a sense* for what the present development may cause at the end of the year" (Interview 23, 00:18:25, my

3 The teams in the institutes vary and the description provided here is an "ideal type" generalization.

emphasis). This brings to light that "mental time traveling" is not just a cognitive but also an emotional activity.

After the phase of working alone on the first forecasts, a further interaction process starts. The five types of internal forecasters meet to discuss their individual results, exchange data, discuss their aggregate-related forecasts, and describe and justify their assumptions. They interact and "foretalk" with each other and try to align their forecasts and harmonize their "mental time travels." Their aim is to create a forecast with no internal contradictions. One of the forecasters describes this step in detail:

> "And if someone sees 'Okay, this doesn't fit here and there', we just start again and take information from the others and go back to our offices and we begin to recalculate – we cut off the corners to make the calculations fit we call it *Rundrechnung*." (Interview 25, 00:35:39; my emphasis)

The notion of *Rundrechnung* is an interesting one as it shows the iterative character of the interaction process. It is barely translatable, but a literal translation may be "round-calculation" or "circle-calculation." It summarizes the process of several re-adjustments of the common forecast until it is a smooth, rounded, and theoretically consistent forecast. This notion describes accurately how economic forecasters adjust, re-adjust, and re-re-adjust their results until they have created a "rounded image" of the future. To them, this notion means that the components of the forecast fit together, that the forecast appears theoretically harmonious, and that there are no internal contradictions, no inconsistent corners, in the image it provides.

For about two to three weeks, the forecasters continue to work individually on their special topic. They then meet again with the others to produce a new forecast that is in line with the views of the other four types of internal forecasts. The process of *Rundrechnung* is based mainly on social interaction and can be understood as a repeated "foretalk" of "mental time travelers," each with a different angle on the economy. Every economist is a specialist in one part of "the economy" and experiences it from a specific perspective. They come together to produce interactionally a common view that could not be produced individually. This clearly delineates that the forecasters are not passive observers of the economy but active participants in constituting the "knowledge" they create.

4. Emotion and Scientific Reasoning

After analyzing the huge interaction network economic forecasters are embedded in and analyzing how forecasters use this network to produce scientific knowledge, I now turn to a second epistemic resource forecasters use that is also beyond numbers and econometric models: Emotion.

Typically, science and emotion are juxtaposed. Traditionally, philosophies of science, such as positivism, argues that emotion has no place in scientific research; it *contaminates* the methodological process of pure science and distorts and disturbs the knowledge produced. Traditionally, science is characterized as a "cool, logical, dispassionate" (Parker and Hackett 2014, 549) activity. In contrast, newer methodological approaches argue that emotion in general helps to understand and interpret the world (e.g., Damasio 1994) – and this is also true for the economic world. These newer approaches criticize and challenge the "myth of dispassionate investigation" (Jaggar 1989, 161).

Within the sociology of science, emotion is an indispensable part of scientific research and scientific knowledge. There, the dichotomy between reason and emotion, a sacred cow in the classic philosophy of science, is strongly challenged. Yet, though the sociology of science and the sociology of emotion grew at the same time, there is no synthesized, homogeneous, and integrated theory of emotion in science. So far, any empirical work on the topic has analyzed the connections between emotion and scientific research in fine detail without joining the dots. In general, that research identifies two levels where emotion plays a role in science: First, there is emotion on the epistemic level, i.e., emotion is part of the process of producing scientific knowledge. And second, emotion plays a role on the institutional level, i.e., emotion forms and stabilizes institutions, e.g., through motivation, solidarity, etc.

Even in classic sociological writings, we find close relations between emotion and scientific reasons. The most prominent example was delivered in the 1930s by Ludwik Fleck (1979 [1935]), who created the famous idea of "thought styles": cognitive frameworks that form the perception of the outer world. Thought styles are characterized by common research questions, by methodological standards, and by a common way to think and speak about both. Scientist with common thought styles build "thought collectives" ("Denkkollektive"), and these groups are harmonized by common emotions. As Fleck argues, these emotions are not an opposite to rational reasoning but a necessary part of the epistemic framework in which every scientist works. Fleck argues that the "concept of emotionless thinking is meaningless. There is no emotionless state or pure rationality as such" (Fleck 1979 [1935], 49). For him, scientific research and scientific perception are deeply social and emotional activities, and emotion is an inevitable resource for analyzing the world.

Fleck's insights were widely neglected until Thomas S. Kuhn re-discovered them in the 1970s. Henceforth, recent sociologies of science have frequently analyzed the role of emotion in science and (as Fleck did in the 1930s) destroyed the dichotomy between reason and emotion. Newer research analyzes, for example, how highly influential scientists describe the emotional aspects of their work and find that there are variations between disciplines (Koppman, Cain, and Leahey 2015) and investigate socio-emotional aspects of scientific collaboration such as trust (e.g., Knorr Cetina 1999; Shapin 1994), solidarity (Collins 1998), job satisfaction (Hermanowicz 2003, 2005), or emotions such as shame, despair, pride, and joy in peer review panels, job meetings, and priority disputes (e.g., Bloch 2012; Lamont 2009).

4.1. Emotions in Economic Forecasting

Drawing on this line in sociological research, I turn now to scientific economic forecasting again to analyze in empirical detail how forecasters mobilize emotions to produce economic forecasts. The interviews show that institutional and social aspects of emotion play only a minor role. Rather, they suggest that scientific economic forecasters emphasize and value emotion as an epistemic resource.

Let me start with an example from an interview with an experienced forecaster who worked for more than 40 years at the heart of German economic forecasting. I asked him if there were any special skills or abilities one needed to be able to forecast the economy.

> "Well, you have to have one: you have to have a *feeling* for numbers, for the statistics, what can the statistics achieve, what can't they achieve? What do we have to *add* to the numbers, so to speak. You also have to have a feeling for developments, let's say, what was the economic development in the past, what

> can we learn from it for the future? [...] A *feeling* for courses and developments." (Interview 37, 00:10:10, my emphasis)

Later in the interview, the forecaster clarifies that, with the notion of "feeling," he does not mean an "empathy for numbers," such as human can have for other humans, but rather a feeling for what is possible to read from the statistics at hand and "how they are to be interpreted." The necessity for a feeling for numbers is a dominant phenomenon in the interviews.[4] Another interviewee, a young forecaster, describes it as follows:

> "[...] even when we do not have to produce a forecast right now to go public, we must, of course, have an idea of what impulse something has now for economic growth, if the government has now decided this or that. Our colleague who focuses on financial policy deals a lot with the numbers we are provided with and asks: What was actually done? And makes a summary of the hard data and facts, which is, so to speak, the fiscal impulse, and then we start different quantitative programs and try to get a *sense of ('Gespür')*, so to speak, what can this year still cause [...]" (Interview 23, 00:18:25, my emphasis)

These interviews show that, for forecasters, the line between emotion and numbers seems to blur. It is an epistemic two-way: It is not only necessary to get a feeling for the numbers, to know how far and in what directions they can be interpreted, and to identify possible errors. The numbers also support the forecasters in developing a feeling for the economy, for possible economic developments, and for what is going on, what the current main problems are in the economy. This is the main two-way epistemic resource of emotion in economic forecasting: Feelings for numbers and numbers as a support for feeling the economy.

How do forecasters develop such feelings for statistics and quantitative-informed feelings for economic developments? This question is especially important as forecasters learn their business mainly on-the-job and, normally, economic forecasting is not taught at universities (Reichmann 2010, 67–73). The interviews show that the ability to develop such emotion is based on experience:

---

4 Furthermore, there is other work that has found the same phenomenon, e.g., Kennedy and Hill (2018).

> "You simply gather experience by joining in. [...] Then, of course, you also start reading the literature; you read the literature about models; you may develop a model yourself and then begin to forecast. *At the beginning, one believes very strongly in the results delivered by econometric models.* If one realizes after a quarter of a year that they were maybe not right, because something happened that was perhaps outside the model world, then you start to also bring in your experiences – and that is exactly this experience I'm talking about. That one knows how to estimate the results correctly against the background of many years of experience and many years of observing cycles." (Interview 39, 00:03:50, my emphasis)

This (very experienced) forecaster creates an opposition between econometric models on the one side and experience on the other. Where the models fail, forecasters bring in other epistemic resources, such as emotion, interaction, or experience. This is exactly the point when forecasters bridge the gap produced by the radical uncertain conditions that frame their epistemic world. The need for experience has another consequence: Normally, young economists who are "rookies" ("Frischlinge," Interview 37, 00:12:00) have to gain experience to develop the right emotions. This takes time, and it is difficult and complex for the more experienced ones to pass on such knowledge.

There is also a different side to mobilizing emotion as an epistemic resource: the control of emotion. One forecaster answers the question of the special skill or abilities differently – but he also refers to emotions:

> "Yes, you have to, once, you have to stay *cool* and not let yourself be thrown off track by every little movement of any time series. So, for example, you've made a forecast and now, the stocks have fallen. Now you have to be very *calm*, let's wait and see [...] So you have to keep calm, stay *firm*." (Interview 36, 00:15:00, my emphasis)

In this case, the forecaster argues that, to make good forecasts, emotions have to be controlled. Forecasters are often confronted with high dynamics, e.g., in financial markets or politics. Such dynamics should not upset forecasters as they have to keep an overview. The control of emotion and "keeping calm" is a further epistemic resource for economic forecasters.

The last case I want to present here is an economist who was deeply involved in producing the System of National Accounts (SNA) in Germany her whole academic life. She told me in great detail about her contributions to the SNA in Germany, about the technical developments, and about conflicts she had with others. After this relatively long part of the interview, she summarizes:

> "Let me say, it was actually a fulfilling program, I had there." I: "Yes, fulfilling in the sense of time consuming ...?" "Yes, but also, I had fun. [laughs] It was really, well, with this 'account of the flow of income' ('Einkommenskreislaufrechnung') you can [...] calculate balances that are not available elsewhere. And I was so crazy that I always found the new results exciting. [laughs] I was really, I really had, I really had fun, and I have to add that, I think that's the way it must be; otherwise you can't do that." (Interview 35, 00:31:45)

The same forecaster said a little later in the interview:

> "[...] for me it was like a crossword puzzle. Every time I was curious about the balances, for example. changes in inventories, or profits. Well, let's say it this way: it was really, like I invested some of my blood, sweat, and tears ('Herzblut') in the whole thing." (Interview 35, 00:32:30)

This interview shows another dimension of the role of emotion in economic forecasting. The work on the data and the development of a "feeling for numbers" mentioned above is "fun," and it needs more than a superficial glance at the data. In the above case, the forecaster even highly identifies with the statistics she produced. And she had great "fun" when working on them.

4.2. Emotion as Epistemic Resource

To sum up, the empirical data from the interviews show that emotion is mobilized in economic forecasting to produce knowledge about the economic future and ensure the quality of economic forecasts. Producing scientific knowledge under radical uncertainty requires investing in emotion that helps to bridge the gap left by the shortcomings of pure reasoning, of economics theory, and of econometric models. Economic forecasts would be worse[5] without the feeling for numbers, without the quantitative-informed feeling for the economy, without a coolness towards the manifold dynamics of economy and politics, and without a kind of fun and "joy" ("Freude") when working with statistics and numbers.

---

5 For, what it may mean to evaluate a forecast to be "good" or "bad," see Reichmann (2018, 251–87).

The interviews furthermore show that the traditional juxtaposition between emotion and reason is untenable. Economic forecasters argue that the future is open and that pure reasoning, statistics, and econometric models cannot fill the uncertain world they work in. Forecasters have to "add" something, and that is feelings, coolness, and passion. In doing so, they make it possible to produce legitimate scientific knowledge under radically uncertain conditions and ensure the quality of their forecasts.

5. Conclusion

Producing scientific economic forecasts involves not just econometric modeling, economic theories, and huge amounts of statistics – it is also full of social interaction and emotion. Forecasts are neither the result of simply feeding econometric models nor the result of pure reasoning in social isolation. Rather, economic forecasting is also based on various forms of social interaction and on mobilizing emotion. The interactional processes enrich and sharpen the expectations and imaginations of the economic future by increasing the forecasts' responsiveness to novelty, their social legitimacy, and their stability. Emotion helps to overcome the shortcomings of data, statistics, and econometric models.

Social interaction is, first of all, a resource for economic forecasters to discover novel imaginaries of the future they would otherwise have missed. It also increases the social legitimacy of their forecasts because they integrate many political and economic actors into their epistemic process. Forecasters are confronted with the problem that the open character of the economic future increases the need to legitimate the knowledge they produce about the economic future. By including as many relevant actors as possible, the interaction process helps to justify forecasts and the political decisions deduced from this knowledge, even if they turn out to be "wrong" afterwards, and therefore improves the stability of the common view to the future. The interaction network provides access to the beliefs of many economic and political actors and enables the forecasters to pick up emerging trends entertained by actors who have a significant chance of performing the future. Economic forecasters mobilize emotion because they are aware of the risks and shortcomings of statistics and econometric models. They argue that they have to "add" something to the models, something that the models alone cannot fulfill. Based on experiences from past forecasting processes, they develop a feeling for numbers, one that helps them to analyze, process, and interpret what econometrics cannot depict. Both interaction and emotion are inevitable epistemic resources in forecasting the non-ergodic part of the economy.

References

Bloch, Charlotte. 2012. *Passion and Paranoia: Emotions and the Culture of Emotion in Academia*. London: Routledge.

Campbell, John L., and Ove K. Pedersen. 2014. *The National Origins of Policy Ideas: Knowledge Regimes in the United States, France, Germany, and Denmark*. Princeton: Princeton University Press.

Clayton, Nicola S., Sérgio P. C. Correia, Caroline R. Raby, Dean M. Alexis, Nathan J. Emery, and Anthony Dickinson. 2008. "Response to Suddendorf & Corballis (2008): In Defence of Animal Foresight." *Animal Behaviour* 76: e9–11.

Collins, Randall. 1998. *The Sociology of Philosophies: A Global Theory of Intellectual Change*. Cambridge: Havard University Press.

Damasio, Antonio R. 1994. *Descartes' Error – Emotion, Reason, and the Human Brain*. New York: Avon Books.

Davidson, Paul. 1996. "Reality and Economic Theory." *Journal of Post Keynesian Economics* 18 (4): 479–508.

Döhrn, Roland. 2014. *Konjunkturdiagnose und -prognose. Eine anwendungsorientierte Einführung*. Berlin & Heidelberg: Springer Gabler.

Evans, Robert. 1997. "Soothsaying or Science? Falsification, Uncertainty and Social Change in Macroeconomic Modeling." *Social Studies of Science* 27 (3): 395–438.

Evans, Robert. 1999. *Macroeconomic Forecasting: A Sociological Appraisal*. London: Routledge.

Evans, Robert. 2007. "Social Networks and Private Spaces in Economic Forecasting." *Studies in History and Philosophy of Science Part A* 38 (4): 686–97.

Fleck, Ludwik. 1979 [1935]. *Genesis and Development of a Scientific Fact*. Chicago & London: The University of Chicago Press.

Friedman, Walter A. 2009. "The Harvard Economic Service and the Problems of Forecasting." *History of Political Economy* 41 (1): 57–88.

Friedman, Walter A. 2014. *Fortune Tellers: The Story of America's First Economic Forecasters*. Princeton & Oxford: Princeton University Press.

Gibson, David R. 2011a. "Avoiding Catastrophe: The Interactional Production of Possibility during the Cuban Missile Crisis." *American Journal of Sociology* 117 (2): 361–419.

Gibson, David R. 2011b. "Speaking of the Future: Contentious Narration during the Cuban Missile Crisis." *Qualitative Sociology* 34 (4): 503–22.

Gibson, David R. 2012. *Talk at the Brink: Deliberation and Decision during the Cuban Missile Crisis*. Princeton: Princeton University Press.

Gilbert, Milton, and George Jaszi. 1944. "National Product and Income Statistics as an Aid in Economic Problems." *Dun's Review* 52 (2): 7–17.

Goffman, Erving. 1983. "The Interaction Order." *American Sociological Review* 48 (1): 1–17.

Hermanowicz, Joseph C. 2003. "Scientists and Satisfaction." *Social Studies of Science* 33 (1): 45–73.

Hermanowicz, Joseph C. 2005. "Scientists and Self-Doubt Across Strata of Academic Science." *Research in Higher Education* 46 (3): 309–26.

Holmes, Douglas R. 2013. *Economy of Words – Communicative Imperatives in Central Banks*. Chicago: The University of Chicago Press.

Jaggar, Alison M. 1989. "Love and Knowledge: Emotion in Feminist Epistemology." *Inquiry* 32 (2): 151–76. https://doi.org/10.1080/00201748908602185.

Kennedy, Helen, and Rosemary Lucy Hill. 2018. "The Feeling of Numbers: Emotions in Everyday Engagements with Data and Their Visualisation." *Sociology* 52 (4): 830–48. https://doi.org/10.1177/0038038516674675.

Knorr Cetina, Karin. 1999. *Epistemic Cultures: How the Sciences Make Knowledge*. Cambridge & London: Harvard University Press.

Koppman, Sharon, Cindy L. Cain, and Erin Leahey. 2015. "The Joy of Science: Disciplinary Diversity in Emotional Accounts." *Science, Technology, & Human Values* 40 (1): 30–70.

Lamont, Michèle. 2009. *How Professors Think. Inside the Curious World of Academic Judgement*. Cambridge: Cambridge University Press.

McNees, Stephen K. 1990. "Man vs. Model? The Role of Judgment in Forecasting." *New England Economic Review*, August, 41–52.

Parker, John N., and Edward J. Hackett. 2014. "The Sociology of Science and Emotions." In *Handbook of the Sociology of Emotions*, Vol. 2, edited by Jan E. Stets and Jonathan H. Turner, 549–72. Dordrecht: Springer Science+Business.

Reichmann, Werner. 2009. „Dauerhaft, Gefestigt und Erfolgreich – Kommunikative Einigkeiten zwischen Konjunkturforschung, Öffentlichkeit und Politik." *Geographische Revue* 11 (2): 39–45.

Reichmann, Werner. 2010. *Die Disziplinierung des ökonomischen Wandels: Soziologische Analysen der Konjunkturforschung in Österreich*. Vol. 37. Geschichte der deutschsprachigen Ökonomie. Marburg: Metropolis-Verlag.

Reichmann, Werner. 2013. "Epistemic Participation – How to Produce Knowledge about the Economic Future." *Social Studies of Science* 43 (6): 852–77. https://doi.org/10.1177/0306312713498641.

Reichmann, Werner. 2018. *Wirtschaftsprognosen – Eine Soziologie des Wissens über die ökonomische Zukunft*. Frankfurt am Main: Campus.

Schutz, Alfred. 1967. *The Phenomenology of the Social World*. Evanston: Northwestern University Press.

Shapin, Steven. 1994. *A Social History of Truth: Civility and Science in Seventeenth-Century England*. Chicago: The University of Chicago Press.

Suddendorf, Thomas. 2013. *The Gap – The Science of What Separates Us from Other Animals*. New York: Basic Books.

Tichy, Gunther. 1994. *Konjunktur: Stilisierte Fakten, Theorie, Prognose*. Berlin: Springer Verlag.

Olivier Pilmis (Centre de Sociologie des Organisations)

The Dynamics of Expectations: A Sequential Perspective on Macroeconomic Forecasting[1]

Abstract: The chapter claims forecasting is a *process* during which forecasts are regularly updates and revised. Paying attention to the dynamics of expectations provides the opportunity to study changes in expectations formed by professionals, and thus give insights into how their labor unfolds. Drawing upon data from a purposely-built database of forecasts running from September 2006 to September 2017, linear and logistic regression models investigate the informational and organizational grounds of forecasts revisions. It suggests that similar forecasts form a consistent sequence, so that revisions mostly consist in the adjustments of 'old' forecasts with respect to newly available information. By and large, forecasting means updating former forecasts. Besides, data shows the core activity of forecasting organizations, and in turn their audience, matter to understand the extent to which they revise their forecasts: despite what forecasters claim in interviews, public institutions, among which the IMF or the OECD, tend to revise their forecasts on a wider scale than private banks or insurance companies. Eventually, scrutinizing how forecasts revisions distribute according to the years during which they are produced, stress that during major economic crises, such as the Great Recession, forecasters not only revise their former expectations downward but also upward. This hints at a Durkheim-inspired interpretation of economic crises as re-opening the future.

Keywords: Macroeconomic forecasting, forecasters, sequence, temporalities, organizations, regression analysis

1. Introduction

While neoclassical economic theories often assume certainty to be a key feature of economies, other social sciences, along with some subfields of economics, have long emphasized the importance of uncertainty in the 'real', or

1 The French National Research Agency (ANR) as part of the "Investissements d'avenir" program within the framework of the LIEPP center of excellence (ANR11LABX0091, ANR 11 IDEX000502) funded this research. I am grateful to Valerie Arnhold (CSO) and Ulrich Fritsche (Universität Hamburg) for their comments on earlier versions of the text.

'empirical', economic world. Uncertainty has been scrutinized from at least three points of view, respectively referring to the properties of commodities, to individual behaviors, and to the ontology of economies. First, uncertainty arises from unobservable qualities of goods and products. (Akerlof 1970) famously shows that asymmetric information implies releasing the theoretical hypotheses of perfect information and homogeneity and, empirically, may lead to sub-optimality and, eventually, to the collapse of markets. Studying a similar topic, namely uncertainty over quality, sociologists highlight it renders obsolete price-based choices and requires turning to judgment devices (Karpik 2010). Secondly, 'boundedly rational' actors face difficulties to analyze complex situations and, as a result, to discern 'optimal' solutions – all the more so as the ultimate consequences of action remain unknown (Simon 1959). Uncertainty here arises from actors' limited computational abilities: Unable to reach the 'best' solution, economic actors pursue 'satisficing', rather than 'optimizing', solutions. Thirdly, uncertainty is a common property of 'real world' situations: The classic distinction between risk and uncertainty (Keynes 1921; Knight 1921) sheds light on the ontological differences between situations where outcomes can be associated to a defined set of probabilities, and those where "there is no scientific basis on which to form any calculable probability whatever. We simply do not know." (Keynes 1937, 214) Whether its sources lie in individuals, objects, or the economic system, uncertainty prevents from attaining the conditions of general equilibrium and therefore makes it impossible to reach optimality, or efficiency (Beckert 2002). In extreme cases, uncertainty prohibits any economic activity.

In a functionalist perspective, forecasting aims at providing economic actors with depictions of the future to enable action. When uncertainty prevails, actors' decisions are necessarily anchored in 'fictions', requiring actors *a priori* to 'suspend disbelief' and adopt an 'as if' convention. When the future has yet to be created and cannot be known at present (Shackle 1972), economic actors can base their action only on 'fictional expectations' – that is, "pretended representations of a future state of affairs" (Beckert 2013, 226). In this perspective, 'instruments of imagination', among which forecasts, fuel actors' imagination – they eventually build the fictional expectations upon which economic action and coordination are based (Beckert 2016).

2. Shifting the Focus from Outcomes to Processes

Most literature on macroeconomic forecasting deals with 'errors', through the comparison between forecasts and actual economic performance. Indeed, assessing such errors relies on the *ex post* comparison between 'what actually happened' and 'what had been predicted' – a reality test forecasters often discard as 'irrelevant' or 'ineffective' (Pilmis 2018). Following for example the outburst of the Great Recession, explanations of collective forecasting failures often focus on econometric models: in particular, economists advocate for new forms of macroeconometric modelling that would include financial cycles (Borio 2014) or reduce the discrepancies between the 'real' world and the one models create (Taleb 2007; Caballero 2010). Other hypotheses stress the importance of cognition and beliefs in the economic world. While behavioral economists emphasize the importance of 'animal spirits' in finance and in the economy (Akerlof and Shiller 2009), it is worth noting that the notion applies to forecasters as well as to 'ordinary' economic actors. Combining Durkheimian and Bourdieusian traditions, sociologists underline that economists' adherence to a dominant vision of the economic order form the common ground upon which similar interpretations of economic situations are built (Lebaron 2010).

Although inspiring, these sets of explanations remain partly unsatisfactory. Approaches dealing with econometric models often share an optimistic, and somehow positivist, belief that improved future models will be robust enough to provide an accurate approximation of economic mechanisms. It claims a continuous 'march towards progress' will eventually put an end to most forecasting mistakes since they result from mere technical problems. Such explanations nonetheless make no reference to the social dynamics within the world of forecasting and concentrate on the sole statistical puzzles econometricians are bound to solve: It thus offers little insight into the actual process of forecasting. Whether they originate from economics or sociology, a major drawback of 'cognitive' explanations lie in their almost tautological nature. One may provocatively summarize them as follows: 'Forecasters make the same predictions because they agree on how the economy works', or even 'They see the same things because they think the same way.' Consensus then becomes self-explanatory, resulting from either socio-historical configurations of the profession of economist (Fourcade 2010), the interwoven theoretical, political and ideological grounds of economic thinking (Lebaron 2000), or herd behavior. Keynes's famous analysis of a 'beauty contest' (Keynes 1936) shows that herding can be a rational strategy for actors facing uncertainty: In a game-theoretical perspective, mutual observation grants access to formerly private information, allowing individual behaviors to adapt accordingly (Chamley 2003). Obviously, forecasters are no exception: among them, consensus partly emerges from the observation of peers and especially from the observations of organizations that are deemed to hold information before earlier than others (major statistical agencies, for instance). However, in addition to reducing social processes to the sole spreading of information, the analysis of rational herds often leaves the issues its production raises in the shade.

Indeed, focusing on 'errors' rules out whole areas of the activity and process of forecasting. It pays attention to the *opus operatum* but provides little information about the *modus operandi*. Shedding light on forecasting as an on-going process rather than on its outcomes departs from how it is usually understood. Moving backstage, sociologists emphasize the collective dimension of forecasting and stress the importance of social networks in its making (Evans 2007) as well as the role of the 'epistemic participation' of the object of forecasters' inquiry, namely the economy, to the very process of forecasting (Reichmann 2013). However, these scholarly works usually pay attention to one singular institution (e.g., one academic research center, or one central bank) rather than to the broader world of forecasting. More, they often implicitly assume forecasts from a same institution are widely unrelated, so that forecasting exercises could be studied independently from each other.

This chapter advocates for a different approach to the forecasting process, which emphasizes forecasting *sequences* made of successive forecasts of a similar object. Indeed, forecasters issue several forecasts for a same horizon, a same country, and a same variable – usually at the end of each quarter. To take an extreme example, the United States Congressional Budget Office (CBO) produced more than twenty different projections of the US GDP (Gross Domestic Product) growth at the end of year 2017 – forecasts being produced twice a year (usually in January and August) up to ten years in advance. For the same variable, country, and horizon, the

International Monetary Fund (IMF) produced ten different projections – at the end of the first and third quarters of year *y-5* (here, 2012), and at the end of each quarter of both years *y-1* (2016) and *y* (2017). Each new forecast revises the preceding one to reflect the incorporation of newly available economic information – the implied changes being sometimes dramatic (see Fig. 1 for an illustration).

Fig. 1: CBO Forecasts of US Real GDP Growth at the End of 2010 and 2017.
Source: Congressional Budget Office, Budget and Economic Outlook (https://www.cbo.gov/about/products/major-recurring-reports#1).

Understanding the process and nature of forecasting requires paying special attention to forecasts revisions. From a theoretical perspective, revisions provide the opportunity to study changes in expectations formed by professionals, and give insights into how their labor unfolds. It allows investigating the weight of various factors, related either to the properties of the forecasted object, to the identity of forecasters, or to the historical and institutional environment of forecasting. This approach differs from Nordhaus's (1987) which, through the analogy with financial markets (Fama 1970), concentrates on forecasts 'efficiency' and makes little, if any, difference between revisions and 'errors'. It obviously conveys normative statements as to the process it evaluates and, because it focuses on the use of information rather than on its availability, misses a key aspect of forecasting. For example, the deepening of economic crises, which the successive releases from statistical bureaus trace, prevents forecast revision at date *t* to be independent from that at date *t*-1 – contrarily to what the efficiency hypothesis implies.

3. Data and Material

The text exposes early results from ongoing research on macroeconomic governance. It draws upon data from a purposely-built database of forecasts running from September 2006 to September 2017 (designated below as 'Forecasts Database'). Firstly, data first drawn from 'Consensus Forecasts',[2] a series of monthly economic forecasts from professional forecasters. In order to match the quarterly pace of actual forecasting, collected forecasts were produced at the end of each quarter (March, June, September and December[3]). In other words, the database contains a sample of all 'Consensus Forecasts' issues over an eleven-year period (size = ⅓), and almost exhaustively represents all the end-of-quarter releases. Secondly, institutional forecasters usually grant access to their publications online, and enable retrieving the IMF *World Economic Outlook*, the Organization for Economic Co-operation and Development (OECD) *Economic Outlook*, the European Commission (EC) *Economic Outlook* or the CBO *Budget and Economic Outlook*.[4] The 'Forecasts database' eventually gathers more than 32,000 forecasts about two macroeconomic variables (GDP growth and inflation, using 'consumer prices' as a proxy in the latter case) and eight countries or group of countries (China, France, Germany, Greece, Japan, United Kingdom, United States, and the Eurozone). Each forecast is further characterized by its point value, its date *t*, its (more or less distant) horizon and, when appropriate, the date and magnitude of its revision between *t*-1 and *t*. The approach taken here

2 Consensus Forecasts™ are publications from Consensus Economics™, a London-based organization established in 1989 which claims to be "the world's leading macroeconomic survey firm" (Consensus Economics website, http://www.consensuseconomics.com, accessed June 25, 2019).

3 This rule suffered only one exception: "Consensus Forecasts" for December 2011 were missing and thus replaced by data from January 2012.

4 Appendix A displays these institutional sources with greater details.

seemingly reduces forecasting to mere calculation, while forecasts encapsulate not only figures but also scenarios. It is assumed here that both go together: Figures may on occasion mitigate scenarios, but they mostly express them in a numerical fashion.

This chapter more specifically relies on a subset of the 'Forecasts database'. In order to keep a balanced panel, analyses exclude forecasts about China and Greece, as well as those whose horizon exceeds 24 months.[5] Besides, forecast organizations are distinguished according to their main activity:

- *Public institutions* gather institutional forecasters, that is organizations such as IMF, OECD, EC, and CBO. They produce closely scrutinized figures and scenarios about a large number of countries.
- *Major banks* are multinational banks whose subsidiaries or national offices produce macroeconomic forecasts for various countries. Here, such banks comprise Bank of America (including Merrill Lynch), Citigroup, Crédit Suisse, Goldman Sachs, HSBC, JP Morgan, Morgan Stanley, UBS and Unicredit.
- *Other banks* designates the remaining organizations of the banking sector.
- *Other organizations* mostly regroup insurance companies (e.g. AIG, Allianz, Axa, Dai-Ichi Life, etc.), business firms with a department devoted to macroeconomic forecasting (among others, DuPont, FedEx, Ford, General Motors, Total or Toyota), research centers, consulting firms, rating companies, etc.

4. Are Predictions Predictable? Forecasting as a Sequence

At some point, the purpose of forecasting is to compute the economic future by means of macroeconomic information, the largest part of which is made available to the community of forecasters by data providers and statistical bureaus. Scheduled press releases and embargos enable a simultaneous access to recent data for all forecasters and economists.

> We forecast continuously: We are equipped with databases to feed Excel spreadsheets. Supply comes straight from databases once the GDP is out – a quarter an hour later,

5 Appendix B provides a more precise account of the panel structure.

> and even sometimes at the same minute. When the US figures are released, they are under embargo but they are already delivered to the press and data providers and, say, the embargo is lifted at 8 or 8:30 NY time, hop!, all the data becomes public at once through press agencies and data providers, and I get them on Excel, like, five or ten minutes later... that depends on the data provider, sometimes it needs maybe an hour. Then, they pour out... I don't know, about one country, you get 20 or 30 entries. I don't use them all but I do get them that way, automatically.
>
> Chief economist, Insurance company, French citizen, born early 1960's, December 2015.[6]

In this regard, the world of macroeconomic forecasting displays some features of quasi-perfect information. Most, if not all, macroeconomic information is available and, what is more, purposely-designed devices implement symmetry and ensure economists and forecasters all get the same information at the same time. Since forecasting often consists in extrapolating recent data to spot economic trends, the nature, amount and accuracy of information is critical to produce forecasts. Even though forecasters willingly compare their activity to some kind of 'art' which would require experience-based intuition to 'feel' the coming tendencies and identify key figures within a large-sized dataset, forecasts values may decisively depend on the information available and their basic properties (e.g. the forecasted variable or country). Provided information is symmetric, the date on which forecasts are produced and previous forecasts values may serve as proxies for new and past information, respectively. Testing such hypotheses requires linear regression modelling of the relationship between forecast value at time t (v_t) and a varying set of independent variables. Tab. 1 displays four different models, which share the same ordinary least square (OLS) method. Model 1 tests the autoregressive vector $v_t = \alpha_0 + \alpha_0 \ v_{t-1} + \varepsilon$. For models 2–4, dummies enable including qualitative independent variables, such as forecasters' activity, country, or forecasted variable. When continuous independent variables are significant, using dummies also allows breaking them into discreet modalities to scrutinize their impact: Especially, in the case of production years, it enables paying attention to specific economic conjuncture, rather than considering 'time' as a mere duration.

---

6 All excerpts are part of a larger qualitative study, made of 48 in-depth interviews. The author has conducted them since June 2014 (average duration: 80 minutes) with economists and forecasters from public (either national or international) and private (banks, insurance companies, and so on) institutions.

Tab. 1: Linear Regression Modelling of Forecast Values[a]

			Model 1	Model 2	Model 3	Model 4
Forecasts	Country	Eurozone		0.036**	-0.734***	-0.741***
		France		n.s.	-0.861***	-0.853***
		Germany		0.062***	-0.581***	-0.582***
		Japan		n.s.	-1.247***	-1.241***
		United Kingdom		0.062***	-0.186***	-0.191***
		United States		*ref*	*ref*	*ref*
	Variable	GDP		*ref*	*ref*	*ref*
		Inflation		0.088***	0.113***	0.114***
	Distance to horizon				0.023***	-0.004***
Forecasters	Bank	Major bank			n.s.	n.s.
		Other bank			*ref*	*ref*
	Public institution				n.s.	n.s.
	Other organization				n.s.	n.s.
Context	Year	2006				0.573***
		2007				0.368***
		2008				0.060*
		2009				-2.050***
		2010				n.s.
		2011		0.005***	-0.014***	0.279***
		2012				-0.291***
		2013				-0.245***
		2014				n.s.
		2015				-0.299***
		2016				-0.379***
		2017				*ref*
	Previous forecast value		0.999***	0.999***		
Intercept			-0.073***	-9.438***	29.594***	1.938***
Adjusted R-squared			0.8199	0.8217	0.1286	0.3794
df			24,737	24,729	29,701	29,691
N			27,739	24,739	29,713	29,713

*Method: OLS. Signif. codes : ***: Pr. < 0.001. **: Pr. < 0.01. *: Pr. < 0.05*

[a]Source: Forecasts Database Subset

Tab. 1 exhibits that simple linear regression modelling, including a small set of independent variables, accurately 'predicts' macroeconomic forecast values. It is noticeable that the identity of forecasting organizations holds little, if any, role: There is no significant difference between banks, public institutions and other organizations. In contrast, the very object of forecasting matters. Regarding countries, the modelled coefficients unsurprisingly reflect the hierarchy of macroeconomic performances, since forecasts are often continuation of past trends into the future. Although not always in a strictly linear manner, the horizon also weighs in forecasts value: All other things kept equal, and the impact of conjuncture being controlled for, longer-term forecasts look more optimistic than shorter-term. In addition, the forecasts are sensitive to their context of production. Here again, the outburst of the Great Recession (especially year 2009) is easy to spot through spectacularly negative coefficients. These results support the claim according to which data providers are decisive actors who disseminate the economic and statistical raw information necessary to produce forecasts. All organizations being granted access to the same information at the same time, their precise nature, singularities and peculiarities make little difference, all the more so as cooperation is a key feature of the social world of forecasting (Evans 2007; Reichmann 2013). Shared economic information lead to fairly similar forecasts. To say it bluntly, forecasters seemingly lack 'imagination', and forecasting appears data-driven to a large extent.

Yet, the most remarkable result lies in the decisive role of previous values to understand newly produced ones. Removing the previous forecast from regression models dramatically diminishes their goodness of fit, as shown by the R^2 dropping from around 0.82 (model 2) to 0.13 (model 3). The finding stresses that forecasting is a process which continuously incorporates new economic information, rather than a series of unrelated operations. Forecasting widely draw upon preceding forecasts which supposedly embrace recent economic trends. That forecasts are actually self-referential is well-known in economics. "Forecasters," Nordhaus (1987, 668) writes, "tend to have a certain consistency (stickiness?) in their views of the world, so that recent forecasts will go far in explaining current forecasts." A broader explanation for such self-reference argues previous forecasts encapsulate, not only forecasters' own views about the future,[7] but also the amount of economic information available at time *t*-1 – the persistence of some information from one period to the next then contributes to the stickiness of forecasts. Indeed, *revising* forecasts by definition implies forecasting exercises seldom start from scratch. The importance of 'post-mortem' in the world of macroeconomic forecasting – that is, the examination of former forecasts at the beginning of a new exercise – demonstrates the connection between past and present forecasts: Improving future forecasts requires spotting flaws in previous similar forecasts. In line with the near-perfect correlation between two successive forecasts,[8] it suggests that similar forecasts form a consistent sequence, so that revisions mostly consist in the adjustments of previous forecasts with respect to newly available information. By and large, forecasting means nothing but updating former forecasts.

5. What Is Updating? The Informational Grounds of Forecasts Revisions

Studying updates sheds light on the practice of forecasting as well as on economic expertise as a whole. It especially suggests expertise not only originates from a defined set of knowledge and techniques, but is also anchored in a particular institutional setting. Indeed, interviewees sometimes relate forecast revisions to the properties of organizations, such as their main activity or the contours of their audience.

> – There is a major difference as to how work is done here [a major French bank] and in the public sector – especially the OECD but the Planning Bureau [Dutch Centraal Planbureau] too. People in those places are very cautious.

---

7 Nordhaus (1987) often regards forecasters' views in a behavioral perspective, drawing from Kahneman and Tversky's depiction of the 'anchoring effect' (Tversky and Kahneman 1981). As most works in psychology-inspired behavioral economics, such under-socialized perspective cannot truly account for social phenomena (Bergeron et al. 2018): Forecasters' views are not just their own personal views, they are also grounded in the epistemology of economics as a whole, in the econometric tools they use, in the categories according to which the economy is described...

8 Autogression Model properties (adjusted $R^2 = 0.8199$, coefficient close to 1 – 0.999) stress the almost perfect correlation between v_t and v_{t-1}. Autocorrelation coefficient for v_t (all t) is 0.91.

When the figures are bad... well, next ones may be good. You don't know if this is the beginning of a new trend. You keep very cautious. And if you look at the forecasts from the Planning Bureau, there is little difference between one forecast and the other. Things are very different here because, here, it is of great importance to get the new trends – and yet, like the others, we missed the [2008] crisis in the US. [...]

- When you said "you keep very cautious", what does it mean? Does it mean saying, when the figures look bad, that they might not be "that bad" and, likewise, when the figures look good, saying they might not be "that good"? Or does...
- [Interrupting] Yes. Well, most importantly, in the case of the OECD and the Planning Bureau, because these institutions are carefully watched. And, when they release something about the US, they fear it will trigger a stock market crash. They want to avoid that. Their goal is not to spread panic. Things are different here because we are not a public institution – we don't bear responsibility to the general public. We assume liability to our investors. And we are under an obligation to warn them that things may turn very bad. Well, if that's our impression, we don't want to spread panic either, but we state "the risks are high". [...] And our forecasts can change far more dramatically. Also, one reason for this is that our clients do not really look backwards. I do. I take a look at what I had forecasted three months earlier. But our clients don't give a damn: they get our forecasts once every three months and that's it. At the OECD, people are far more cautious when it comes to changing forecasts dramatically.

Forecaster, French Bank, Dutch Citizen, born mid-1950s.

In addition to stating a testable hypothesis, the interviewee highlights the role of revisions as a means for forecasters to check their own work. As a practical category, forecast 'revisions' encompass a variety of situations, so that several proxies may capture their intensity. As numerical re-assessments of coming economic evolutions, their measure is three-fold:

1. A revision can first equate to the *deviation*, i.e. to the arithmetic difference, between the values v of forecast at time t and at time t-1: $(v_t - v_{t-1})$ – called below 'revisions' without any further specification.
2. The *squared deviation* allows studying the magnitude of revisions, whatever their sign: $(v_t - v_{t-1}/v_{t-1})^2$– designated below as 'squared revisions'.
3. Finally, *squared relative deviation* provide a same scale for all revisions and, accordingly, enables comparing them despite widely different face values:

Tab. 2: Distribution of Forecasts Revisions (Overview)[a]

	Mean	Median	Std Dev	Skewness	Kurtosis
Deviation	-0.08	0.00	0.55	-2.29	20.84
Squared Deviation	0.30	0.04	1.38	16.52	410.49

[a]Source: Forecasts Database subset

$(v_t - v_{t-1}/v_{t-1})^2$. However, as forecasters often anticipate unchanged macroeconomic situations (meaning $v_{t-1}=0$), using such an index poses difficulties.

Tabs. 2 and 3 expose the statistical distribution of forecasts revisions and squared revisions. Whatever the measure considered, forecasts revisions are not normally distributed. First, forecasters more often revise downward than upward (mean and skewness are both negative) and revisions concentrate around the mean (kurtosis is over 20 in the case of revisions, and over 400 in the case of squared revisions). The distribution of squared revisions is especially spectacular, whose median (0.04) almost equals the minimal value (0 per definition) – meaning half revisions belong to the interval [–0.2; 0.2]. However, more than one fifth of all revisions exceed 0.5 point in absolute value, and more than 1 in 15 exceed 1.0 point. The implementation of linear regression models deepens the understanding of the impact of forecasts properties on the magnitude of their revisions. Tab. 4 exposes the results of three models, which share the same dependent variable (above-defined forecasts revisions). Models 5–7 implement the

Tab. 3: Forecast Revisions by Type and Magnitude[a]

Type	Negative		Positive		Null		Total	
Magnitude	N	%	N	%	N	%	N	%
[0–0.5[	8,449	*34.15*	7,454	*30.13*	3,552	*14.36*	19,455	*78.64*
[0.5–1[	2,065	*8.35*	1,685	*6.81*			3,750	*15.16*
[1-max]	1,100	*4.44*	434	*1.75*			1,534	*6.20*
Total	11,614	*46.95*	9,573	*38.70*	3,552	*14.36*	24,739	*100*

[a]Source: Forecasts Database subset. With null revisions excluded, $\chi^2 = 195.11$, df = 2, $p<2.2e-16$

same method (OLS) as models 1–4, and dummies intervene in the same way. Tab. 5 displays the results from another series of linear regressions (models 8–10), which are identical to models 5–7 except for the dependent variable –then, squared revisions.

In a seemingly unsurprising manner, Tabs. 4 and 5 show that the higher the value of preceding forecasts, the larger their downward revisions. As to the distance to horizon, dummies hint at a partly non-linear effect, suggesting lower revisions occur on the shortest- (less than six months) and the longest-term (more than 18 months). Both tables stress the impact of macroeconomic conjuncture, as years 2008 and 2009 are associated to increased downward revisions (Tab. 4) and higher squared revisions (Tab. 5). Last but not least, all models show a close positive association between (either squared or not) revisions at time *t* and at time *t*-1. As mentioned earlier, this hints at a (more or less) deliberate forecast smoothing, but it also relates to the informational structure of forecasting and to the well-known difficulties to assess economic turns, during which actors encounter difficulties to reach diagnosis of either economic crisis or recovery. The relationship between forecasts revisions in *t* and *t*-1 partly reflects the release of new information which gradually confirms what previously appeared only as a possibility: In the end, data corroborates forecasters' previous judgments and interpretations.

More interestingly, Tabs. 4 and 5 provide little support to the aforementioned claim that 'public organizations' would be especially cautious as compared to the private banking system. Considering either revisions or squared revisions, public institutions differ from the other forecasting organizations by a tendency to revise their own forecasts more strongly. Conversely, professional forecasters more easily smooth their forecasts than institutional forecasters. This obviously contradicts the above-quoted forecaster. On the other hand, it reminds of what other forecasters state: "One forecaster told me that he smoothed his forecasts because a more accurate but jumpy forecast would 'drive his customers crazy.' President Carter indeed complained about the 'inconsistency' of his economic advisers, stating he was tempted to prefer the fortune teller at the Georgia State Fair. Another reader commented that too-quick forecast revisions would entail reversing decisions about investment plans too often." (Nordhaus 1987, 673) Besides supporting this claim, such results raise two additional

Tab. 4: Linear Regression Modelling of Forecast Revisions[a]

			Model 5	Model 6	Model 7
Forecasts	Country	Eurozone			0.030*
		France			n.s.
		Germany			0.052***
		Japan			n.s.
		United Kingdom			0.045***
		United States			*ref*
	Distance to horizon	0 to 5 months		-0.008***	*ref*
		6 to 12 months			-0.097***
		13 to 18 months			-0.079***
		19 to 24 months			n.s.
Forecasters	Bank	Major Bank			n.s.
		Other bank			*ref*
	Public institution				-0.071***
	Other organization				n.s.
Context	Year	2007		0.005***	-0.044*
		2008			-0.326***
		2009			-0.242***
		2010			n.s.
		2011			-0.101***
		2012			-0.131***
		2013			-0.073***
		2014			-0.195***
		2015			-0.173***
		2016			-0.156***
		2017			*ref*
	Previous forecast value	Q1		-0.039***	*ref*
		Q2			-0.166***
		Q3			-0.272***
		Q4			-0.455***
	Previous forecast revision		0.178***	0.217***	0.183***
Intercept			-0.069***	-0.105***	0.314***
Adjusted R-squared			0.0329	0.0467	0.1524
df			19,659	19,656	16,635
N			19,661	19,661	19,661

*Method: OLS. Signif. codes : ***: Pr. < 0.001. **: Pr. < 0.01. *: Pr. < 0.05.*
Note: The inclusion of the previous revision requires taking into account three successive forecasts, therefore excluding forecasts produced during Year 2006.

[a]Source: Forecasts Database Subset

Tab. 5: Linear Regression Modelling of Squared Forecast Revisions[a]

			Model 8	Model 9	Model 10
Forecasts	Country	Eurozone			-0.131***
		France			-0.163***
		Germany			n.s.
		Japan			0.156***
		United Kingdom			n.s.
		United States			*ref*
	Distance to horizon	0 to 5 months		0.021***	*ref*
		6 to 12 months			0.379***
		13 to 18 months			0.085**
		19 to 24 months			n.s.
Forecasters	Bank	Major Bank			n.s.
		Other bank			*ref*
	Public institution				0.263***
	Other organization				n.s.
Context	Year	2007		-0.057***	n.s.
		2008			0.720***
		2009			1.156***
		2010			0.155**
		2011			0.370***
		2012			0.129**
		2013			n.s.
		2014			n.s.
		2015			n.s.
		2016			n.s.
		2017			*ref*
	Previous forecast value	Q1		-0.085***	*ref*
		Q2			n.s.
		Q3			n.s.
		Q4			0.181***
	Squared previous forecast revision		0.139***	0.101***	0.061***
Intercept			0.284***	115.01***	-0.150**
Adjusted R-squared			0.0205	0.0422	0.0926
df			19,659	19,656	19,635
N			19,661	19,661	19,661

*Method: OLS. Signif. codes : ***: Pr. < 0.001. **: Pr. < 0.01. *: Pr. < 0.05.*
Note: The inclusion of the previous revision requires taking into account three successive forecasts, therefore excluding forecasts produced during Year 2006 (see Appendix A).

[a]Source: Forecasts Database Subset

issues for future research. It first requires explaining the discrepancies between forecasters' discourses: How come professionals from a same field hold so widely contrasting views of its functioning? Secondly, both discourses stress the importance of audiences to understand the process of forecasting. It challenges the usually admitted idea that forecasting is *solely* data-driven and instead suggests studying forecasts and forecasters in their broader social environment, taking into account the specific needs and demands of their own audience.

A further investigation of the institutional setting of forecasting implies defining revisions as 'events' rather than 'calculations'. Indeed, each forecast revision holds a singular meaning, with respect to its sign ('negative' or 'positive') and magnitude ('more or less than 0.5 point'). Some of these events are frequent enough to be modelled using logistic regression modelling (see Tab. 3). Each model then studies a specific binary dependent variable (coded 0/1): negative revisions (model 11), positive revisions (model 12), and revisions over 0.5 point (model 13). All models rely on Maximum Likelihood Estimation (MLE) and propose the same set of independent variables:

- Country (6 modalities: Eurozone, France, Germany, Japan, UK and US)
- Forecasted variable (2 modalities: GDP and Inflation)
- Distance to horizon (4 modalities: 0–5, 6–12, 13–18, and 19–24 months)
- Forecasting organization (4 modalities: major banks, other banks, public institutions, other organizations)
- Production year (12 modalities: 2006 to 2017)
- Forecast value in *t*-1 (4 modalities: quartiles by year)

Results from Tab. 6 are consistent with the preceding linear regression models. They do not support the hypothesis that banks would more likely overreact to new information in order to warn their clients of coming downturns, while public institutions would be more cautious to avoid spreading panic. Indeed, public institutions are more prone to revise their forecasts downward (model 11) and to revise them strongly (model 13) than any other organization in the panel. On the contrary, major banks lean toward rising successive forecasts, which further weakens the claim according to which they would mainly (or at least, more than other forecasting institutions) commit to alerting their clients

Tab. 6: Logistic Regression Modelling of Forecast Revisions (odds ratio)[a]

			Model 11 Dependent variable: Negative Revision	Model 12 Dependent variable: Positive Revision	Model 13 Dependent variable: Abs. Revision ≥ 0.5 pt
Forecasts	Country	Eurozone	0.745***	n.s.	0.531***
		France	0.851***	0.722***	0.544***
		Germany	0.599***	0.902*	0.784***
		Japan	0.823***	n.s.	n.s.
		United Kingdom	0.670***	n.s.	n.s.
		United States	*ref*	*ref*	*ref*
	Variable	GDP	*ref*	*ref*	*ref*
		Inflation	0.895***	n.s.	0.689***
	Distance to horizon	0 to 5 months	*ref*	*ref*	*ref*
		6 to 12 months	1.115**	1.086*	2.992***
		13 to 18 months	n.s.	0.847***	1.276***
		19 to 24 months	n.s.	0.739**	n.s.
Forecasters	Bank	Major Bank	n.s.	1.149***	n.s.
		Other bank	*ref*	*ref*	*ref*
	Public institution		1.523***	0.778***	2.051***
	Other organization		n.s.	n.s.	n.s.
Context	Year	2006	1.685***	0.560***	0.575***
		2007	0.619***	1.394***	0.606***
		2008	1.573***	n.s.	3.945***
		2009	n.s.	1.200**	3.367***
		2010	0.490***	2.021***	n.s.
		2011	0.781***	1.791***	2.696***
		2012	*ref*	*ref*	*ref*
		2013	n.s.	n.s.	0.601***
		2014	1.738***	0.639***	0.618***
		2015	1.541***	0.684***	0.664***
		2016	1.351***	0.720***	0.730***
		2017	0.563***	1.834***	0.264***
	Previous forecast value	Q1	*ref*	*ref*	*ref*
		Q2	1.815***	0.529***	0.668***
		Q3	2.764***	0.346***	0.665***
		Q4	5.686***	0.169***	1.194***

Tab. 6: Continued

	Model 11 Dependent variable: Negative Revision	Model 12 Dependent variable: Positive Revision	Model 13 Dependent variable: Abs. Revision ≥ 0.5 pt
Intercept	0.272***	2.449***	0.214***
Pseudo R^2 (MacFadden/ Nagelkerke)	0.0927/ 0.1605	0.0889/ 0.1518	0.1445/ 0.2156
Confusion Matrix Accuracy	64.84 %	66.70 %	79.87 %
df	24,712	24,712	24,712
N	24,739	24,739	24,739

*Method: MLE. Signif. codes : ***: Pr. < 0.001. **: Pr. < 0.01. *: Pr. < 0.05*

[a]Source: Forecasts Database Subset

of coming economic bursts (model 10). Distance to horizon as well as production year also bear salient outcomes. First, the distance to horizon once again hints at a non-linear temporality in forecasting. Indeed, the 6 to 12-month-ahead period is the most closely associated with forecast revision, whatever its sign, as well as, by far, with stronger revisions. Secondly, considering odds ratio, 2008 and 2009 appear as years during which forecasts underwent massive revisions. Yet, while many negative revisions occurred in 2008, the following year 2009 is associated to positive revisions. Interestingly, odds ratio for positive revisions are not significant in the case of 2008, neither are those for negative revisions in the case of 2009. This contrasts with all other years included in the analysis, for which a negative association (odds ratio <1) with one particular type of revisions (either positive or negative) comes along a positive association (odds ratio >1) with the other. That more upward (respectively, downward) forecast revisions than expected occurred in 2009 (respectively, 2008) does not mean that, the same year, fewer downward (respectively, upward) revisions were observed. It reminds that moments of economic crises jeopardize former conventions and habits, thus opening the field of possibilities: Both deep recession and dazzling recovery seem possible, if not likely.

6. Discussion and Conclusion

These early results shall be considered with caution. They require consolidation through further analyses. In particular, testing hypotheses on smaller subsets would allow restraining the analysis to one country at a time, excluding some years, and would therefore prevent an overdetermination of statistical results by some singular socio-historical configurations. Besides, factor analyses would enable studying forecast revisions with a different stance, emphasizing a '*mutatis mutandis*' rather than a '*ceteris paribus*' perspective to shed light on the congruence and correlation between variables.

The inquiry however highlights some features of forecasters' work. First, and unsurprisingly, forecasting is partly data-driven. Indeed, forecasting organizations do not hold an instrumental role *per se*. The homogeneity of models and methods amongst organizations demonstrates the similarities of economic reasoning across the world of forecasting. Economic information is treated in such similar ways that little differences arise between forecasting organizations. Forecast revisions trace shifts in expectations and representations of the future, whether major or minor. Mostly are they nothing but adjustments, which marks the incorporation of new, though sometimes significant, data. Studying the kind of data leading to such changes is a promising lead for further research, as it may enable investigating the categories of thought according to which forecasters apprehend the economy. Forecasters have to identify what is supposedly relevant within a plethoric and ever-growing economic information, so that not all data can serve as input to econometric models. The analysis of how forecasters select information, and how their selection principles evolve across time, would give the opportunity to understand macroeconomic thinking in the making and, eventually, to study together both the narrative and calculative dimensions of forecasting. How expectations form and change arises from the dynamics of forecasting, i.e. from forecasters' working practices, which involve the tasks of selecting, questioning, interpreting and incorporating newly available economic information to produce forecasts for a certain type of clientele or audience. In the end, expecting means revising, adjusting, or updating former expectations.

Paying attention to forecast revisions also emphasizes a two-fold non-linearity of economic forecasting. Obviously, it first reflects the non-linearity of economic evolutions, especially in the case of crises and downturns, by definition disruptive. The Lehman Brothers collapse and its aftermath led to huge forecast revisions, especially during years 2008 and 2009. Secondly, it has to do with the very nature of forecasting and economic expertise. One would expect the distance to horizon to be inversely related to the amount of available economic information, so that most forecast revisions would happen in the final months, when it accumulates and grows more precise. The collected data highlights on the contrary that forecasts revisions are more likely to occur earlier during the sequence of forecasting. Everything goes as if the main features of macroeconomic forecasts were fixed between six and twelve months prior to the horizon, leaving just some details to set. In line with an informational perspective on forecasting, it raises questions as to the nature of the economic data that is made available at that precise moment. Altogether, these results remind that the time is not a continuous but a discreet variable, whether in the economy or within economics.

A Durkheimian perspective on economic evolutions provides a theoretical frame to understand how fictions about the economy change. "Crises," Durkheim writes in his seminal study on *Suicide*, "[are] disturbances of the collective order" (Durkheim 2005, 206). Such 'anomy,' as he names it, has widespread consequences.

> The [social] scale is upset; but a new scale cannot be immediately improvised. Time is required for the public conscience to reclassify men and things. So long as the social forces thus freed have not regained equilibrium, their respective values are unknown and so all regulation is lacking for a time. The limits are unknown between the possible and the impossible, what is just and what is unjust, legitimate claims and hopes and those which are immoderate. Consequently, there is no restraint upon aspirations.
>
> (Durkheim 2005, 213)

That forecast revisions, in times of crisis, go both upwards and downwards seem to confirm the Durkheimian intuition of a widening range of possibilities. Major crises contribute to (re-)open the future, by making possible or thinkable what was not. Fictions, i.e. representations of the future, change. Again, switching narratives eventually alter point forecasts.

Yet, another complimentary way to draw on such an argument instead considers the combination of downward and upward revisions of forecasts as a way to keep the future unchanged. Forecasters indeed distribute and, through the notion of ‘horizon’, categorize a continuous time into discreet temporalities (short-, medium- and long-term), and assign each of them to differing explanatory models. Investigating forecasters’ practices shows that each horizon involves a singular bundle of concepts and techniques. The analysis of economic conditions in the last few months of an on-going year makes use of economic data about the first quarter or semester of the same year, which have then been made public by national statistical agencies. Conversely, economic conjuncture cannot take part in longer-term forecasting, which provides statements about economic structures – Non-Accelerating Inflation Rate of Unemployment (NAIRU), potential GDP, or potential growth are then crucial notions. Revising long-term forecasts therefore means re-investigating how economic structures translate into numbers. Provided that, in times of crisis, downward revisions are more closely associated to short-term forecasts and upward revisions to medium-term forecasts, their combination brings about a same depiction of the long-term economic future as prior to the crisis. In this perspective, crises are nothing but temporary perturbations. Medium term would then matches what Durkheim defines as the “required time to regain equilibrium.” In times of crisis, fictions about the economic future, for the shaping of which forecasting is instrumental, change dramatically. Yet, forecasters still share a same belief: that, in the long run, equilibrium will prevail, and that the potential output will only slightly change. In this respect, economic theories would operate less as “instruments of imagination” fueling actors’ imagination (Beckert 2016, 245–68) than as constraints restraining forecasters’.

Appendix A: Forecasts Publication Date

Tab. 7: Source: 'Forecasts Database'

	Consensus Forecasts	CBO Budget and Economic Outlook	EC Economic Forecasts	IMF World Economic Outlook	OECD Economic Outlook
2006	Sept./ Dec.	Aug.	Nov.	Sept.	Jun./ Dec.
2007	Mar./ Jun./ Sept./ Dec.	Jan./ Aug.	Feb./ May/ Sept./ Nov.	Mar./ Sept.	Jun./ Dec.
2008	Mar./ Jun./ Sept./ Dec.	Jan./ Sept.	Feb./ May/ Sept./ Nov.	Mar./ Sept.	Jun./ Sept./ Dec.
2009	Mar./ Jun./ Sept./ Dec.	Jan./ Mar./ Aug.	May/ Sept./ Nov.	Mar./ Sept.	Mar./ Jun./ Sept./ Nov.
2010	Mar./ Jun./ Sept./ Dec.	Jan./ Aug.	Feb./ May/ Sept./ Nov.	Mar./ Sept.	May/ Nov.
2011	Mar./ Jun/ Sept.	Jan./ Aug.	Feb./ May/ Nov.	Mar./ Sept.	May/ Nov.
2012	Jan./ Mar./ Jun/ Sept./ Dec.	Jan./ Aug.	May/ Nov.	Mar./ Sept.	May/ Sept./ Nov.
2013	Mar./ Jun./ Sept./ Dec.	Feb.	Feb./ May/ Nov.	Mar./ Sept.	May/ Sept./ Nov.
2014	Mar./ Jun./ Sept./ Dec.	Feb./ Aug.	Feb./ May/ Nov.	Mar./ Sept.	Sept./ Nov.
2015	Mar./ Jun./ Sept./ Dec.	Jan./ Aug.	Feb./ May/ Nov.	Mar./ Sept.	Mar./ Jun./ Sept./ Nov.
2016	Mar./ Jun./ Sept./ Dec.	Jan./ Aug.	Feb./ May/ Nov.	Mar./ Sept.	Feb./ Jun./ Sept./ Nov.
2017	Mar./ Jun./ Sept./ Dec.	Jan./ Jun.	Feb./ May/ Nov.	Mar./ Sept.	Mar./ Jun./ Sept.

Appendix B: Panel Overview

Tab. 8: Source: 'Forecasts Database' Subset

Variable and Modalities	N	%
Country	**29,713**	**100**
Eurozone	5,538	18.6
France	4,109	13.8
Germany	5,570	18.7
Japan	4,153	14.0
United Kingdom	4,876	16.4
United States	5,467	18.4
Macroeconomic Aggregate	**29,713**	**100**
GDP	14,988	50.4
Inflation	14,725	49.6
Distance to Horizon	**29,713**	**100**
0 to 5 months	7,313	24.6
6 to 12 months	10,692	36.0
13 to 18 months	7,621	25.6
19 to 24 months	4,087	13.8
Forecasters	**29,713**	**100**
Major Banks	7,137	24.0
Bank of America – Merrill Lynch	1,026	3.5
Citigroup	910	3.1
Crédit Suisse	530	1.8
Goldman Sachs	1,004	3.4
HSBC	899	3.0
JP Morgan	726	2.4
Morgan Stanley	654	2.2
UBS	868	2.9
Unicredit	520	1.8
Other banks	8,997	30.3
Public institutions	2,096	7.1
Congressional Budget Office	92	0.3
European Commission	736	2.5
IMF	550	1.9
OECD	718	2.4
Other organizations	11,483	38.6

Tab. 8: Continued

Variable and Modalities	N	%
Production year	**29,713**	**100**
2006	1,342	4.5
2007	2,647	8.9
2008	2,643	8.9
2009	2,514	8.5
2010	2,506	8.4
2011	1,896	6.4
2012	3,107	10.5
2013	2,658	8.9
2014	2,684	9.0
2015	2,779	9.4
2016	2,792	9.4
2017	2,145	7.2

References

Akerlof, George A. 1970. "The Market for 'Lemons': Quality Uncertainty and the Market Mechanism." *Quarterly Journal of Economics* 84 (3): 488–500.

Akerlof, George A, and Robert J. Shiller. 2009. *Animal Spirits. How Human Psychology Drives the Economy, and Why It Matters for Global Capitalism*. Princeton, NJ: Princeton University Press.

Beckert, Jens. 2002. *Beyond the Market. The Social Foundations of Economic Efficiency*. Princeton, NJ: Princeton University Press.

Beckert, Jens. 2013. "Imagined Futures: Fictional Expectations in the Economy." *Theory and Society* 42 (3): 219–40.

Beckert, Jens. 2016. *Imagined Futures. Fictional Expectations and Capitalist Dynamics*. Cambridge, MA: Harvard University Press.

Bergeron, Henri, Patrick Castel, Sophie Dubuisson-Quellier, Jeanne Lazarus, Etienne Nouguez, and Olivier Pilmis. 2018. *Le Biais comportementaliste*. Paris: Presses de Sciences Po.

Borio, Claudio. 2014. "The Financial Cycle and Macroeconomics: What Have We Learnt?" *Journal of Banking & Finance* 45: 182–98.

Caballero, Ricardo J. 2010. “Macroeconomics after the Crisis: Time to Deal with the Pretense-of-Knowledge Syndrome.” *Journal of Economic Perspectives* 24 (4): 85–102.

Chamley, Christophe P. 2003. *Rational Herds: Economic Models of Social Learning*. Cambridge: Cambridge University Press.

Durkheim, Emile. 2005 [1897]. *Suicide. A Study in Sociology*. London; New York: Routledge.

Evans, Robert. 2007. “Social Networks and Private Spaces in Economic Forecasting.” *Studies in History and Philosophy of Science Part A* 38 (4): 686–97.

Fama, Eugene F. 1970. “Efficient Capital Markets: A Review of Theory and Empirical Work.” *The Journal of Finance* 25 (2): 383–417.

Fourcade, Marion. 2010. *Economists and Societies. Discipline and Profession in the United States, Britain, and France, 1890s to 1990s*. Princeton, NJ: Princeton University Press.

Karpik, Lucien. 2010. *Valuing the Unique. The Economics of Singularities*. Princeton, NJ: Princeton University Press.

Keynes, John M. 1921. *A Treatise On Probability*. London: MacMillan.

Keynes, John M. 1936. *The General Theory of Employment, Interest, and Money*. London: Palgrave Macmillan.

Keynes, John M.. 1937. “The General Theory of Employment.” *Quarterly Journal of Economics* 51 (2): 209–23.

Knight, Frank H. 1921. *Risk, Uncertainty and Profit*. Boston; New York: Houghton Mifflin.

Lebaron, Frédéric. 2000. *La croyance économique. Les économistes entre science et politique*. Liber. Paris: Seuil.

Lebaron, Frédéric. 2010. *La crise de la croyance économique*. Bellecombe-en-Bauges: Editions du Croquant.

Nordhaus, William D. 1987. “Forecasting Efficiency: Concepts and Applications.” *Review of Economics and Statistics* 69 (4): 667–74.

Pilmis, Olivier. 2018. “Escaping the Reality Test: How Macroeconomic Forecasters Deal With ‘Errors’.” In *Uncertain Futures. Imaginaries, Narratives, and Calculation in the Economy*, by Jens Beckert and Richard Bronk, 124–43. Oxford: Oxford University Press.

Reichmann, Werner. 2013. “Epistemic Participation: How to Produce Knowledge about the Economic Future.” *Social Studies of Science* 43 (6): 852–77.

Shackle, George L. S. 1972. *Epistemics and Economics : A Critique of Economic Doctrines*. New York, NY: Transaction Publishers.

Simon, Herbert A. 1959. “Theories of Decision-Making in Economics and Behavioral Science.” *American Economic Review* 49 (3): 253–83.

Taleb, Nassim Nicholas. 2007. *The Black Swan: The Impact of the Highly Improbable*. New York, NY: Random House.

Tversky, Amos, and Daniel Kahneman. 1981. “The Framing of Decisions and the Psychology of Choice.” *Science* 211 (4481): 453–58.

Jörg Döpke (Hochschule Merseburg), Ulrich Fritsche (Universität Hamburg), and Gabi Waldhof (Martin-Luther-Universität Halle-Wittenberg)

Never Change a Losing Horse?: On Adaptations in German Forecasting after the Great Financial Crisis

Abstract: Using data from a recent survey among German professional macroeconomic forecasters, we analyze whether their (self-reported) behavior and attitude towards new methods has changed since the *Great Recession*. We find that several forecasters claim to use new methods and some known methods more frequently. By contrast, forecasters do not report to have changed their loss function after the *Great Recession*. Although linking forecasters´ attitudes towards a change in methods to socio-demographic variables (age, gender, nature of the institution) did not yield precise estimates, point estimates still suggest that the openness towards new methods is negatively related to medium-run forecasting success. Forecasters with good medium-term track record seem to be more reluctant to change technology whereas forecasters with a bad record seem to be more open for new methods.

Keywords: Forecast error evaluation, questionnaire, survey, business cycle forecasts, professional forecaster

1. Introduction

The *Great Financial Crisis* (GFC) is related to a huge macroeconomic forecast error of the *Great Recession* (GR) which tremendously impaired the reputation of the entire macroeconomic forecasting guild and the economics profession as a whole (see for example Besly and Hennessy 2009; Nienhaus 2009; Gaffney 2011; Bezemer 2010). Consequently, intensive debates have emerged, e.g. over probate macroeconomic modelling strategies (Aghion et al. 2002 Krugman 2018; Reis 2018; Stiglitz (2018); Vines and Wills 2018), as well as about updating stylized business cycle facts following the GFC (see S. Ng and Wright 2013, for a survey). On the academic side, there is a ongoing discussion about the necessity to re-formulate macroeconomic models after the GFC. Positions range from fundamental criticism of the road macroeconomics has taken since Sargent and Lucas (1979) (see Romer 2016, for a long and detailed discussion) to moderate arguments in Vines and Wills (2018) or Reis (2018) to a defence of established models Christiano, Eichenbaum, and Trabandt (2018).[1] The idea that the academic discourse is influenced by real-world development is supported by Lüdering and Winker (2016), who undertook a text-mining analysis of the *Jahrbücher für Nationalökonomie und Statistik*, a German economic scholarly journal.

We contribute to these debates by asking, whether the behavior of professional macroeconomic forecasters and the discussion within the economic profession has changed. Furthermore, we investigate what determines forecasters' openness to apply new methods or models. Although at first glance it may seem unlikely that there is a direct relationship between a single but huge macroeconomic forecast error and the behavior and the toolkit used by macroeconomic forecasters, the academic debate draws a very distinct picture.

As Friedman (1953) argued, the ultimate goal of economic models in a non-normative, i.e. positive way is to deliver "predictions" of phenomena unknown in advance. In this methodological tradition based on Hempel (1942), there is often an implicit parallelism between conditional (i.e. model-based with a priori assumptions) forecast and the scope of explanation of a certain model/ method/ paradigm. The implicit parallelism can be found e.g. in the arguments of Sargent and Lucas (1979).

1 It is beyond the scope of the paper to document all discussions in detail but a look at the grants and projects of the "Institute for New Economic Thinking" reveals that there is an ongoing and lively debate about the re-formulation of traditional macroeconomic modelling after the GFC.

Box 1: Quotes Highlighting the Role of Forecast Errors in the Evolution of Macroeconomic Theory

"Thus, the logical structure of a scientific prediction is the same as that of a scientific explanation."

(Hempel 1994 [1942], p. 38)

"Judging econometric models by their forecasting success seems such a natural procedure that it might occasion surprise to question its usefulness."

(Hendry 1986)

"[The Keynesian models, UF, JD, GW] predictions were wildly incorrect and that the doctrine on which they were fundamentally awed are now simple matters of fact, involving no novelties of economic theory."

(Sargent and Lucas 1979)

"Nonetheless, I remember the 1970s quite well, and stagnation did indeed play a role in the rise of New Classical macroeconomics, albeit in a subtler way than the caricature that it proved Keynes wrong, or something like that. What mattered instead was the fact that stagnation had in effect been predicted by Friedman and Phelps; and the way they made that prediction was by taking a step in the direction of microfoundations."

(Krugman 2014)

"The stagnation of the 1970s, when both inflation and unemployment rose, is one of the greatest successes of out-of-sample forecasting by a macroeconomist."

(Mankiw and Reis 2018)

"This analysis shows that a valid model can forecast badly, and a poor model can forecast successfully."

(Castle and Hendry 2011)

Box 1 shows some quotes of influential scholars representing different viewpoints on the relation between forecast errors and macroeconomic thinking.

The research question of this chapter can be stated as follows: *Did the experience of the GFC and the GR lead to changes in the way macroeconomic forecasts are produced in Germany?* This question could be addressed in several ways: For example, Frenkel, Lis, and Rülke (2011) analyse the expectation formation process of professional forecasters before and after the recession. The authors argue that certain important relations of applied macroeconomics, namely an Okun relation, a Phillips curve, and a Taylor rule have not changed in the eyes of professional forecasters. Döpke, Fritsche, and Waldhof (2019) evaluate forecasting errors before and after the recession and conclude that forecast accuracy has not changed, but that there are some signs of a change in the loss functions of the forecasters before and after the financial crisis. Pain et al. find that the OECD has learned from the crisis, since they subsequently re-thought their forecasting practice and now pay more attention to global economic or financial developments. Heilemann and Schnorr-Bäcker (2017) provide an in-depth *post-mortem* analysis of the failed forecasts of the downturn after the financial crisis in Germany and remain more sceptical on the possibility of learning effects from the GR. Forecasters, they argue, had low priors about the probability of a recession in the first place. Drechsel and Scheufele (2012) take a different perspective and argue that, based on leading indicators, forecasters had little chances to correctly predict the recession. While the combination of forecasts provides same gains of accuracy, the forecasts made in the dawning of the recession came pretty close to the best indicator based forecasts. Thus, there are only small incentives to look for better indicators. Based on a structural model of the U.S. economy, Fair (2012) finds that a large share of forecasts uncertainty is based on fluctuations of asset prices, which – as the author argues – are almost unpredictable. Therefore, one might see the financial crisis and the subsequent recession as a "perfect storm" that teaches not much lessons to improve forecasts in the future.

Common to all approaches is an indirect way of assessing the behavior of the forecasters: observed forecasts, forecast errors, and information over the available information at the forecasting date are used. The literature, however, also suggests a more direct way to collect relevant information: ask the forecasters. Surveys among professional forecasters have frequently been used to analyze a range of problems. To name just a few: D. Batchelor and Dua (1990a) and R. Batchelor and Dua (1990b) analyze how divergent theories and models are across different forecasting institutions and do not find a strong impact of theoretical positions and forecasting techniques on the accuracy of the forecasts. In a similar vein, Ashiya (2006) cannot find a respective connection based on Japanese data. The European Central Bank (2009) and European Central Bank (2014) has conducted special surveys among participants of the regular "Survey of Professional Forecasters." The results confirm a great importance of judgemental forecasting as opposed to model-based forecasting

(Fildes and Stekler 2002; Lawrence et al. 2006). Furthermore, they find a very low "relative weight" of use of modern macroeconomic (i.e. DSGE) models, which contrasts to the high academic reputation of these models (see, e.g., Wieland and Wolters 2013). Stark (2013) presents results based on a special survey among the U.S. "Survey of Professional Forecasters." According to his results, forecasters use a combination of methods with a high degree of judgemental methods.

In the following, we are going to argue that astonishingly little has changed after 2008. We find only weak evidence that the (self-reported) behavior of forecasters has changed substantially since the GR. While some forecasters claim that they use new methods or known methods more frequently, they remain silent on the question of what methods are meant by these statements. The vast majority of forecasters reject the idea of a changed loss function. Linking the attitude of the forecasters towards a change in methods or theories to demographic information on the forecasters (age, gender, nature of the institution) yield only highly imprecise estimates and rests heavily on the assumption of a linear probability model.

In the course of the paper, we discuss several hypotheses and lines of arguments why this might be the case. Briefly:

- First, in line with the hypothesis in Mankiw (2006) we can interpret macroeconomic forecasting as a task of macroeconomists in their role as "engineers." Colander (2017) takes up this notion and extends the methodology of engineering to a general role model for economists. This might explain the de-coupling of academic and theory-related discussions from the "business-as-usual" in macroeconomic forecasting.
- Second, the populations in the academic "camp" seem to differ from the people living in the forecaster's "camp" (Geiger, Sauter, and Schmid 2009). The differences mostly refer to the "schools of thought" people sympathize with and to the models people have in mind when asked about how the economy functions.
- Third, in contrast to the period mentioned in Sargent and Lucas (1979), macroeconomic forecasters were not (scientifically and personally) discredited in the scientific community – which in turn is related to the first argument – but in the general public. This provoked several

"self-evaluation" and "re-assessment" studies but no pressing need for a fundamental change of methodology.

The chapter is organized as follows: Section 2 describes the survey we have conducted among German forecasters. In Section 3 we present the empirical analysis with respect to whether the forecasting process has changed since the GFC and the Great Recession. Section 4 will provide arguments and evidence for the de-coupling hypothesis and Section 5 concludes.

2. The Survey

Included in our statistical population are forecasters that meet the following criteria: The institution the forecaster is working at is based in Germany or provides forecasts for the German economy. These forecasts are quantitative, i.e. includes at least a prediction for real Gross Domestic Product (GDP) growth. Additionally, we only included macroeconomic forecasters, i.e. we exclude institutions that provide forecasts for individual sectors, branches, or regions only from our sample. The institution forecasts on a regular basis. We refer to short-run, i.e. mostly to one-year-ahead or at best two-year-ahead forecasts. We include only forecasts that are – at least in part – offered as a public good. Some institutions provide a detailed explanation of the forecasts only for their customers, but are counted in public rankings with their "headline" numbers of, say, real GDP growth. Our net-based search strategy, however, will miss firms that provide their forecasts exclusively for their customers, although we are not aware of such a firm. In contrast to previous studies, our basic statistical unit are not the forecasting institutions, but the individual forecasters. We refer to currently active forecasters.[2]

Relying on publicly available information, we have identified 266 persons that match the above-mentioned criteria. We have taken into account institutions that have been listed in the ranking of Fricke (2016) and the

2 We have asked retired forecasters and individuals, who are still active as economist, but not as a forecaster for comments on a pre-test version of the questionnaire.

Tab. 1: Some Demographic Information. In Brackets: 25 % and 75 % Quartiles. Source: Döpke, Fritsche, and Waldhof (2019)

Median age of respondent	43	49 [37; 52.5]
Median years experience as a forecaster	50	10 [5; 18]
Share of female forecasters	54	13 %
Academic degree or position	56	Diplom: 9 Master of Science: 4 Dr.: 39 Professor: 3 Other: 1
Field of studies	57	Economics: 53 Mathematics: 1 Others: 2
Group of institutions	81	Public institutes: 18 Private institutes: 12 Policy related institutions: 19 Private firms: 31

regular reports of Consensus Forecast ™ (2016). We contacted 266 persons. The overall response rate was 34 % with respect to the invited persons and 67 % with respect to the invited institutions, which is relatively high compared to other online surveys.

Tab. 1 provides some demographic information regarding the respondents. The median years of experience as a forecaster is of particular interest for our topic, since it makes clear that roughly half of the forecasters have no personal professional experience that includes the time span leading to the GR. Therefore, we have specifically asked for the changes within the institution, the respondent might be aware of.[3]

3. Empirical Results

3.1. Responses to Pre-Formulated Statements

Fig. 1 shows the responses to a question exploring changes in the forecasting process that might have happened following the recent financial crisis and the subsequent GR. The most popular answer is that the

3 Further details, analyses, and a list of all relevant institutions can be found in Döpke, Fritsche, and Waldhof (2019).

institutions now use "new" methods in forecasting. However, we offered the possibility to answer a free-text question to provide more information which new models have been used. In this question, it was possible to add "additional" methods that have been used for forecasting in the institution as answer categories. Hence, the "new" method mentioned should shine up in the answers for that question, but this was generally not the case.

While there is some evidence for the use of new methods or the more frequent use of already known methods, or "other" changes in the forecasting process, the overall impression is that there have been little changes in response to the crisis and the subsequent forecast errors. In particular, it seems intuitively reasonable that forecasters might have changed their loss function and, e.g., try to forecast more cautiously. We find, however, no hint to a changed loss function in either direction. In addition, only a minority of the forecasters report that their institution takes dissenting opinions more seriously into account than before. Again, this statement seems to be plausible in advance.

Interestingly, the statement favoring new methods in forecasting is much more popular than the idea of new theoretical models. On the one hand, this is in line with previous findings that applied macroeconomic forecasting prefers data-driven to theory-driven forecasts. For example, Meyler and Rubene. report – based on the Survey of Professional Forecasters conducted by the European Central Bank – that more than 35 % of the respondents refer to judgemental forecasting in short-term forecasting GDP growth. Additional by about 45 % refer to time series methods. These numbers contrast sharply to the share of less than 20 % who use traditional large-scale econometric models, and markedly less than 5 % who use DSGE models. Similarly, Stark (2013) documents – albeit on a small sample – for data from the U.S. Survey of Professional Forecasters that models with subjective adjustment and "No Model – Experience and Intuition" alone dominate mathematical and computer models. On the other hand, it might be a hint that more recent theoretical models are not very popular among forecasters.

Question: In the aftermath of the Financial Crisis 2008/09 economic forecasts have been criticized (again). This leads to the possibility that your institution may have changed its forecasting process. Which statements apply to your institution?

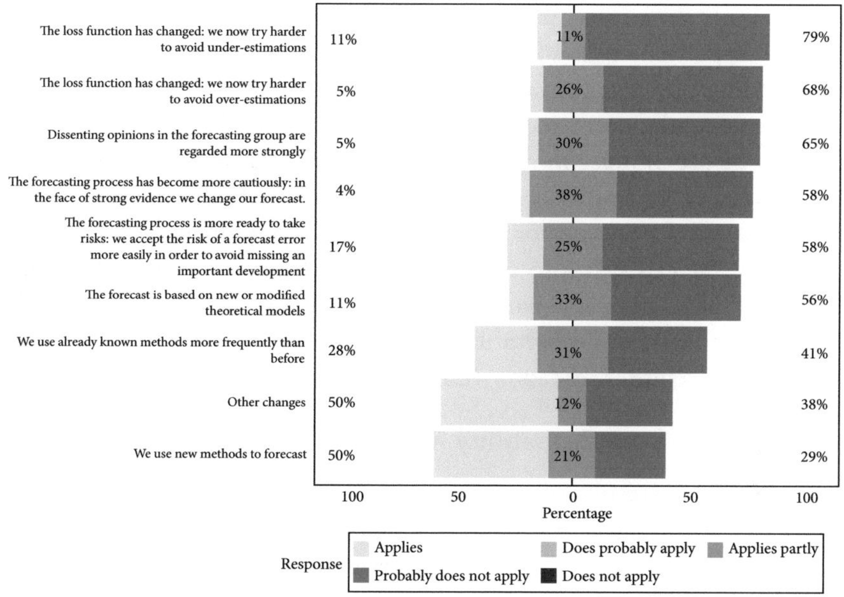

Fig. 1: Consequences of the Great Recession.
Source: Own Survey and Calculation

3.2. Answers to Free Questions

Respondents also had the opportunity to answer to a free-text question and provide information about what has changed in the forecasting process due to the Financial Crisis. One person reported that the respective institution has undertaken *an overhaul of existing and estimation of new econometric models, in particular new indicators, and now uses methods of model averaging*. Another respondent argues that the institution *looks more strongly on measures of uncertainty* that rely on market prices. Moreover, they consider more strongly the balance sheets of both firms and households, because they feel that balance sheet adjustments have weakened growth after the crisis. Finally, according to the results, this institution finds that *bubbles have become more important*. A third forecaster argues that his or her institution takes now into account a *broader diversity of forecasting methods and models as well as forecast combination*. A forecaster from an institution that relies on own surveys among firms to build their forecasts reports on changes in the methodology of the surveys, in particular an adjustment of the own survey technique (shorter survey period, faster publication).

More generally, one forecaster observes for his/her institution that they are *more aware of inaccuracy, think in broader bandwidths*. Furthermore, they place greater emphasis on *risk scenarios*. One forecaster also points to "systematic forecast error evaluation" as a consequence of the failed forecast of the crisis. It also seems that at least some forecasters feel that their business has become harder: For example, one person points to his/her impression that the literature regarding forecasts has become more complex and requires in-depth studies.

3.3. Evidence from Probability Models

Tab. 2 shows the results of some estimations of determinants of the probability that a certain forecaster responds positively to a certain item. We chose the two answers that led to the most pronounced average support by the respondents:

(i) Agreement to the statement "We use new methods to forecast." ("New method" for short),
(ii) Agreement to the statement "We use already known methods more frequently than before." ("More often").

All answers are recoded to a numerically scale such as "5" denotes full agreement, whereas "1" represents no agreement at all. Thus, we check, whether a forecaster is more open to changes after the GFC.

Fig. 2 shows, for example, the agreement to the statement "Our institution uses new methods" by age group. Forecasters with an age under 35 are rare and have mostly no opinion on whether their institution has changed their forecasting methods. For the two other groups of older forecasters, there is no noticeable difference. As possible determinants for openness to change, we consider the following variables:

- Forecaster Age: An older age might make him or her less open for models that are more recent. However, increased age might have different implications for the usage of models. Although forecasters might be unwilling to learn new methods, at the same time their perceived

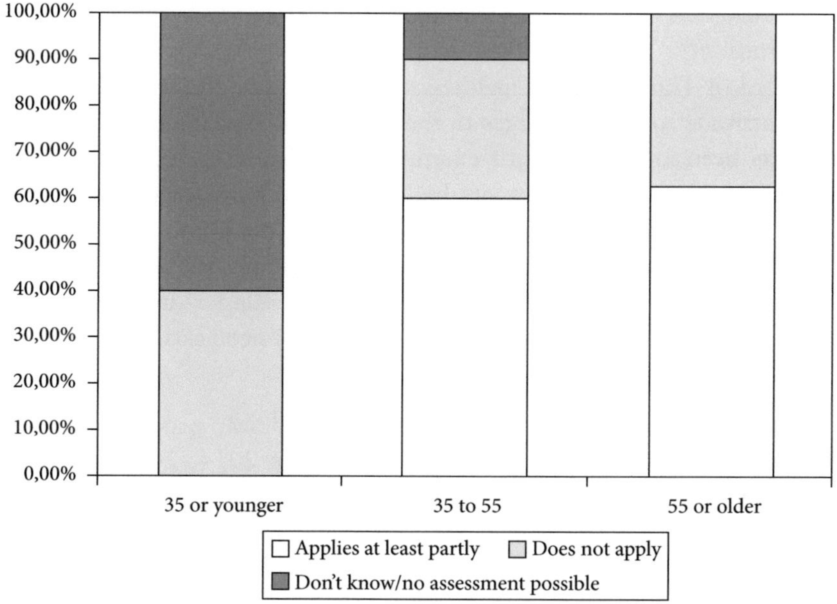

Fig. 2: Agreement to the Use of New Methods by Age Group.
Source: Own Survey and Calculation

pressure to conform to standards in the field might decrease with experience and confidence. Lamont (2002) argues that forecasters become more established with age and therefore have incentives to stick to the consensus, since they face an increased risk of a reputation loss. Therefore, his model predicts that forecasts of older forecaster are less accurate. As the relation of age and the probability of using new methods might be non-linear, we take also into account squared age.

- Type of Institution: We include a dummy variable that assumes the value 1, if the institution of the forecasters is a private one, 0 otherwise.
- Gender: We test with the help of a dummy variable, whether the gender of the forecaster is important for the probability of interest.
- Previous Success of the Institution: We also suspect a possible influence of the previous success of the forecasting institution. Hence, we include the rank of the forecasting institution according to the ranking

of Fricke (2016). A lower value indicates a more successful forecasting institution.[4]

- School of Thought and Openness to Change: Finally, we tried to link the attitude towards changes to the theoretical position of a forecaster. It has been argued (see, for example, Farrell and Quiggin 2017) that certain macroeconomic events had been challenges for different macroeconomic schools of thought, in particular, the Great Recession has been a problem for neoclassical models. Therefore, we test for a difference in the attitude towards new models by using a dummy variable that equals 1, if a forecaster leans more to a neoclassical position, 0 otherwise.[5]

We estimate the relation both by means of the linear probability model (Angrist and Pischke 2008, 101 ff.; Wooldridge 2014, 209 ff.) and by means of a multinomial Logit model.[6]The results do not provide much support to the view that forecasters' attributes may explain a lot of the variation of their openness to change. Of course, our sample is very small and, consequently, parameters can be estimated very imprecisely only. Furthermore, the results of columns 1 and 3 of Tab. 2 heavily depend on the assumption of a linear probability model. Note that most results have to be interpreted with care due to relatively high standard errors. Given these caveats, it is still worthwhile to have a brief look at the results:

- *Forecaster Age*:_According to the point estimates, the probability to use new methods increases with experience, but up to a certain point only. After this point in time, forecasters tend to stick with their already known methods.

---

4 Note that the ranking does not exclusively rely on the accuracy of the growth rate forecast. Rather, the ranking takes also into account whether the directional change of some central components of final demand (consumption, exports, investment) have correctly been anticipated. For details please refer to https://neuewirtschaftswunder.de/

5 Details on how this dummy is constructed can again be found in Döpke, Fritsche, and Waldhof (2019).

6 The relative merits of both estimation strategies are discussed in Hippel (2015) and Schaffler (2012).

Tab. 2: Probability Models for the Likelihood to Change the Forecasting Process. Robust Standard Errors in Parentheses. Source: Own Survey and Calculation

Constant	–3,80		–0,17	
	(10,04)		(6,35)	
Age	0,26	0,34	0,13	0,19
	(0,40)	(0,83)	(0,28)	(0,78)
Age^2	–0,00	–0,00	–0,00	–0,00
	(0,00)	(0,01)	(0,00)	(0,01)
Institution	0,96	1,59*	–0,23	–0,54
	(0,59)	(0,95)	(0,43)	(0,92)
Gender	–0,28	–0,59	0,43	0,87
	(0,72)	(1,66)	(0,27)	(0,69)
Success	0,10**	0,16**	0,08*	0,16*
	(0,04)	(0,06)	(0,04)	(0,09)
Theory	0,78	1,20	–0,13	–0,33
	(0,49)	(0,80)	(0,49)	(0,89)
Cut_1		6,41		2,15
		(22,14)		(16,62)
Cut_2		8,93		4,12
		(21,85)		(16,83)
Cut_3		9,52		5,77
		(21,77)		(16,72)
Cut_4		10,34		7,91
		(21,56)		(16,59)
n	27	27	26	26
R^2	0,12		0,09	

- *Type of Institution*: Working in a private institution makes it more likely to use new methods, but less likely to use known methods more frequently.
- *Previous Success of the Institution:* The impact of success, i.e. a good rank in the ranking of the institutions is the largest single effect and also (at least at the 10 % level) statistically significant in all models: the lower the rank of the forecaster (which corresponds to a relatively bad prediction record) the higher the probability that a respondent reports the use of new methods.

- *Neoclassical Positions and Openness to Change*: Tending to a neoclassical position goes hand in hand with a higher probability of using new methods and a lower probability of using existing methods more often.

4. Decoupling of Academia and Macroeconomic Forecasting Camp

As pointed out above, we consider the possibility that academic work on forecasting and practical forecasting processes do not overlap by very much. We are, of course, not the first, who see important gaps between different spheres of forecasting. For example, Tichy (1976) diagnosed what he labelled the "Great Dichotomy" between business cycle theory, business cycle empirics, and the receptive policy. He argues that, after the initial large interest in business cycle theory related to the *Great Depression* the 1960s and 1970s had been a phase with substantial progress in empirical methods and forecasting, but little interest in related theory. Later, he argues in retrospect (Tichy 2013), the picture changed: empirical business cycle research stagnated while interest in business cycle theory increased again.

In a similar vein, we have argued that active forecasters and academic economists, who work on related questions, are likely a rather distinct groups of persons. To give a first impression on how distinct these groups are, we compare our underlying sample – the forecasters we have invited to our survey – with a subgroup of the *Verein für Socialpolitik* – the German Economic Association.

In particular, we referred to all members that have singled out either the JEL code E3:"Prices, Business Fluctuations, and Cycles" or the JEL code C53: "Forecasting and Prediction Methods, Simulation Methods" as their main scientific area. The overlap of these two groups was very small: while our sample includes 252 persons, and the subgroup of the academic association consist of 109 persons, we have found only 5 persons that are members of both groups. More generally, only 25 subjects from our invited sample have been found in the database of the members of the *Verein für Socialpolitik* – by about 10 %.

Additional to institutional differences, survey results point to substantially different views on particular economic schools of thought. To illustrate this point, we compare the results of Schneider, Frey, and Humbert (2007), who surveyed the members of the *Verein für Socialpolitik* with our

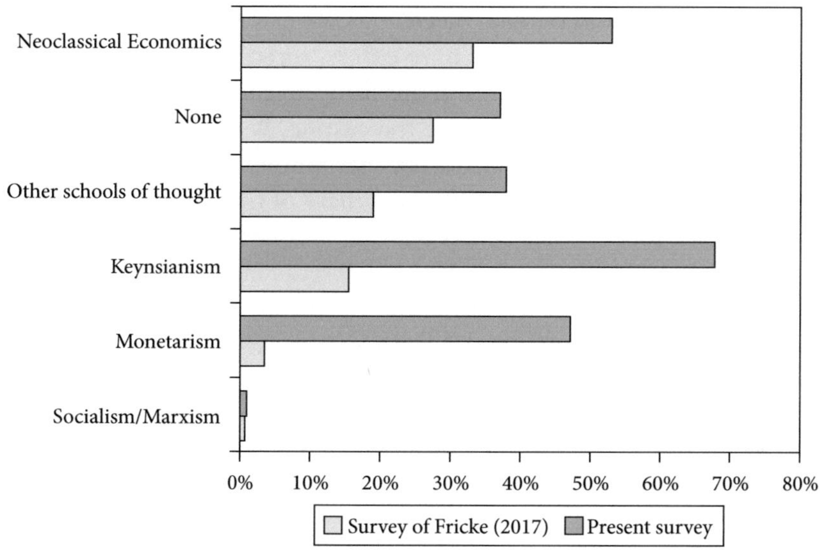

Fig. 3: Comparison of Survey Answers of Döpke, Fritsche, and Waldhof (2019) and Fricke (2017).

Notes: For the present survey the bars represent the share of respondents that see a particular school of thought as either as "extremely important," "very important," or "relatively important" personally. For the present survey "Neoclassical economics" is "Neoclassical economics" and "New classical economics," "Keynesianism" is the average of "Keynesianism (neoclassical synthesis)" and "New Keynesianism," and "Public choice etc." represents "Theory of political business cycles." "Socialism/Marxism" has been no answer option in the present survey (but possible as a free-text answer). Note that the answer options in to Fricke (2017) survey have been exclusively, whereas in Döpke, Fritsche, and Waldhof (2019) respondents have been allowed to choose more than one answer.

Source: own survey and calculation; Fricke (2017)

more recent survey. As can be seen from Fig. 3, the popularity of certain schools of thought is markedly different.

The possible decoupling might also in part reflect a changed importance of macroeconomic forecasting for academic research. For example, in 1962, the German Economic Association (Verein für Socialpolitik) devoted a complete annual conference to the problem of forecasting Giersch and Borchardt (1962). Thus, we wonder whether forecasting plays a similar prominent role in broad academic cycles today. Evidence in favor of the decoupling hypothesis might be seen in the frequency of papers in general-interest scholarly journals that are devoted to study related topics.

Taking the *German Economic Review* as an example, we searched the IDEAS-database for papers that have either "forecast*" or "predict*" or "macro*" in title or abstract. From this list we picked the papers arguably directly relevant for macroeconomic forecasting. We end up with 7 papers out of 461 (by about 1.5 %) listed for that journal in IDEAS recently. In a similar vein, we use the ECONBIZ database of the Leibniz Information Centre for Economics, Kiel to check for the frequency of papers that deal with questions related to macroeconomic forecasting.

Fig. 4 reveals that the scientific interest in business cycle forecasting in Germany indeed reacts to the financial crisis, but temporarily only. Of course, this is a first illustration of this point only. We therefore test this hypothesis with the help of a broader dataset: the texts of the papers presented at the annual meeting of the *Verein für Socialpolitik*.

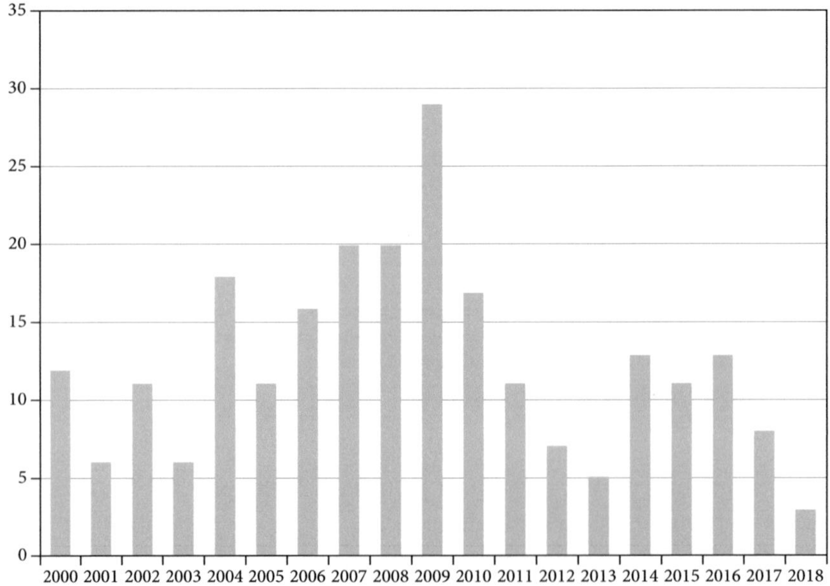

Fig. 4: Hits for Search "Konjunkturprognose* + fehler*"[1)] in ECONBIZ Database per Year.

Source: Own Calculation Based on https://www.econbiz.de/Search/Results?type=AllFields
1) "Business cycle forecast*+ error*", * represents truncation and "+" a logical "and".

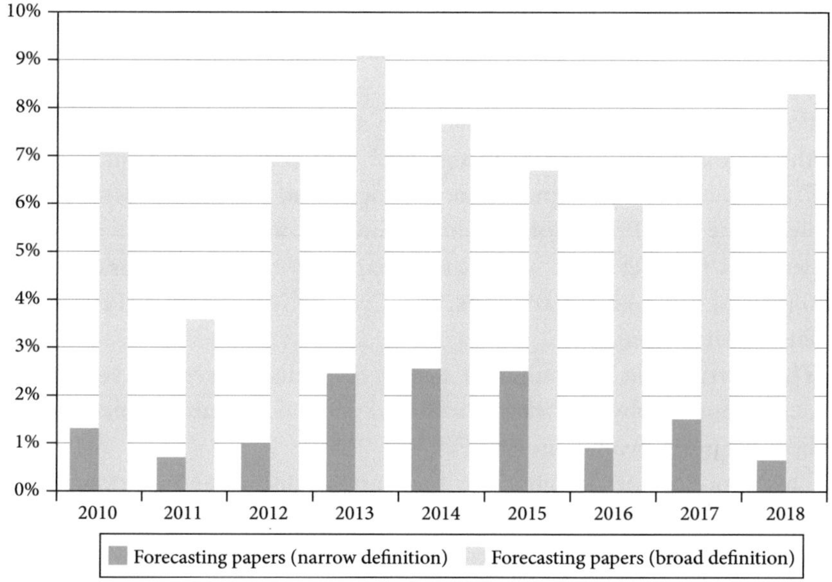

Fig. 5: Share of Forecasting Papers Presented at the Annual Meeting of the German Economic Association.
Source: Own Calculation

We furthermore used the abstracts of the papers presented at the open sessions of the annual meetings of the "Verein für Socialpolitik" to fit a Latent Dirichlet Allocation (LDA) topic model on the abstracts (Blei, A. Y. Ng, and Jordan 2003; Blei 2012). Unfortunately, data are only available from 2010 to 2018 in the ECONBIZ database. LDA stands for "Latent Dirichlet Allocation" and describes a mixed membership model where all word with certain probabilities belong to topics and all topics with certain probabilities appear in documents. The Dirichlet distribution in fact is the conjugate prior to the multinomial distribution in Bayesian statistics. The LDA model – despite its analytical non-tractability – can be estimated using variants of Gibbs sampling or variational inference (Heinrich 2005; Hornik and Grün 2011) conditional the number of topics is fixed a priori. Several criteria were proposed in the literature to deal with that issue. We used the criteria proposed by Arun et al. (2010), Cao et al. (2009), Deveaud, SanJuan, and Bellot (2014) and Griffiths and Steyvers (2004) to determine the number of topics. We fixed the number of topics to 15. Inspection of the most probable words in the topics revealed that two of the identified topics are possibly strongly related to the GFC and GR: topic 1 (risk, banking, finance) and topic 7 (macroeconomics, monetary policy)

Forecasting papers in a narrow sense are papers that have at least on of the following JEL-classifications: E32 (Business Fluctuations, Cycles), E37(Forecasting and Simulation: Models and Applications) or C53 (Forecasting and Prediction Methods, Simulation Methods). Forecasting papers in a broader sense also include papers with the JEL-classifications E30 (Prices, Business Fluctuations, and Cycles, General), E31 (Price Level, Inflation, Deflation).

The distribution of estimated topics over time reveals a very stable structure but no obvious trend for the GFC- or GR-related topics 1 and 7 to become more prominent (see Fig. 8).

This data provides insights into the German discourse. Additionally, we searched international data, or data for the Anglosaxon research community. We searched the *American Economic Review* articles indexed in the JSTOR database and again focused on papers that have either "forecast*"

Fig. 6: Topic 1: Wordcloud Figure.

Source: Own Calculation. LDA topic model fitted with number of topics k = 15

Fig. 7: Topic 7: Wordcloud Figure.

Source: Own Calculation. LDA topic model fitted with number of topics k = 15

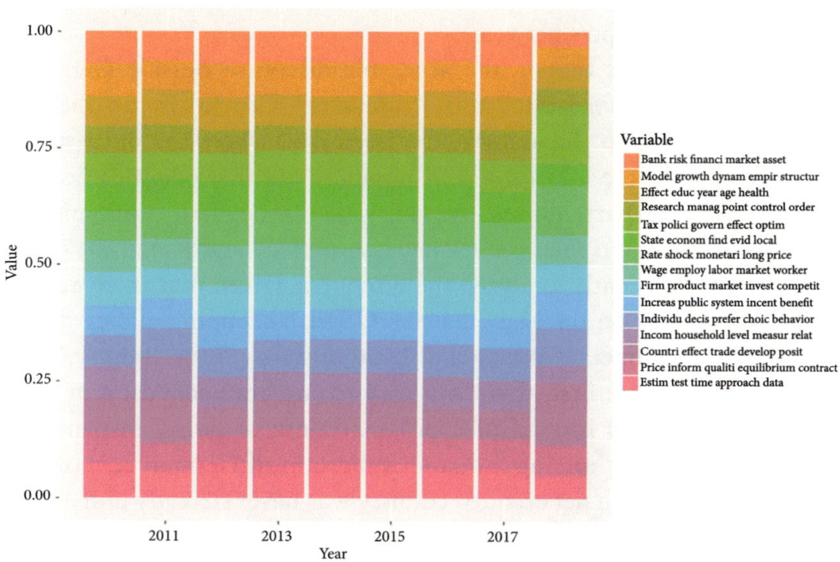

Fig. 8: Abstracts of Papers Presented at Annual Meetings of "Verein für Socialpolitik": Distribution of Estimated Topics over Time 2011 to 2018

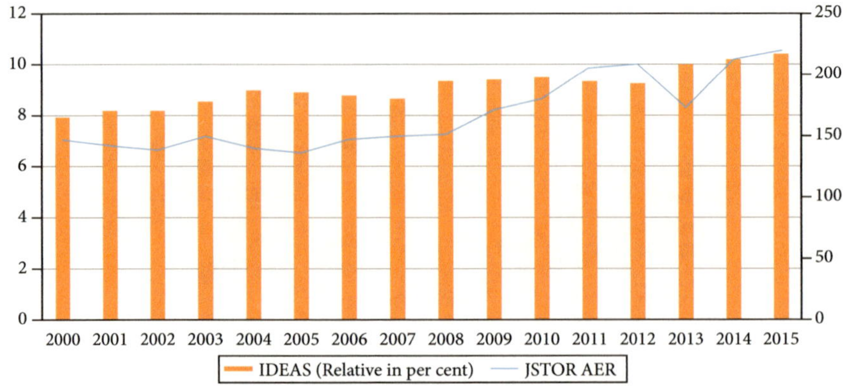

Fig. 9: AER and IDEAS Key Word Search Results.

Source: Own Calculation. Count of JSTOR-indexed AER papers that have either "forecast*" or "predict*" or "macro*" in title or abstract. The same search was done for the full IDEAS database (data are scaled relative to all IDEAS-indexed papers per year).

or "predict*" or "macro*" in title or abstract. We applied the same search string to the full IDEAS database (data are scaled relative to all IDEAS-indexed economic papers per year).

The figures reveal that in the academic discourse outside Germany, the topics "macroeconomics" and "forecasts" seem to be on the rise. This is in contrast to the analysis for Germany, where the interest rose only shortly after the GFC/ GR and points to another (second) decoupling problem: the particularity or oddity of the German economic discourse with respect to macroeconomic issues. Beck and Kotz (2017) and Winkler (2018) recently analyzed the discourse. Given that there are different perspectives on the issue that the German economic policy debate with respect to monetary policy and fiscal austerity is an "oddity," two observations remain: first, there is a very strong argumentation in favor of general principles instead of a pragmatic use of policy instruments. The latter is popular among a certain subgroup of German economists. Second, Germany as a net creditor country was never strongly under pressure to adjust or use harsh austerity.

To sum up: On an international level we can observe that the importance of research devoted to macroeconomics and forecasting issues increased over the last couple of years with the German academic scene as an exception.

Glandon et al. (2018) also report that macroeconomics has responded to the crisis at least to a certain extend. While, on the one hand, they find that the share of theoretical papers has increased at the expense of empirically orientated contributions, the role of financial intermediation in the papers, on the other hand, has increased (again) after the crisis. Still, the gap to the forecasting practitioners has probably increased, since the share of general equilibrium models has become much larger in their sample, while partial equilibrium models, which are more relevant for forecasting, have become less important over time.

5. Conclusion

Relying on data from a recent survey among professional macroeconomic forecasters in Germany, we conclude that changes in the forecasting process are at best modest. While forecasters claim to use new methods and some known methods more frequently, they remain unspecific which methods they mean by these statements. Forecasters do not report to have changed their loss function after the recession. Linking the attitude of forecasters towards a change in methods or theories to demographic information on the forecasters (age, gender, nature of the institution) yield only highly imprecise estimates. A longer-term bad forecasting record, which exceeds the single event of the GFC, is the single most influential factor explaining the openness for new methods. However, we can infer some tendencies from the open question part: Some forecasters seem to combine forecasts from different methods more often, and re-evaluated their existing toolbox after the GR. Furthermore, the sources of forecast errors are evaluated more often in some cases and measuring macroeconomic uncertainty seems to be more important for the forecast.

This is in contrast to the debate on macroeconomics on the international level but not necessarily on the German level. The astonishingly little reaction of the forecasting community on the macroeconomic turbulences after 2008 in our interpretation might be due to a mixture of facts:

Macroeconomic forecasting is to a very large extent "engineering" and only loosely related to theoretical debates about the "right" theory or school of thought. Consider, for example, the German "oddity" of neglecting the need for active macroeconomic policy or opposing the idea of active policy at all, which is common to a relevant subgroup of German economists and parts of the public discourse. This point of view might have decreased the pressure on forecasters to use more modern theoretical models (at least for the German sub-population we analyzed).

These conclusions are obviously based on a small database only, which future research will have to extend. One possible way to do so might be seen in an analysis of citations. Based on such an analysis Fourcade, Ollion, and Algan (2015) show that economics shows a larger degree of insularity as compared to other parts of the social sciences. If our decoupling hypothesis is true, a similar picture should be visible for the forecasters camp. Another way to gain further insights might be a closer look at personal relations and biographies of forecasters. As they are academically trained, it would be interesting to look at their origins in this respect and to check whether they come from certain universities and/or other institutions. This link may well establish social networks (Grimm, Kapeller, and Pühringer 2017), which in turn may explain how certain positions evolve during time.

References

Aghion, Phillipe, Roman Frydman, Joseph E. Stiglitz, and Michael Woodford, eds. 2002. *Knowledge, Information, and Expectations in Modern Macroeconomics: In Honor of Edmund S. Phelps*. Princeton, NJ: Princeton University Press.

Angrist, Joshua D., and Jörn-Steffen Pischke. 2008. *Mostly Harmless Econometrics: An Empiricist's Companion*. Princeton, NJ: Princeton University Press.

Arun, R., V. Suresh, C. V. Madhavan, and M. N. Murthy. 2010. "On finding the natural number of topics with latent dirichlet allocation: Some observations." In *Advances in Knowledge Discovery and Data Mining*, edited by M. J. Zaki, J. X. Yu, B. Ravindran, and V. Pudi, 391–402, Berlin: Springer.

Ashiya, Masahiro. 2006. "Forecast accuracy and product differentiation of Japanese institutional forecasters." *International Journal of Forecasting* 22 (2): 395–401.

Batchelor, Roy., and Pami Dua. 1990a. "All forecasters are equal." *Journal of Business and Economic Statistics* 8: 143–44.

Batchelor, Roy, and Pami Dua. 1990b. "Forecaster ideology, forecasting technique, and the accuracy of economic forecasts." *International Journal of Forecasting* 6 (1): 3–10.

Beck, Thorsten, and Hans-Helmut Kotz, eds. 2017. *Ordoliberalism: A German Oddity?* A VoxEU.org eBook. London: CEPR Press. https://voxeu.org/system/files/epublication/Ordoliberalism_Nov22.pdf (last access: 8/13/2019).

Besly, Tim, and Peter Hennessy. 2009. *Letter to the Queen*. https://www.euroresidentes.com/empresa_empresas/carta-reina.pdf (last access: 8/13/2019).

Bezemer, Dirk J. 2010. "No one saw this coming: Understanding financial crisis through accounting models." *Accounting, Organizations and Society* 35 (7): 676–88.

Blei, David M. 2012. "Probabilistic topic models." *Commun. ACM* 55 (4): 77–84.

Blei, David M., Andrew Y. Ng, and Michael I. Jordan. 2003. "Latent dirichlet allocation." *Journal of Machine Learning research* 3 (Jan): 993–1022.

Cao, Juan, Tian Xia, Jintao Li, Yongdong Zhang, and Sheng Tang. 2009. "A density-based method for adaptive LDA model selection." *Neurocomputing* 72 (7–9): 1775–81.

Castle, Jennifer, and David F. Hendry. 2011. "On not evaluating economic models by forecast outcomes." *Istanbul Business Research* 40 (1): 1–14.

Christiano, Lawrence J., Martin S. Eichenbaum, and Mathias Trabandt. 2018. "On DSGE models." *The Journal of Economic Perspectives* 32 (3): 113–40.

Colander, Dave. 2017. "Economists should stop doing it with models (and start doing it with heuristics)." *Eastern Economic Journal* 43 (4): 729–33.

Consensus Forecast ™. 2016. "G7 and Western Europe.".

Deveaud, Romain, Eric SanJuan, and Patrice Bellot. 2014. "Accurate and effective latent concept modeling for ad hoc information retrieval." *Document numérique* 17 (1): 61–84.

Döpke, Jörg, Ulrich Fritsche, and Gabi Waldhof. 2019. "Theories, techniques and the formation of German business cycle forecasts." *Jahrbücher für Nationalökonomie und Statistik* 239 (2): 203–41.

Drechsel, Katja, and Rolf Scheufele. 2012. "The performance of short-term forecasts of the German economy before and during the 2008/2009 Recession." *International Journal of Forecasting* 28 (2): 428–45.

European Central Bank. 2009. "Results of a special questionnaire for participants in the ECB Survey of Professional Forecasters (SPF)." *Monthly Bulletin* April: 1–16.

European Central Bank. 2014. "Results of the second special questionnaire for participants in the ECB Survey of Professional Forecasters." *Monthly Bulletin* January: 1–28.

Fair, Ray C. 2012. "Analyzing macroeconomic forecastability." *Journal of Forecasting* 31 (2): 99–108.

Farrell, Henry, and John Quiggin. 2017. "Consensus, dissensus, and economic ideas: Economic crisis and the rise and fall of Keynesianism." *International Studies Quarterly* 61 (2): 269–83.

Fildes, Robert, and Herman Stekler. 2002. "The state of macroeconomic forecasting." *Journal of Macroeconomics* 24 (4): 435–68.

Fourcade, Marion, Etienne Ollion, and Yann Algan. 2015. "The superiority of economists." *Journal of Economic Perspectives* 29 (1): 89–119.

Frenkel, Michael, Eliza M. Lis, and Jan-Christoph Rülke. 2011. "Has the economic crisis of 2007–2009 changed the expectation formation process in the Euro area?" *Economic Modelling* 28 (4): 1808–14.

Fricke, Thomas. 2016. *Prognostiker des Jahres 2016 – die Langzeitauswertung*. https://neuewirtschaftswunder.de/ (last access: 8/13/2019).

Fricke, Thomas. 2017. "Altes Einheitsdenken oder neue Vielfalt? Eine systematische Auswertung der großen Umfragen unter Deutschlands Wirtschaftswissenschaftler_innen." *FGW-Studien* 3: 2017. https://www.fgw-nrw.de/fileadmin/user_upload/NOED-Studie-03-Fricke-A1-Web-komplett.pdf (last access: 8/13/2019).

Friedman, Milton. 1953. *Essays in Positive Economics*. Chicago, IL: University of Chicago Press.

Gaffney, Mason. 2011. "An award for calling the crash." *Econ Journal Watch* 8 (2): 185–92. https://econjwatch.org/articles/an-award-for-calling-the-crash (last access: 8/13/2019).

Geiger, Felix, Oliver Sauter, and Kai D. Schmid. 2009. "The camp view of inflation forecasts." *Hohenheimer Dikussionsbeiträge* 320/2009.

Giersch, Herbert, and Knut Borchardt, eds. 1962. *Diagnose Und Prognose Als Wirtschaftswissenschaftliche Methodenprobleme: Verhandlungen Auf Der Arbeitstagung Des Vereins Für Socialpolitik, Gesellschaft Für Wirtschafts- Und Sozialwissenschaften in Garmisch-Partenkirchen 1961*. Arbeitstagungen zur Erörterung der Aufgaben und Methoden der Wirtschaftswissenschaft in unserer Zeit 1,1961. Berlin: Duncker & Humblot.

Glandon, Philip, Kenneth N. Kuttner, Sandeep Mazumder, and Caleb Stroup. 2018. "Macroeconomic research, present and past." Unpublished manuscript, https://papers.ssrn.com/sol3/papers.cfm?abstract_id=3225417 (last access: 8/13/2019).

Griffiths, Thomas L., and Mark Steyvers. 2004. "Finding scientific topics." *Proceedings of the National academy of Sciences* 101 (suppl 1): 5228–35.

Grimm, Christian, Jakob Kapeller, and Stephan Pühringer. 2017. "Zum Profil der deutschsprachigen Volkswirtschaftslehre: Paradigmatische Ausrichtung und politische Orientierung deutschsprachiger Ökonom_innen." ICAE working paper series. Unpublished manuscript, http://hdl.handle.net/10419/171445 (last access: 8/13/2019).

Heilemann, Ullrich, and Susanne Schnorr-Bäcker. 2017. "Could the start of the German recession 2008-2009 have been foreseen? Evidence from Real-Time Data." *Jahrbücher für Nationalökonomie und Statistik* 237 (1): 29–62.

Heinrich, Gregor. 2005. "Parameter estimation for text analysis." Technical report Universität Leipzig. Unpublished manuscript, http://www.arbylon.net/publications/text-est.pdf (last access: 8/13/2019).

Hempel, Carl G. 1994 [1942]. "The function of general laws in history." In *Readings in the Philosophy of Social Science*, edited by Michael Martin and Lee C. McIntyre, 43–53. Cambridge, MA: MIT Press.

Hendry, David. F. 1986. "The role of prediction in evaluating econometric models." *Proceedings of the Royal Society A: Mathematical, Physical and Engineering Sciences* 407 (1832): 25–34.

Hippel, Paul von. 2015. "Linear vs. Logistic probability models: Which is better, and when?" https://statisticalhorizons.com/linear-vs-logistic (last access: 8/13/2019).

Hornik, Kurt, and Bettina Grün. 2011. "topicmodels: An R package for fitting topic models." *Journal of Statistical Software* 40 (13): 1–30.

Krugman, Paul R. 2014. "Stagflation and the fall of macroeconomics." https://krugman.blogs.nytimes.com/2014/06/ 28/stagflation-and-the-fall-of-macroeconomics/ (last access: 8/13/2019).

Krugman, Paul R. 2018. "Good enough for government work? Macroeconomics since the crisis." *Oxford Review of Economic Policy* 34 (1/2): 156–68.

Lamont, Owen A. 2002. "Macroeconomic forecasts and microeconomic forecasters." *Journal of Economic Behavior & Organization* 48 (3): 265–80.

Lawrence, Michael, Paul Goodwin, O' Conno, Onkal, Marcusr, and Dilek Onkal. 2006. "Judgmental forecasting: A review of progress over the last 25 years." *International Journal of Forecasting* 22 (3): 493–518.

Lüdering, Jochen, and Peter Winker. 2016. "Forward or backward looking? The economic discourse and the observed reality." *Jahrbücher für Nationalökonomie und Statistik* 236 (4): 483–515.

Mankiw, N. Gregory. 2006. "The macroeconomist as scientist and engineer." *The Journal of Economic Perspectives* 20 (4): 29–46.

Mankiw, N. Gregory, and Ricardo Reis. 2018. "Friedman's Presidential address in the evolution of macroeconomic thought." *The Journal of Economic Perspectives* 32 (1): 81–96.

Meyler, Aidan, and Ieva Rubene. "Results of a special questionnaire for participants in the ECB Survey of Professional Forecasters (SPF)." Unpublished manuscript, https://www.ecb.europa.eu/stats/prices/indic/forecast/shared/files/quest_summary.pdf (last access: 8/13/2019).

Ng, Serena, and Jonathan H. Wright. 2013. "Facts and challenges from the great recession for forecasting and macroeconomic modeling." *Journal of Economic Literature* 51 (4): 1120–54.

Nienhaus, Lisa. 2009. *Die Blindgänger: Warum die Ökonomen auch künftige Krisen nicht erkennen werden*: Frankfurt; New York: Campus Verlag.

Pain, Nigel, Christine Lewis, Thai-Thanh Dang, Yosuke Jin, and Pete Richardson. 2014."OECD forecasts during and after the financial crisis." OECD Economics Department Working Papers 1107.

Reis, Ricardo. 2018. "Is something Rreally wrong with macroeconomics?" *Oxford Review of Economic Policy* 34 (1/2): 132–55.

Romer, Paul. 2016. "The trouble with macroeconomics." *The American Economist* 20: 1–20.

Sargent, Thomas J., and Robert E. Lucas. 1979. "After Keynesian macroeconomics." *Federal Reserve Bank of Minneapolis Quarterly Review* 3 (2): 295–319.

Schaffler, Mark. 2012. *Probit Better than LPM?* http://www.mostlyharmlesseconometrics.com/2012/07/probit-better-than-lpm/ (last access: 8/13/2019).

Schneider, Friedrich, Bruno Frey, and Silke Humbert. 2007. "Was denken deutsche Ökonomen? Eine empirische Auswertung einer Internetbefragung unter den Mitgliedern des Vereins für Socialpolitik im Sommer 2006." *Perspektiven der Wirtschaftspolitik* 8 (4): 359–77.

Stark, Tom. 2013. "SPF panelists forecasting methods: A note on the aggregate results of a November 2009 special survey." *Federal Reserve Bank of Philadelphia*. https://www.philadelphiafed.org/-/media/research-and-data/real-time-center/survey-of-professional-forecasters/spf-special-survey-on-forecast-methods.pdf?la=en (last access: 8/13/2019).

Stiglitz, Joseph E. 2018. "Where modern macroeconomics went wrong." *Oxford Review of Economic Policy* 34 (1/2): 70–106.

Tichy, Gunther. 1976. *Konjunkturschwankungen: Theorie, Messung, Prognose. Heidelberger Taschenbücher 174*. Berlin: Springer.

Tichy, Gunther J. 2013. *Konjunkturschwankungen: Theorie, Messung, Prognose*: Berlin: Springer-Verlag.

Vines, David, and Samuel Wills. 2018. "The rebuilding macroeconomic theory project: An analytical assessment." *Oxford Review of Economic Policy* 34 (1/2): 1–42.

Wieland, Volker, and Maik Wolters. 2013. "Forecasting and policy making." In *Handbook of Economic Forecasting*, Vol 8, edited by

Graham Elliott, Clive Granger, and Alan B. Timmermann, 239–325. Amsterdam: Elsevier.

Winkler, Adalbert. 2018. "Zehn Jahre nach dem Konkurs von Lehman Brothers: Ordnungspolitische Irrtümer in der Bewegung der EZB-Geldpolitik seit der globalen Finanzkrise." *Perspektiven der Wirtschaftspolitik* 19 (2): 141–62.

Wooldridge, Jeffrey M. 2014. *Introduction to Econometrics: Europe, Middle East and Africa Edition*: Andover, Hampshire: Cengage Learning.

Literatur – Kultur – Ökonomie
Literature – Culture – Economy

Herausgegeben von / Edited by
Christine Künzel, Axel Haunschild, Birger P. Priddat,
Thomas Rommel, Franziska Schößler und / and Yvette Sánchez

Bd./Vol. 1 Franziska Schößler: Femina Oeconomica: Arbeit, Konsum und Geschlecht in der Literatur. Von Goethe bis Händler. 2017.

Bd./Vol. 2 Yvette Sánchez (Hrsg.): Business-Fiktionen und Management-Inszenierungen. 2018.

Bd./Vol. 3 Manuel Pombo: Trueques discursivos entre Literatura y *Management*. 2019.

Bd./Vol. 4 Franziska Jekel / Anna-Katharina Krüger / Myriam-Naomi Walburg (eds.): Writing (for) the Market. Narratives of Global Economy. 2020.

Bd./Vol. 5 Ulrich Fritsche / Roman Köster / Laetitia Lenel (eds.): Futures Past. Economic Forecasting in the 20th and 21st Century. 2020.

www.peterlang.com